Forgotten Power

BYZANTIUM

Bulwark of Christianity

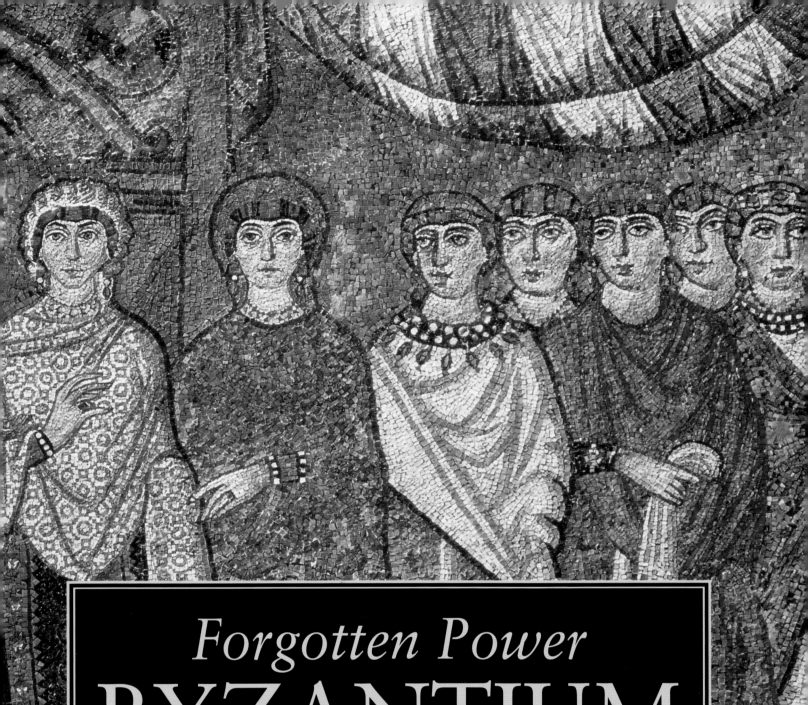

Forgotten Power
BYZANTIUM
Bulwark of Christianity

Roger Michael Kean

THALAMUS
PUBLISHING

PICTURE CREDITS

Previous page: Detail of a Byzantine mosaic showing Empress Theodora and her courtly retinue.

Title page: Portrait of mounted John VIII Palaeologus in Italy.

Contents

Introduction

It is food for thought that until almost the end of the 20th century, most historians considered the Byzantine Empire to be little more than an after-taste of the Roman Empire, a side order to Medieval Europe and an indifferent appetiser to the splendour of the Renaissance. At best, it was a stopping-off place on the crusading route to the Holy Land. In his celebrated trilogy of books on the subject published in 1988–95, John Julius Norwich made amends for the attitudes of earlier historians, or what he called the empire's 'atrocious press'. This is typified by the entry for Byzantium in W.E.H. Lecky's *History of European Morals*, published in 1869, quoted by Norwich. This is just a taste:

> *Of that Byzantine Empire the universal verdict of history is that it constitutes, without a single exception, the most thoroughly base and despicable form that civilisation has yet assumed…. The history of the Empire is a monotonous story of the intrigues of priests, eunuchs and women, of poisonings, of conspiracies, of uniform ingratitude, of perpetual fratricides.*

Actually, this makes it sound just like any other history – if anything, more exciting than many. And it sweepingly ignores almost one thousand years of human endeavour. The ancient Roman Empire which preceeded it, and from which it sprang, almost fully formed, was never remiss in providing murders, intrigues and generous portions of ingratitude. But the Byzantine emperors, their courtiers and clerics carried off these matters of daily historical life with a flair for the theatrical that their more dour and serious forebears never managed.

Lecky and his ilk also overlooked what the Byzantine Empire accomplished. In its heyday, Constantinople ruled over a vast mercantile empire whose commerce fuelled the development of the barbarian successor states of the collapsed Roman Empire. Under Byzantium, the monastic movement flourished, spread throughout Europe and often acted as a welcome counter-balance to the overbearing power of the established Latin Church. Byzantium gave the emerging medieval Europe many of its laws, enshrined in the codifications of emperors like Justinian I, Basil I and Leo VI. It preserved the skills of art and literature through the sixth to thirteenth centuries – largely a dark period elsewhere in Europe – and its scholars developed humanist thinking, the very mainspring of the Renaissance.

Perhaps most importantly, Byzantium acted as a bulwark of Christianity against the tide of Islam that otherwise threatened to overwhelm all of Europe from the mid-seventh century onwards. And this book explodes the popular myth that the Byzantine Empire survived in a vacuum – far from it, for many European states at the time it was much too involved in European matters.

But that is what makes for exciting history. And this one begins early in the fourth century as – having defeated Maxentius, the usurping 'emperor' of Italy, in 312 at the battle of the Milvian Bridge, and his legitimate colleague Licinius, ruler of the East in 324 – Constantine the Great becomes the Roman Empire's uncontested sole and absolute ruler.

Roger Michael Kean

The Conquest of Trebizond, painting by an unknown Florentine artist, late 15th century. An important Byzantine trading centre, the Black Sea port of Trebizond became isolated from the rest of the empire after the crusader's sack of Constantinople in 1204. It remained an independent empire of its own under the rule of the Byzantine Comneni family. Trebizond outlasted Constantinople's fall to the Ottoman Turks in 1453 by eight years. On 15 August 1461 David Comnenus, last emperor of Trebizond, surrendered the last throne of the Byzantine world to Sultan Mehmet II.

List of maps

Justinian I (r.527–65) is often referred to as last of the 'Roman' emperors, but during his reign all the social and cultural features we associate with the Byzantine Empire were established.

Byzantium – A New Centre

In the first half of the fourth century, two profound changes affected the Roman Empire that would have a tremendous impact on the future development of the East. One was the adoption of Christianity as the official state religion, the other was the eclipse of Rome as the empire's capital. Both were the designs of one man, Emperor Constantine the Great.

Constantine (r.306–337) changed the course of first-millennium history. Because of his policies Christianity was spread throughout the Roman Empire, and so became the faith that fired the civilised world. The political expediencies that persuaded the ambitious emperor to embrace Christianity are largely forgotten. Nor did his conduct in later life always appear appropriate for a humble servant of Christ. But Constantine, by playing the religious card, united the empire – fractured by civil war – under one standard: the Christian *Chi-Rho*.

However, the undisputed ruler of the empire had no desire to set up his court in the city of Rome. He had spent many of his 50 years in the Gallic tetrarchic capital of Treveri (Trier), but all his impressionable youth at Byzantium. And he was aware that the West was now eclipsed in the imperial partnership. Trade and culture buzzed in the East as Asia grew in importance. Making his new capital in the East was a logical step, and where better than the city that had nurtured his youth? To this point, Byzantium had been only a modestly important trading centre, and was little larger than the town rebuilt by Septimius Severus after he had torn it down in 196. But Constantine determined that it should become his new capital.

The great city that was to bear Constantine's name for more than a thousand years was begun in 324, shortly after his victory over Licinius. It should be doubted that Constantine actually dedicated Constantinopolis to his own name, or that he was building a city to supersede Rome in scope. More to the point, in contrast to Rome, this was to be the Christian capital of the world.

The new city was styled Roma Nova and probably only became known as Constantinopolis after the emperor's death. However, it is convenient to refer to Byzantium

Clean-cut, honest and ruthless, Constantine I the Great changed the religious temper and the political centre of the empire forever. In so doing he laid the foundation for what would become the Byzantine Empire.

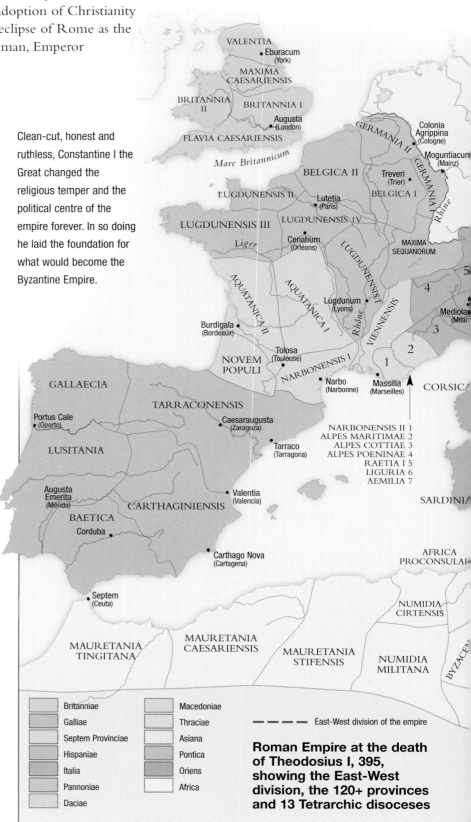

Roman Empire at the death of Theodosius I, 395, showing the East-West division, the 120+ provinces and 13 Tetrarchic disoceses

Britanniae	Macedoniae	
Galliae	Thraciae	– – – – – East-West division of the empire
Septem Provinciae	Asiana	
Hispaniae	Pontica	
Italia	Oriens	
Pannoniae	Africa	
Daciae		

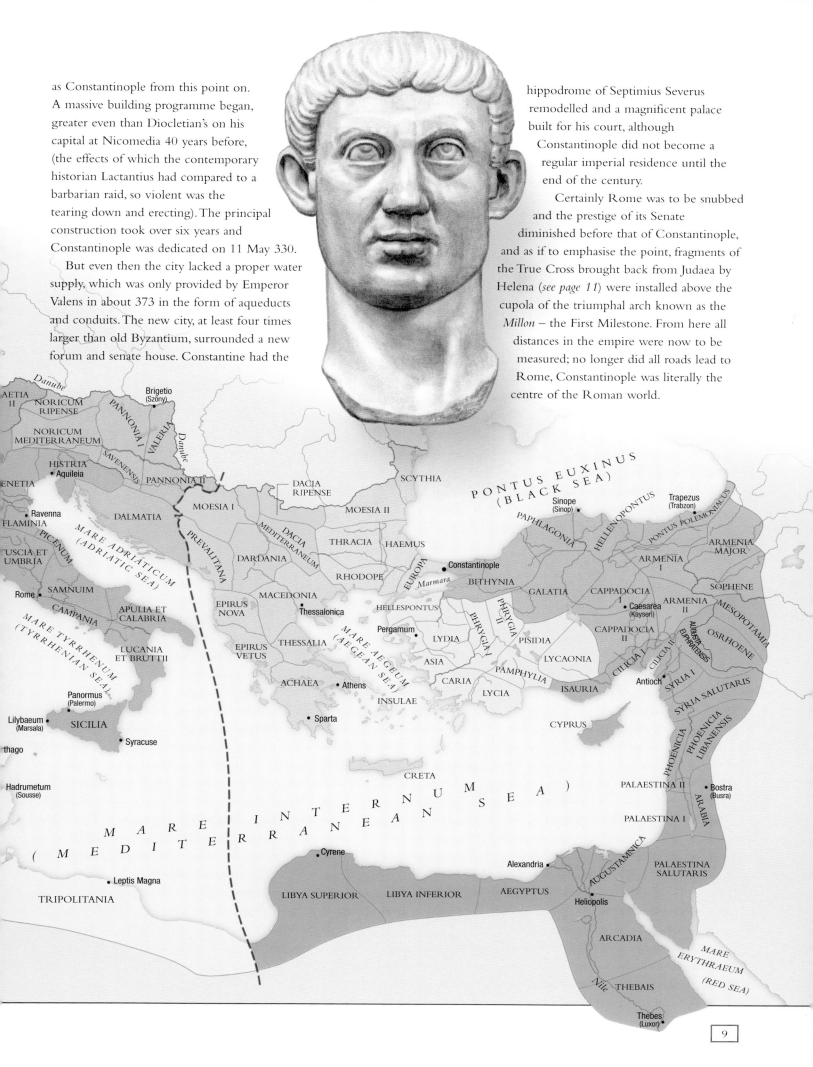

as Constantinople from this point on. A massive building programme began, greater even than Diocletian's on his capital at Nicomedia 40 years before, (the effects of which the contemporary historian Lactantius had compared to a barbarian raid, so violent was the tearing down and erecting). The principal construction took over six years and Constantinople was dedicated on 11 May 330.

But even then the city lacked a proper water supply, which was only provided by Emperor Valens in about 373 in the form of aqueducts and conduits. The new city, at least four times larger than old Byzantium, surrounded a new forum and senate house. Constantine had the hippodrome of Septimius Severus remodelled and a magnificent palace built for his court, although Constantinople did not become a regular imperial residence until the end of the century.

Certainly Rome was to be snubbed and the prestige of its Senate diminished before that of Constantinople, and as if to emphasise the point, fragments of the True Cross brought back from Judaea by Helena (*see page 11*) were installed above the cupola of the triumphal arch known as the *Millon* – the First Milestone. From here all distances in the empire were now to be measured; no longer did all roads lead to Rome, Constantinople was literally the centre of the Roman world.

Establishment of the State Church

When Constantine won his victory against Maxentius outside Rome in 312, his army marched for the first time under the Christian banner, but the establishment of Christianity as first the state religion, and then the only permitted faith was not a straightforward matter.

Right: A triumphant Constantine is depicted on a gold solidus gazing up to heaven.

Below: The Christian *Chi-Rho* symbol soon replaced the traditional sun disk image on late Roman coinage.

Right: The theologian Arius of Alexandria evolved a creed that was to split the Roman Church for over a century – and its echoes never entirely faded. There is no contemporary portrait of Arius, this is from a 14th-century painting by Andrea di Buonaioto.

Despite the declaration of faith professed by the waving banners of Constantine's armies, it should be doubted that the emperor was an overnight convert. Indeed, he remained without baptism until his deathbed. Like his soldiers – probably pagan to a man – Constantine was happy to have a powerful talisman on his side. Championing Christianity, for instance, did not prevent him from holding the ancient office of *pontifex maximus*, chief priest of the pagan Roman state religion.

Previous emperors had regarded Christianity as divisive to national unity, whereas Constantine wielded its power as a unifying movement. Since most of the army and the upper classes were convinced pagans, it was not practical to unite the Christian Church to the State, but he wanted to utilise its moral and economic advantages for the State's benefit.

In 318 he issued an edict that recognised the jurisdiction of the episcopal courts and, where by mutual agreement the litigants brought a case before the bishops, accorded their decision the same validity as that of the civil magistrates.

Although he was more concerned with the building of Constantinople, Rome was not ignored. An extensive programme of religious building began, including a basilica for the pope on the site of what had been the camp of the mounted imperial guard, and many other churches, among them the first St Peter's. To the people he presented himself as the champion of Christians everywhere.

But even among Christians there was disunity. As early as 313 Constantine became embroiled in what is known as the Donatist schism. Donatists argued that those Christians who had recanted or had given up sacred books to the inquisitions of Emperor Diocletian were sinners, and that their readmittance to the communion should be qualified. They argued with the more tolerant over how far the Church should be a mixed body of sinners and the righteous.

In the East an even more divisive schism occurred, one which was to dog Christian unity for decades. A deacon and presbyter of Alexandria

of Judaea as Christ's birthplace and the land of his mission. Having the mother of the empire's Christian ruler endorse the validity of the shrines she visited established the Holy Land as the essential place of pilgrimage.

During her journey Helena proclaimed the Via Dolorosa, identified all 14 Stations of the Cross, the place where Jesus fed the five thousand and where he preached his Sermon on the Mount, the place of the Annunciation and Joseph's carpentry workshop. She also discovered several pieces of the True Cross, and thus started the passion for hunting down relics.

At the place of Jesus' crucifixion she started building the Church of the Holy Sepulchre, although this is usually credited to Constantine. Vitally, her pilgrimage established a bond between Constantinople and Jerusalem that would endure and become one cause of the bitter Crusades in the 12th century.

Left: Helena began the mania for collecting relics. This mosaic depicts Helena and Constantine with the True Cross.

Below: A 14th-century painting of the Church of the Holy Sepulchre, founded in Jerusalem by Helena and Constantine.

called Arius (c.250–336) had professed a heresy which stated that Christ was 'God's Creature', whereas the orthodox held that Christ was also God. Arianism became the adopted creed of choice for incoming barbarians, and the heresy came close to destroying the empire before its final eradication.

Starting the relics trade

Schismatic activity within the Church was bound to annoy Constantine, who required a unified clergy whose authority was recognised by all, otherwise the partnership between Church and State would be undermined. Towards non-Christians Constantine had promised religious toleration: 'Let no one molest another,' he had written in the so-called Edict of Milan. But the edict contained a warning for pagans that the wise would do well 'to be persuaded that purity and holiness can only be obtained by submission to the Holy Laws of God'.

In 326 the emperor's mother Helena undertook a pilgrimage to the Holy Land. Her journey was remarkable in so far as few Christians to this point had taken much notice

A Divided Empire

Tradition holds that the Roman Empire was divided into two halves – East and West – on the death of Theodosius I in 395, but in effect the split was predicated by Constantine's creation of Constantinople, and after his death the administration of the eastern and western provinces was rarely unified. As the West declined, the East was already turning into what would become the Byzantine Empire.

In the years following Constantine the Great's death, the city he founded grew and outshone ancient Rome. Nevertheless, links between the two great Roman cities were maintained at consular level, as this diptych with 'Rome' on the left and 'Constantinople' on the right indicates.

During his reign Constantine had unified the empire, secured the frontiers and safeguarded the provinces from civil war. On the debit side, most inhabitants of the empire were neither happy nor prosperous. Ground down by taxes, condemned to the unremitting drudgery of compulsory service in their fathers' trades, most were no better than slaves of the state. The massive weight of imperial bureaucracy that was to characterise the Byzantine Empire had now come into being, together with the evils of corruption through the choice of imperial favourites for the many offices and dignitary titles established. Rome had lost its pre-eminence and the old gods were almost gone.

Constantine's death on 22 May 337 was the precursor to first a brutal cull of his nephews Dalmatius and Hannibalianus, and then a bloody civil war between his three sons. All named Flavius, they are known as Constantine II (aged 21), Constantius II (20) and Constans, who was aged about 15 or 16 at the time. There was uncertainty in the three-month interregnum that followed, during which Constantine's body was laid to rest in the great basilica he had built, the Church of the Holy Apostles (and in peeved Rome, the Senate voted him divine honours and made a pagan god of the first Christian emperor). And then the army made a decision – the soldiers would only accept Constantine's sons, ruling jointly.

They divided the empire between them: Constantine II held sway over Britain, Gaul and Spain; Constantius took the eastern provinces and Egypt; while Constans received the largest patrimony: Africa, Italy, Illyricum, Macedonia and Thrace. This gave him control of Constantinople, although in the event it was of little significance. The joint reign began badly, with the massacre of virtually all the male descendants of Constantine the Great's extended family, removing at one stroke any further claimants to the throne. Only two young boys survived, Claudius Gallus and Flavius Julianus, the sons of Constantine's half-brother.

Rebellion and disaffection

Unfortunately for the empire, none of Constantine's sons was the man his father had been. Constantine II attempted to exert his authority over the others, especially Constans, still little more than a child. But Constans refused to submit to his will and late in 339 asked Constantius for his help in return for giving him authority over Constantinople. Constantine II invaded Italy in 340, but he was slain in a battle near Aquileia and his body thrown into a river. Constans assumed command of the western and central parts of the empire. But Constans, spoiled child of an autocratic court, swamped by pomp and ceremony, turned into a degenerate, 'a leader in avarice'.†

† Sextus Aurelius Victor, *History of the Caesars*

At the start of 350, an officer of British extraction named Magnentius seized the purple, and Constans was executed. Constantius, as the surviving Augustus, turned to his distant cousin Gallus, one of the two boys who survived the dynastic massacre, and raised him to the rank of caesar. He married his sister Constantia to Gallus, gave him control of the East and prepared to tackle the usurper. The armies met on 28 September 351 at Mursa (Osijek). Constantius was victorious, but Magnentius managed to escape with a part of his force and return to Gaul to raise another army. The emperor tracked across Europe in pursuit, and after several inconclusive skirmishes, defeated Magnentius at Lyons in 353, after which the usurper fell on his own sword.

However, peace remained elusive. In the East Gallus had caused havoc with his incompetent rule. Having connived at the removal of the praetorian prefect sent to Antioch to keep an eye

on him, Gallus found himself recalled to meet Constantius at Sirmium on the Danube in 354. But he never reached his destination. When Constantius heard that Gallus was placing all the blame for the unrest he had caused in the East on Constantia, the Augustus lost his patience and ordered his Caesar's execution, turning instead to the younger brother of Gallus, Julianus.

Above: Claudius Gallus Caesar married Constantius's ambitious sister Constantina. But their irresponsible behaviour in Asia aroused the emperor's ire and led to Gallus's doom.

Division of the empire in the last years of Constantine between his sons and nephews

Hannibalianus was king of Armenia and governor of Pontica (sometimes erroneously called King of Pontica).

BRITANNIAE
Treveri
GALLIAE
Mediolanum
PANNONIAE
THRACIAE
PONTUS EXUINUS
Armenia
Constantinople
PONTICA
ITALIA
MOESIAE
Thessalonica
ASIANA
HISPANIAE
Antiochia
Carthago
MARE INTERNUM
AFRICA
Alexandria
ORIENS

Constantine's sons
Constantine II
Constantius II
Constans
Constantine's nephews
Dalmatius
Hannibalianus

Julian Apostate

Julian's reign is significant for his attempt to return a unified empire to the worship of the ancient Roman and Greek gods. His failure to do so ensured that from henceforward Christianity would gain in force, and that the prelates of the faith would become increasingly the power behind the empire's throne.

Right: Flavius Claudius Julianus: the austere face of the man who decided to reinstate the pagan gods of old.

Below: Coin of the young Julian. The scholarly young Caesar's military abilities were underestimated by Constantius.

Facing: Once Julian was emperor, he instituted radical reforms at court. The thousands of flunkeys were reduced to a skeleton staff, and frugal simplicity ruled daily life. His political and religious reforms were just as drastic.

As a child, Julian had been tutored by Bishop Eusebius of Nicomedia and brought up as a good Christian. However, in his adolescence he became enamoured of Greek philosophy and enrolled at the school of Libanius, a teacher who had rejected Christianity and re-embraced classical paganism; Julian soon followed suit. Fearing the wrath of his cousin Constantius, Julian kept his apostasy to himself, and watched the downfall of his brother Gallus with trepidation. Julian was even more alarmed when Constantius summoned him to court.

Bookish Julian was a shy and socially dysfunctional young man whose speech was halting and whose laughter when provoked was described as being 'nervous and uncontrolled'. Disdainful of his scholarship, Constantius had Julian's student beard shaved, his long hair cut in short trooper style, his out-of-condition body stuffed into a military uniform and, on 6 November 355, paraded him before the troops and acclaimed him as caesar.

Julian was to be a leader only in name. After appointing all his ministers and generals, Constantius dispatched him to Gaul to deal with the increasing attacks of German tribes across the Rhine. But Constantius had underestimated him. Always conscientious, Julian made it his business to learn soldiering fast. So it was that the successful lightning campaign of 356 resulted as much from his efforts as those of his cautious generals.

In 360, the Sassanian Empire threatened the East, but when Constantius requested reinforcements from Julian he was refused. The 28-year-old was no longer a shy scholar, but a solid Roman with a mission: to re-establish the true ancient faith and avenge the murder of his family by Constantius in 337. In March 360,

Julian was acclaimed by his troops, and in the following year he marched on Constantinople. However, Julian won a bloodless victory by the hand of fate. Constantius had moved from the Syrian frontier to Antioch and was setting out to cross Anatolia when he was stricken by a fever and died at the age of 44 in the small village of Mopuscrenae on 3 November 361. His army clamoured for Julian to lead them.

A sluggish revival

With great rapidity Julian established a new virtuous court. Out went the flummery of Diocletian and Constantine I: 'There were a thousand cooks,' said Libanius, 'as many barbers, and even more butlers… the eunuchs were more in number than flies around the flocks in spring….' None remained when Julian was finished, and he furnished himself with little more than a skeleton staff for his own austere needs.

Julian had no intention of reverting to the days of Christian persecution, not just because he was a merciful man – he had learned that martyrs seemed to have an opposite effect on the Christian Church to that intended. He repealed the decrees by which the pagan temples had been closed down and their sacrifices declared illegal, and issued an edict of religious tolerance. He then set about reviving pagan cults but organised along Christian lines: charitable and social

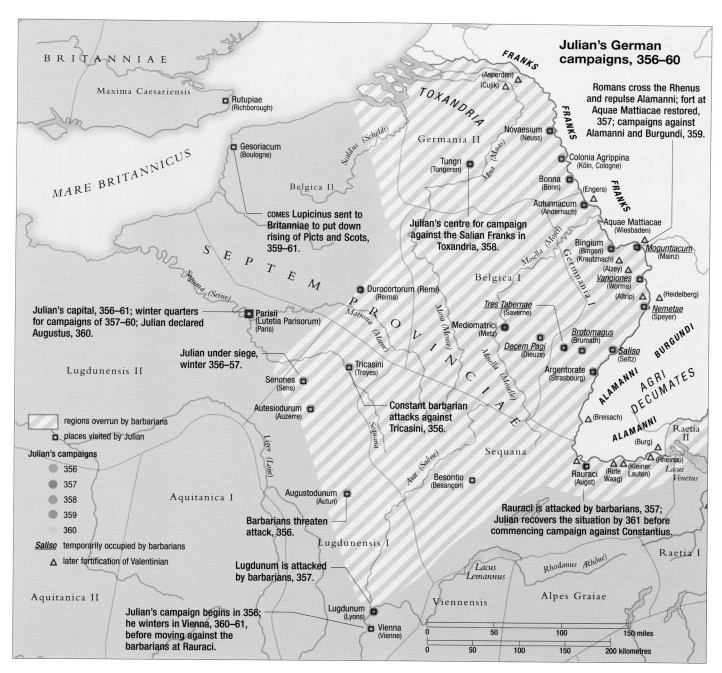

Julian's German campaigns, 356–60

Romans cross the Rhenus and repulse Alamanni; fort at Aquae Mattiacae restored, 357; campaigns against Alamanni and Burgundi, 359.

BRITANNIAE

Maxima Caesariensis

Rutupiae (Richborough)

MARE BRITANNICUS

Gesoriacum (Boulogne)

COMES Lupicinus sent to Britanniae to put down rising of Picts and Scots, 359–61.

TOXANDRIA

FRANKS

(Asperden)
(Cujik)

Germania II

Belgica II

Saldus (Scheldt)

Tungri (Tongeren)

Mosa (Maas)

Novaesium (Neuss)

FRANKS

Colonia Agrippina (Köln, Cologne)

Bonna (Bonn)

(Engers)

Autunnacum (Andernach)

FRANKS

Aquae Mattiacae (Wiesbaden)

Julian's centre for campaign against the Salian Franks in Toxandria, 358.

Moguntiacum (Mainz)

Bingium (Bingen) (Kreutznach)

(Alzey)

Vangiones (Worms)

(Altrip)

(Heidelberg)

Germania I

Belgica I

Mosella (Mosel)

SEPTEM

Sequana (Seine)

Julian's capital, 356–61; winter quarters for campaigns of 357–60; Julian declared Augustus, 360.

Parisii (Lutetia Parisorum) (Paris)

Julian under siege, winter 356–57.

Durocortorum (Remi) (Reima)

Matrona (Marne)

Mosa (Meuse)

PROVINCIAE

Mediomatrici (Metz)

Tres Tabernae (Saverne)

Nemetae (Speyer)

Decem Pagi (Dieuze)

Brotomagus (Brumath)

Saliso (Seltz)

BURGUNDI

Argentorate (Strasbourg)

AGRI DECUMATES

ALAMANNI

Lugdunensis II

Senones (Sens)

Tricasini (Troyes)

Constant barbarian attacks against Tricasini, 356.

Mosella (Mosel)

Liger (Loire)

Autesiodurum (Auzerre)

Sequana

(Breisach)

(Burg)

ALAMANNI

Raetia II

(Rheinau)

Lacus Venetus

regions overrun by barbarians

places visited by Julian

Julian's campaigns

356
357
358
359
360

Saliso temporarily occupied by barbarians

△ later fortification of Valentinian

Aquitanica I

Augustodunum (Autun)

Barbarians threaten attack, 356.

Arar (Saône)

Besontio (Besançon)

Sequana

Rauraci (Augst)

(Rote Waag)

(Kleiner Lauten)

Rauraci is attacked by barbarians, 357; Julian recovers the situation by 361 before commencing campaign against Constantius.

Lugdunensis I

Raetia I

Aquitanica II

Lugdunum is attacked by barbarians, 357.

Julian's campaign begins in 356; he winters in Vienna, 360–61, before moving against the barbarians at Rauraci.

Lugdunum (Lyons)

Vienna (Vienne)

Viennensis

Lacus Lemannus

Rhodanus (Rhône)

Alpes Graiae

0   50   100   150 miles
0   50   100   150   200 kilometres

---

institutions like those offered by the Christian churches would be founded for the support of widows, orphans and the sick.

Julian's dislike of Christianity was deep-seated. He blamed all the ills of the empire on the faith. It was an effete creed that insidiously robbed Romans of their solid virtues by preaching the feminine qualities of meekness, gentleness and charity. No wonder the army was barely capable any longer of manning the frontiers if Christian fifth-columnists were telling the soldiers to turn the other cheek. It was a simplistic view – as late as the fifth century Mithras remained the preferred deity of the frontier troops. But for all his efforts paganism seemed in no hurry to revive.

In the summer of 362 Julian moved to Antioch in preparation for war against Persia. In the six weeks he travelled across Anatolia he discovered to his dismay that the many Christian communities he passed appeared to be flourishing, while those of the pagans seemed to be no stronger than in Constantine's day.

Vowing to take tougher measures against Christianity once the war with Persia was concluded, he began the invasion. But Julian was never to return. After an initially successful campaign, he was wounded retreating from the Sassanian capital Ctesiphon, and died on 26 June 363. The widespread Christian community breathed a sigh of relief.

Theodosius the Great

Apart from a brief eight-month reign by the ineffectual Jovian, the empire was once again divided into East and West spheres between a succession of weak and cruel emperors. Their internal divisions made them incapable of stemming the increasing waves of barbarian attacks from every quarter.

Theodosius I, the last emperor to rule the whole of the empire, is called 'Great' for his establishment of the Roman Catholic Church.

The soldier brothers Valentinian I (r.364–75) in the West and Valens (r.364–78) in the East were almost exclusively involved in fighting frontier wars. When he died of an apoplectic fit brought on by his anger at a barbarian embassy, Valentinian left the West in the hands of his sons, the 17-year-old Gratian (r.375–83) and infant Valentinian II (r.375–92). In the year of their joint accession, their uncle Valens faced a dilemma. He was preparing to make war on the Sassanian Persians when a vast horde of Visigoths, encamped on the opposite side of the Danube, asked for asylum from the ravening Huns who had recently swept into the region. Unwilling to postpone his Persian war, Valens agreed to let them cross the river and settle in Moesia in return for converting to his Christian creed of Arianism and providing him with military service.

Unfortunately the two officers sent to supervise the crossing and settlement preferred to use the opportunity to line their own pockets. In fury, the Goths turned on the light Roman garrisons and began laying waste all of the Balkans. Valens rushed his forces west, and unwisely refusing to wait for aid from his nephew Gratian, rashly attacked the combined armies of Visigoths and Ostrogoths at Adrianople on 9 August 378. The result was a disaster of proportions not seen since Hannibal wiped out the Roman legions at Cannae in 216 BC. Valens was killed, and almost two-thirds of the Eastern army wiped out.

Gratian, aware that his military skills were unequal to the task of recovering the East, called on his father's most distinguished general, Flavius Theodosius (r.379–95), and made him co-Augustus on 19 January 379. He was to be the last great ruler of the Western Empire.

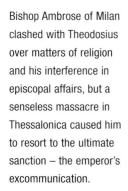

Bishop Ambrose of Milan clashed with Theodosius over matters of religion and his interference in episcopal affairs, but a senseless massacre in Thessalonica caused him to resort to the ultimate sanction – the emperor's excommunication.

For the better part of two years, Theodosius recovered army morale and gradually beat the Goths into submission, eventually absorbing many of their number into the army, and settling the remainder peacefully on Moesian farmland. During his reign, Theodosius resided both in his capital of Constantinople, but also in the western capital of Milan – the city had eclipsed Rome several decades before – dealing with various rebellions against the nominal rule of Valentinian II after Gratian's death in battle against one of the rebels.

It was while he was in Milan during 389 that

an event occurred that was to have lasting consequences for the future relationship in the West between the Christian Church and the State. At Thessalonica in Macedonia an unruly mob had cut down the governor. When Theodosius was given the news he flew into a rage and ordered a mass slaughter of the citizens. Having calmed down, he thought better and sent another order countermanding the first, but it arrived too late and the garrison slaughtered some 7,000 people.

Power of the Western Church

A mass murder undertaken without even the semblance of Roman justice could not be overlooked, and Ambrose, the powerful bishop of Milan, would not. Ambrose insisted on a public repentance and until such was forthcoming, the bishop told his emperor, he would withhold communion from him. Astonishingly, Theodosius meekly accepted his blame, and when it became apparent that Ambrose would not back down, the emperor agreed to the bishop's terms. Accordingly, he presented himself, dressed only in sackcloth and without his imperial diadem, to prostrate himself before the high altar and do penance.

But when he was finished, Ambrose refused the emperor communion unless he removed himself beyond the altar railing because the

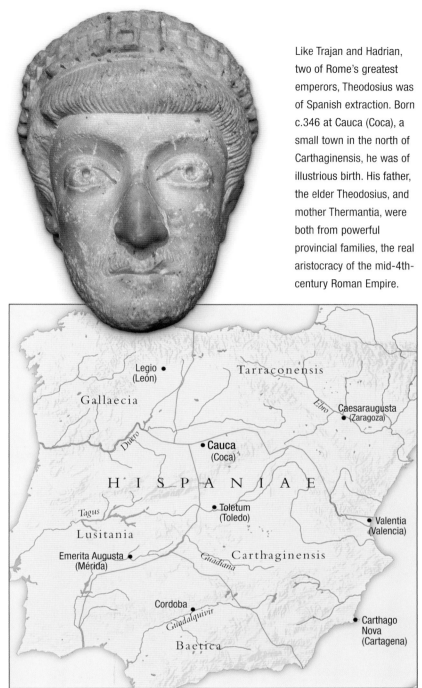

Like Trajan and Hadrian, two of Rome's greatest emperors, Theodosius was of Spanish extraction. Born c.346 at Cauca (Coca), a small town in the north of Carthaginensis, he was of illustrious birth. His father, the elder Theodosius, and mother Thermantia, were both from powerful provincial families, the real aristocracy of the mid-4th-century Roman Empire.

sacred enclosure was reserved for priests. Although Theodosius was only following the procedure of Constantinople, where the emperor celebrated communion at the altar apart from the mass of citizens, he quietly obeyed Ambrose and accepted his words: 'The purple only makes emperors, not priests.'

It was a turning point for Christendom. A cleric had asserted the rights of the spiritual over the temporal power of the ruler, and in accepting the condemnation and punishment of a priest, the emperor had for the first time recognised an authority greater than his own. It was not, however, a relationship that would be copied in Constantinople.

Left: Detail from one face on the base of Theodosius's obelisk which originally stood in the hippodrome. The emperor is shown watching the races, a victor's crown ready in his hand for the winning charioteer.

The First Religious Split

When he died in January 395, Theodosius I left a stable empire, largely at peace with its neighbours, and if not exactly secure on the northern frontiers at least quiet. Yet within another 80 years barbarians would overwhelm the Western Empire, leaving the East to develop in its own oriental, Byzantine way.

Theodosius left the Western Empire in the hands of his youngest son Honorius (r.395–423) in Milan (and later Ravenna) and the Eastern to the older Arcadius (r.395–408). Since Honorius was only ten, Theodosius had appointed his trusted general, the Vandal Stilicho, to the regency. Arcadius, now 18 but sluggish of temperament and mind, was under the thumb of the praetorian prefect Rufinus, a ruthless and ambitious schemer.

The battle of wills between Stilicho – who claimed that Theodosius had placed both sons under his care – and Rufinus greatly damaged Roman ability to respond to the opportunist new leader of the settled Visigoths, a cunning warrior named Alaric. Exploiting the weakness of a divided empire, Alaric played the East off against the West, threatening first one side then the other. The outcome suited the Goths well when Arcadius finally handed over control of all Illyricum to Alaric to spite Stilicho and create a buffer state between the squabbling empires. Stilicho took his revenge by having Rufinus assassinated, but the killer soon became the new power behind the Arcadian throne.

Despite facing Alaric several times in inconclusive battle, Stilicho the Vandal remained on cordial terms with the self-styled Gothic king, and determined to use him as an ally in a conquest of Constantinople. A religious dispute became his pretext for an attack. Two months after his father's death, Arcadius married a sophisticated and ambitious Greek woman named

Eudoxia, whose lascivious behaviour soon earned her the anger of the outspoken bishop of Constantinople, John Chrysostom (b.398–404). He openly referred to her from the pulpit as a 'Jezebel', and she had him exiled for his temerity.

However, the common people loved their saintly prelate and rioted so threateningly that Arcadius hastily recalled Chrysostom. Unfortunately exile had not silvered his pious but insufferable tongue. Fearing further riots if he again banished the troublesome bishop, the emperor compromised by having Chrysostom barred from his churches. At Easter 404, when

Above: In nominal control of the Western Empire, Honorius was a moral destitute, whose one passion was rearing chickens. The real power behind the throne was the Vandal general Stilicho, seen here (**right**) in an ivory relief. Stilicho argued that Theodosius had given him the regency of both Honorius and Arcadius, a claim that led to continual strife between both sides.

312 Constantine I defeats Maxentius at Pons Milvius and enters Rome in triumph	**318** Arius promulgates the notion that Christ is not divine; the heresy is called Arianism	**324** Constantine I defeats rival Licinius to become undisputed ruler of Rome	**325** The first ecumenical Church Council is held at Nicaea and denounces Arianism	**326** Constantine's mother Helena visits Jerusalem and 'discovers' the Holy Land	**330** Nova Roma, the old city of Byzantium, is dedicated as Constantinople	**337** Death of Constantine I the Great. His three sons divide the empire	**361** Constantius dies, leaving his cousin Julian sole ruler; Julian revives the old pagan religion

some two thousand catechumens, unable to take their baptism in a church gathered instead at the Baths of Constantine and became unruly, soldiers were called in to restore order. After the resulting slaughter, Chrysostom was again banished.

A thwarted assault

Chrysostom appealed to Pope Innocent I in Rome, who convoked a Latin synod that unanimously agreed to overturn the banishment. Innocent and Honorius insisted that Arcadius restore Chrysostom to his see. Arcadius made no reply beyond gravely insulting a delegation of Latin bishops dispatched to attempt a settlement and subjecting them to humiliation before sending them back empty-handed.

In the West, the Church had triumphed over the State when the indomitable Ambrose humbled mighty Theodosius. However, in Constantinople the clash of wills between the weakling Arcadius and his bishop had a very different outcome. The humbling of John Chrysostom before the emperor came to characterise the place of the Church in the eastern orthodoxy as being subservient to the

earthly power of the divinely empowered emperor. In turn, this led to the Byzantine emperor becoming head of the Church as well as the State. Chrysostom was never recalled and died in his place of exile in September 407.

The East–West rift was now complete, but Stilicho's campaign never materialised. In the particularly harsh winter of 406/7 the massed tribes of Vandals, Alani, Suevi and Burgundi crossed the frozen Rhine and overwhelmed the severely weakened Roman garrisons. Within days a horde of barbarians was rampaging through central Gaul. A few weeks later, the troops in Britain proclaimed one of their officers emperor, with the name Constantine III. His army crossed to Gaul, battled through the barbarian raiders and set up court at Arles.

Alaric also took matters into his own hands, invading Italy on the grounds that Stilicho had promised payment for Gothic services in the war against Arcadius, which the Senate now refused. Stilicho's abilities as soldier and politician may still have saved the day, but within a year he lay dead, executed on trumped up charges of treason. From this point, the tottering Western Roman Empire was to take a 60-year stuttering plunge into oblivion.

Young Arcadius was slothful, and weak both of intellect and character. His clash of wills with the Bishop of Constantinople, the saintly but outspoken John Chrysostom (**top left**), established the emperor's supremacy over Church affairs in the East, in stark contrast to the pope's position in the West.

Fall of the West

The last 70 years of the Western Roman Empire were blighted by a sorry series of emperors dominated by strong regents, most of them barbarians by birth. It was also a time during which increasing numbers of barbarians took service in the legions that had once protected the empire and made the army's loyalties fragile.

With Stilicho dead, Alaric's Goths invaded Italy and, ignoring the capital Ravenna, besieged Rome in 408. He was paid off, only to return in 409. Although he was kept outside the walls, he managed to set up a short-lived puppet emperor. But when he failed to wring a favourable treaty out of Honorius in 410, the Goths broke in and pillaged Rome, which had not been taken by a foreign foe for over 800 years. During the sack the Goths seized the emperor's half-sister, Galla Placidia, who was staying there, and carried her off as a hostage.

She appears to have been reconciled to her capture, and later married Alaric's half-brother Athaulf, who had become king of the Goths after Alaric's sudden death at the end of 410. Athaulf fell to an assassin's sword in 415 and, as part of a treaty completed by 418, Galla Placidia was sent to Ravenna in return for the Goths being allowed to settle in southwestern France, with their capital at Toulouse. The man who had brought about the treaty through force and negotiation, was named Flavius Constantius. His first service to Honorius had been the defeat of the usurping Emperor Constantine III in 411. Now, as a reward, he was allowed to marry Placidia (whom he had always loved), and Honorius elevated him in 421 to co-Augustus as Constantius III.

However, Theodosius II, now ruling in Constantinople since the death of his father Arcadius in 408, refused to recognise Constantius as a co-ruler. War between the two empires loomed, but was again averted when Constantius died of natural causes only seven months after his elevation to the purple.

Two years later, ineffectual Honorius also lay dead, and Galla Placidia ruled in the West as regent to her infant son by Constantius, Valentinian III. Despite her vigorous determination, Placidia was unable to prevent endless squabbling between her generals, the loss of Africa to invading Vandals under King Gaiseric,

A coin of the Visigoth Alaric, scourge of Italy.

Gaiseric moves the Vandal nation from Baetica to Africa in 428.

first capital of Vandal kingdom

	Italy and territory owing allegiance to Ravenna		Vandal kingdom
	nominal Roman allegiance in urban centres		Eastern Roman Empire
	Visigothic kingdom	→	campaign of Attila, 451–52
	Frankish kingdoms	→	initial Vandal sea-raids on Italia
	Burgundian kingdom	- - -	East-West division of empire
	Suevic kingdom		

or the depradations of the Huns under their leader Attila – the 'Scourge of Christendom'. She died in 450, only months after a combined army of Visigoths and Romans had defeated Attila's horde in the battle of the Catalaunian Plain, near modern Châlons-sur-Marne. Attila took his revenge on northern Italy in the following year, and was only prevented from sacking Rome by the intervention of saintly Pope Leo I. Attila retired from Italy and began planning an assault on Constantinople, but died in 453, after which his nation of Huns dispersed and faded from history, having wreaked havoc on all of Europe.

The final collapse

Valentinian III, his mother's puppet, followed her to the grave with the assistance of two assassins in 455, and with no males of the Theodosian dynasty left, the Western Empire fell into the hands of a series of 'shadow' emperors. Except for the first two, these were creatures of the barbarian warlords of the army, Ricimer and later the Burgundian prince, Gundobad. The first, Petronius Maximus (r.455), was torn limb from limb by his rioting guards just before the Vandal Gaiseric landed and sacked poor Rome for its second time.

Only the third, Majorian (r.457–61) showed any spirit and calibre. The ninth and last was a 14-year-old boy named Romulus Augustulus, who was proclaimed emperor in 475. His father Orestes, who had succeeded Gundobad as king-maker, was a true Roman by birth, which perhaps explains the loathing he felt for the barbarian army that now paraded under Roman arms. When the soldiers demanded a similar settlement for themselves as had been given to the Visigoths, Orestes refused them. He had reason – the Visigoths had settled out of the way in Gaul; Orestes' men wanted one-third of all Italy.

Led by a Herulian Goth named Odoacer, the troops rebelled. Orestes was taken and slain at Piacenza and a few days later Romulus Augustulus was captured at Ravenna. Moved to pity at the boy's plight, on 4 September 476, Odoacer retired the last emperor of the West, and declared himself King of Italy and Illyricum.

Above: The Vandal Gaiseric was to be the bane of the Roman Empire for another 22 years.

Majorian was the first army man to head the West in 70 years. His military and administrative skills worked against him, and Ricimer was soon casting about for a more amenable puppet ruler.

The child Romulus Augustulus was the last Roman 'ruler' of the Western Empire.

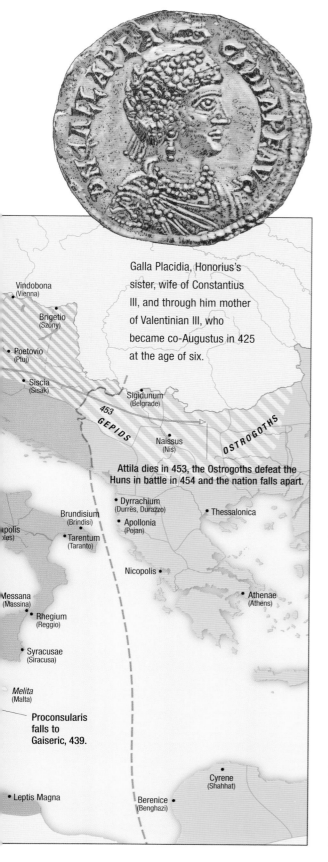

Galla Placidia, Honorius's sister, wife of Constantius III, and through him mother of Valentinian III, who became co-Augustus in 425 at the age of six.

Vindobona (Vienna)
Brigetio (Szöny)
Poetovio (Ptuj)
Siscia (Sisak)
Sigidunum (Belgrade)
453 GEPIDS
Naissus (Nis)
OSTROGOTHS

Attila dies in 453, the Ostrogoths defeat the Huns in battle in 454 and the nation falls apart.

Dyrrachium (Durrës, Durazzo)
Brundisium (Brindisi)
Apollonia (Pojan)
Thessalonica
...apolis ...les)
Tarentum (Taranto)
Nicopolis
Messana (Massina)
Rhegium (Reggio)
Athenae (Athens)
Syracusae (Siracusa)
Melita (Malta)
Proconsularis falls to Gaiseric, 439.
Cyrene (Shahhat)
Leptis Magna
Berenice (Benghazi)

Rome – Retaken and Lost

As the Western Roman Empire declined, Constantinople grew in power through the efforts of a series of non-dynastic emperors and a strong army commanded by German generals of capability.

In the East Theodosius II (r.408–450), who was only seven, succeeded his dull father Arcadius. Initially under the regency of his high-principled praetorian prefect Anthemius and, after Anthemius died in 414, under the influence of his older sister, the Augusta Aelia Pulcheria, he provided Constantinople with a relatively settled reign. Although weak and easily led, Theodosius possessed the charm his father had lacked. He was an earnest student in Latin and Greek classics, mathematics, natural sciences and in art, and became such an adept at illuminating manuscripts that he was given the Greek nickname *Kalligraphos*.

His greatest legacy was the publication of the first great pandect of Roman law. In the age since Diocletian, when the last comprehensive law code had been issued, a large number of general constitutions had been published. Some were no longer relevant, and many more were unworkable or contradictory. After nine years' work, the *Codex Theodosianus* was finally promulgated on 15 February 438 jointly in the senates of Rome and Constantinople (Rome still having the status of the centre of Western jurisprudence).

The code had enormous influence, both in itself and in future legal history. Together with the work of the early third-century Hadrianic jurists Ulpian, Papinian and Julius Paulus, it became the basis for Justinian's much more ambitious judicial reforms in the following century (*see page 30*). It is also possible to trace considerable portions of King Alaric II's *Lex Romana Visigothorum* of 507 to the *Codex Theodosianus*.

An open question

At peace with the Sassanian Empire, the major concern for Theodosius was Attila, who had been receiving tribute for several years. When Attila demanded a doubling of the tribute in 447, Theodosius refused. The Huns invaded and laid waste entire swathes of Macedonia, Moesia and Thrace, eventually being halted by the massive new walls around Constantinople that prescient Anthemius had completed only years before. In the end, the situation was resolved by Attila's

determination to invade the West, and Constantinople was left to begin the provincial reconstruction. Attila's removal coincided with the death of Theodosius, who was killed by a fall from his horse while out hunting on 28 July 450.

His sudden death left the question of the succession open for the first time in over sixty years, since his only surviving child, Licinia Eudoxia, had married Valentinian III. As the Augusta, Theodosius's sister Aelia Pulcheria was

Theodosius II (**his coin above**) was studious and weak. Secluded in a court dominated by the pursuit of religion, he was content to leave the running of

Map labels

SA[...]

Noviodunu
(Soissons)

KINGDOM OF SYAGRIUS

Lutetia
(Paris)

ARMORICANI

Cenabum Aureliani
(Orléans)

469 ✗
Visigothic king Euric defeats Riothamus of Amorica.

Liger (Loire)

Avernum
(Auvergne)
to Visigoths, 474/5

Augustonemetum
(Clermont-Ferrand)

Duranius (Dordogne)

Burdigala
(Bordeaux)

Garumna (Garonne)

Tolosa ▣
(Toulouse)

Narbo
(Narbonne)

PYRENEES

Urbicus (Orbigo)

VASCONI
(Basques)

Brigantium
(La Coruña)

SUEVI

Asturica Augusta
(Astorga)

Legio (León)

456 Urbicus
Visigoths destroy Suevic power in Hispania.

Gallicia

Portus Cale
(Oporto)

Durius (Duero)

Cauca
(Coca)

Caesaraugusta
(Zaragoza)

Iberus (Ebro)

Tarraco
(Tarragona)

VISIGOTHIC KINGDOM

Tagus

Toletum
(Toledo)

Valentia
(Valencia)

Balearic Islands
to Vandal kingdom

Olisipo
(Lisbon)

Anas (Guadiana)

Emerita Augusta
(Mérida)

Baetis (Guadalquivir)

Corduba

Hispalis
(Sevilla)

Baetica

Carthago Nova
(Cartagena)

Gades
(Cadiz)

Malaca
(Málaga)

Cartennae
(Ténès)

Caesarea
(Cherchell)

Tingis
(Tangier)

Septem
(Ceuta)

Siga
(Takembrit)

The Western Roman Empire at the deposition of Romulus Augustulus, 476

	Western 'Roman' kingdom of Odoacer
	'Roman' kingdom of Aegidius and Syagrius 462–86
	Visigothic kingdom and Ostrogoths in the East
	Frankish kingdoms
	Burgundian kingdom
	Suevic kingdom (under Visigothic domination)
	Vandal kingdom
	Eastern Roman Empire

East-West division of Empire

◼ capital city

FRANKS

Colonia (Köln, Cologne)

Moguntiacum (Mainz)

◼ Treveri (Trier) **RIPURARIAN FRANKS**

Rhenus

rocatalauni (álons-sur-Marne)

Argentorate (Strasbourg)

Danuvius **THURINGII**

ALAMANNI

ALAMANNI

(Saône) **RGUNDIAN KINGDOM**

Aventicum (Avenches)

Rhodanus Raetia

Lugdunum Vienna (Vienne)

Augusta Taurinorum (Turin)

Ticinum (Pavia)

Mediolanum (Milan)

Liguria

Verona

Placentia (Piacenza)

Aemilia

Alpes Cottiae

Valentia (Valence)

vennio (Avignon)

ate

Nicaea (Nice)

Sinus Ligusticus (Ligurian Sea)

Massilia (Marseilles)

LANGOBARDI (Lombards)

Vindobona (Vienna)

Brigetio (Szőny)

OSTROGOTHIC KINGDOM

Only nominal Roman control

Virinum (Maria Saal)

Poetovio (Ptuj)

Dravus

Histria

P a n n o n i a

Venetia

Aquileia

Siscia (Sisak)

Savus

◼ Ravenna

Flaminia

Dalmatia effective control to Eastern empire

Salonae (Solin)

GEPIDAE

Sigidunum (Beograd, Belgrade)

OSTROGOTHS

Danuvius

OSTROGOTHS

GEPIDAE

Praevalitana

Naissus (Niš)

Only nominal Roman control

Dacia

Moesia II

Thracia

Rhodope

Corsica to Vandal kingdom

Aleria (Aléria)

✗ **456** Ricimer's fleet destroys the Vandal navy.

Tuscia et Umbria

Tiberis

Picenum

Sámnium

Roma

Campania

MARE ADRIATICUM (ADRIATIC SEA)

Dyrrachium (Durrës, Durazzo)

Macedonia

Thessalonica

Apollonia (Pojan)

Epirus

Sardinia to Vandal kingdom

Neapolis (Napoli, Naples)

Apulia et Calabria

MARE TYRRHENUM (TYRRHENIAN SEA)

Lucania et Brutti

Brundisium (Brindisi)

Tarentum (Taranto)

Nicopolis

Thessalia

Achaea

MARE AEGEUM (AEGEAN SEA)

Caralis (Cagliari)

to Vandal kingdom

Panormus (Palermo)

Messana (Massina)

Rhegium (Reggio)

Athenae (Athens)

MARE IONI-UM (IONIAN SEA)

Lilybaeum (Marsala)

Sicilia

Agrigentum (Agrigento) ✗

Syracusae (Siracusa)

456 Ricimer regains most of Sicilia after defeating the occupying Vandal army.

Creta

Hippo Regius (Annaba)

◼ Carthago

Melita (Malta)

VANDAL KINGDOM

Hadrumetum (Sousse)

M A R E   I N T E R N U M (M E D I T E R R A N E A N   S E A)

Cyrene (Shahhat)

Libya Inferior

Oea (Tripoli)

Leptis Magna

Berenice (Banghazi)

Libya Superior

affairs of state to his strong-willed sister, Empress Aelia Pulcheria, **(her coin above)**.

the logical choice for the throne. She was not, however, the obvious candidate – no woman had ever succeeded to the Roman Empire. Flavius Aspar – son of Theodosius the Great's German general Ardaburius – who had attained the supreme rank of patrician and enjoyed a similar position at Constantinople to that of Ricimer in

Italy – solved the problem. He selected a staff officer named Marcian (r.450–57) and married him to Pulcheria. Marcian received the acclamation of the Senate and the army on 25 August, when the bishop of Constantinople placed the imperial diadem on his head – it was the first instance of a religious coronation.

Council of Chalcedon

Marcian's seven-year reign was something of a golden age.
He secured the political and financial security of the East, established
the orthodox line that future Byzantine emperors would support and
achieved a remarkable degree of political stability. Religious unrest,
however, was another matter.

Right: Coin of Marcian.
His policy of denying Attila
paid off, and the Huns left
Constantinople alone as
they went to ravage the
Western Empire. But his
freedom was largely
illusory, since he was as
much the creature of his
Patrician, the Teutonic
Aspar, as was Majorian of
Ricimer in Ravenna.

Much of Marcian's success was down to
luck. Instead of having to face down Attila
the Hun – who had departed for his campaign
against the West – Marcian's treasury filled up
without the drain of barbarian tribute Theodosius
had had to pay. Consequently he was able to
relieve the populace and the nobility of many
hated taxes, further grace the capital with fine
new buildings, and attend to the proper
administration of justice. Marcian also saved
money by actively avoiding confrontation: the
assassination of Valentinian III and the subsequent
Vandal sack of Rome in 455 were met with
silence from the East.

The chief event of his reign was the Council
of Chalcedon convened in 451 to end the violent
quarrel between the Christians of Alexandria
(known as monophysites) and those of Antioch.
The monophysites stressed Christ's singular
divinity, while those of Antioch insisted that
Christ had a human nature because he needed to
be truly human if he were to be considered the
saviour of humankind. The council's outcome
was a compromise in that it combined both
concepts. However, in the statement known as
the Chalcedonian Definition, it also declared
monophysitism a heresy – the quarrel was not
ended, it was just beginning.

At the same council the outnumbered papal
legates were forced to accept a decree known as
Canon Twenty-Eight. This stated that the see of
Constantinople should rank second only to that
of Rome, that its bishop be given the title

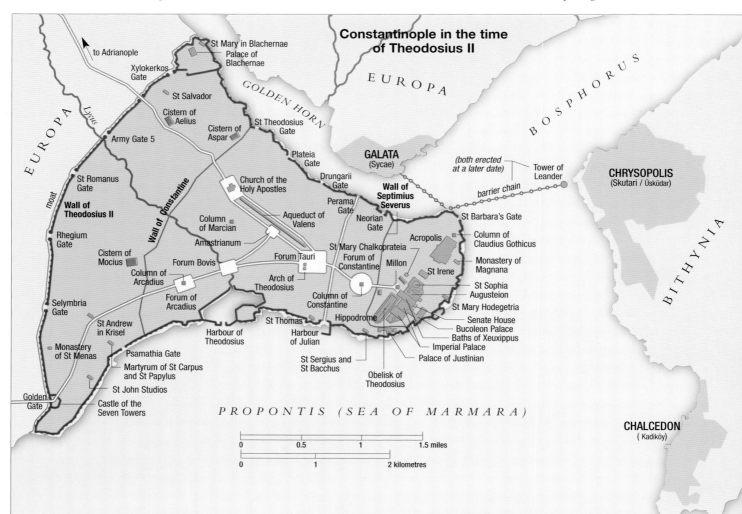

**Constantinople in the time
of Theodosius II**

to Adrianople

St Mary in Blachernae
Palace of
Blachernae

Xylokerkos
Gate

EUROPA

GOLDEN HORN

St Salvador

Cistern of
Aelius

Cistern of
Aspar

St Theodosius
Gate

Army Gate 5

Plateia
Gate

GALATA
(Sycae)

BOSPHORUS

(both erected
at a later date)

Tower of
Leander

CHRYSOPOLIS
(Skutari / Üsküdar)

Lycus

EUROPA

St Romanus
Gate

moat

Wall of
Theodosius II

Wall of Constantine

Church of the
Holy Apostles

Drungarii
Gate

Wall of
Septimius
Severus

barrier chain

St Barbara's Gate

Rhegium
Gate

Column
of Marcian

Aqueduct of
Valens

Perama
Gate

Neorian
Gate

Acropolis

Column of
Claudius Gothicus

Cistern of
Mocius

Amastrianum

Forum Tauri

St Mary Chalkoprateia

Forum of
Constantine

Millon

St Irene

Monastery of
Magnana

Column of
Arcadius

Forum Bovis

Arch of
Theodosius

St Sophia
Augusteion

Selymbria
Gate

Forum of
Arcadius

Column of
Constantine

St Mary Hodegetria

St Andrew
in Krisel

St Thomas

Harbour of
Theodosius

Harbour
of Julian

Hippodrome

Senate House
Bucoleon Palace
Baths of Xeuxippus
Imperial Palace
Palace of Justinian

BITHYNIA

Monastery
of St Menas

Psamathia Gate

Martyrum of St Carpus
and St Papylus

St Sergius and
St Bacchus

Obelisk of
Theodosius

Golden
Gate

St John Studios

Castle of the
Seven Towers

PROPONTIS (SEA OF MARMARA)

CHALCEDON
(Kadiköy)

0   0.5   1   1.5 miles

0   1   2 kilometres

'patriarch', and its control be extended to cover the whole Eastern Empire. The implication was clear: from now on the pope's supremacy would be titular, and that the two sees would in reality be equal. It was the beginning of the rivalry between the Latin and Orthodox Churches that would grow increasingly bitter over the centuries.

Pulcheria died in 453 and Marcian followed her aged 65 in January 457. With no son to succeed him, it was widely believed that the Patrician would declare for himself, but two things counted against Aspar: his barbarian birth and, worse, he professed the Arian creed. Like Ricimer, he contented himself with being a king-maker, and dipped again into his military staff to produce the orthodox Flavius Valerius Leo (r.457–74).

However, Leo – possessed of sound common sense and an independent mind – was no puppet ruler. He quickly learned how to play the various factions at court off against each other and drew the confidence to resist the too imperious edicts of Aspar. A row soon developed between them, and Leo determined to rid Constantinople of the powerful Teutonic faction of which Aspar was the most distinguished member. In purging the army of Germans, Leo recruited from among the wild mountain tribes of Isauria, and made his chief advisor a chieftain named Tarasicodissa Rusumbladeotus. The mouthful of a name was conveniently changed to Zeno when he married Leo's daughter Ariadne. This honour indicated that Zeno was the head of the anti-Aspar party and that – after Ariadne gave birth to a son also named Leo – he would secure the succession either for himself or his son.

A battle for the throne

But there was another contender, Basiliscus, the brother of Leo's wife, the Augusta Aelia Verina. Basiliscus was a buffoon with only one thought in his limited mind – to one day have his brother-in-law's diadem. In his search for glory, through the offices of his sister, Basiliscus had himself appointed commander of the joint East-West expedition to regain Africa from Gaiseric

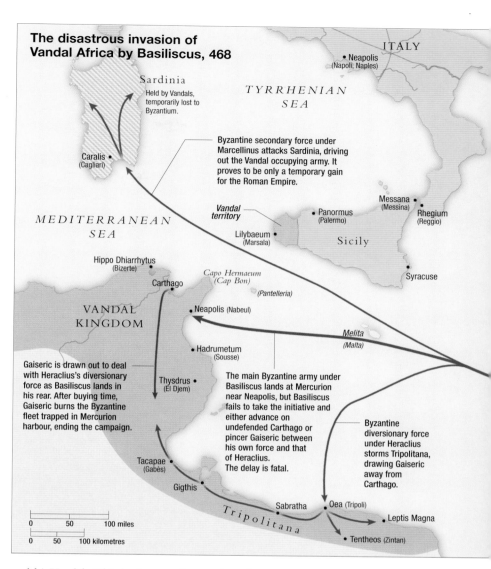

The disastrous invasion of Vandal Africa by Basiliscus, 468

ITALY

Neapolis (Napoli; Naples)

Sardinia
Held by Vandals, temporarily lost to Byzantium.

TYRRHENIAN SEA

Byzantine secondary force under Marcellinus attacks Sardinia, driving out the Vandal occupying army. It proves to be only a temporary gain for the Roman Empire.

Caralis (Cagliari)

MEDITERRANEAN SEA

Vandal territory

Messana (Messina)

Rhegium (Reggio)

Panormus (Palermo)

Lilybaeum (Marsala)

Sicily

Syracuse

Hippo Dhiarrhytus (Bizerte)

Carthago

Capo Hermaeum (Cap Bon)

(Pantelleria)

VANDAL KINGDOM

Neapolis (Nabeul)

Melita (Malta)

Gaiseric is drawn out to deal with Heraclius's diversionary force as Basiliscus lands in his rear. After buying time, Gaiseric burns the Byzantine fleet trapped in Mercurion harbour, ending the campaign.

Hadrumetum (Sousse)

Thysdrus (El Djem)

The main Byzantine army under Basiliscus lands at Mercurion near Neapolis, but Basiliscus fails to take the initiative and either advance on undefended Carthago or pincer Gaiseric between his own force and that of Heraclius. The delay is fatal.

Byzantine diversionary force under Heraclius storms Tripolitana, drawing Gaiseric away from Carthago.

Tacapae (Gabès)

Gigthis

Tripolitana

Sabratha

Oea (Tripoli)

Leptis Magna

Tentheos (Zintan)

0   50   100 miles
0   50   100 kilometres

and his Vandals. This had come about when the puppet-emperor Severus died in 467 and Ricimer suggested Leo's son-in-law Anthemius as the next emperor for the West in return for Leo funding the campaign. But Basiliscus bungled everything. Wily Gaiseric ran rings around him, and the costly enterprise foundered in disaster off the Carthaginian coast in 468.

Basiliscus was spared, but eclipsed by the increasingly powerful Zeno who finally brought down Aspar and with him the German faction. Zeno looked to the septuagenarian Leo's gratitude in the succession but unwilling to give too much direct power to the Isaurian faction, when Leo died in February 474, the throne went to his grandson, Leo II. Nevertheless, Zeno had himself proclaimed co-Augustus, and when his infant son fell ill and died nine months later, he became sole emperor. It was not a situation that the dowager Empress Verina and her brother Basiliscus would tolerate. They conspired successfully with anti-Zeno elements in the court to bring him down. In November 475, fearing for his life, Zeno packed up and fled the capital with his family to Cilicia, leaving Basiliscus to proclaim himself Augustus.

Left above: Bust and coin of Leo I, another man raised to supreme power by Aspar, but one who proved to be no puppet in the Patrician's hands.

The Great Schism

The monophysite quarrel with orthodoxy was to dog the twin reigns of Basiliscus and Zeno. The former was an ardent monophysite, while the latter paid only lip service to the orthodox creed. Constantine the Great's insistence on a unified Church and State came crumbling down in bitter recriminations on all sides of the debate.

Right: An early coin of Zeno bears the simple inscription LEO ET ZENO, as Leo's son-in-law Zeno expected to be next in line but was passed over for his own young son Leo II. However, through the offices of his mother Ariadne, he raised his father to be co-Augustus with him – and died shortly afterwards.

Basiliscus (**below**) – an ineffective and clumsy ruler – was usually at loggerheads with his far more able but meddlesome sister, the empress-dowager Aelia Verina (**bottom**).

Basiliscus was as useless a ruler as general. In short order he had every Isaurian in the capital slaughtered, lost Verina's backing by having her ambitious senatorial lover executed, levied swingeing taxes on every class of society and angered the Church by openly expressing his heretical monophysite opinions.

The monophysite bishop Timotheus Ailouros (the Weasel) had been expelled from his see of Alexandria in 460 after the Council of Chalcedon and Constantinople installed the orthodox Timotheus Solophaciolus in his place. In 475 Basiliscus removed Solophaciolus and returned the see to Timotheus, who promptly demanded the abrogation of the Council's decrees and the abolishment of the patriarchate of Constantinople. Basiliscus was only dissuaded from carrying out this outrageous programme by Daniel, the city's famous *stylite* (*see pages 36–7*). He descended from his pillar for the first (and only) time in 15 years to intercede by haranguing the emperor and terrifying him into withdrawing his edict.

When, in the following year, a disastrous fire swept through the city, destroying the marvellous library of Julian in the process, people saw it as retribution for their evil emperor's actions, and his days were numbered. In July 477, Zeno was swept back into power by popular acclaim, and Basiliscus banished to the wilds of Cappadocia where he later died of starvation; meddlesome Verina was locked up in an Isaurian convent.

In the same year, Timothy the Weasel also died. At this point there were two contenders for the see of Alexandria: the orthodox John Talaia and the monophysite Peter Mongos (the Stammerer). But Zeno returned the vacant see to Solophaciolus, which he held until his death in 481, despite enormous unrest from the numerically superior monophysites. In 482 Zeno and Acacius, the patriarch of Constantinople, attempted to heal the breach between the dangerously disaffected monophysite eastern provinces and the Church through an edict known as the Act of Union, or *Henoticon*. It sought to mend the differences by affirming that Christ was both God and man, but it conspicuously avoided the delicate word 'nature'. As a compromise it was unsuccessful, predictably arousing the ire of all parties. In Rome, Pope Simplicius and his successor Felix III were particularly outraged.

For years Zeno had held John Talaia in esteem, but for some reason Acacius hated him. When the Alexandrian Catholics elected Talaia to the see, he announced his succession to Rome and Antioch, according to custom, but he sent no message to Acacius in Constantinople. The patriarch seized his chance to poison Zeno against Talaia, championing instead Mongos. In the following year the unimpeachably orthodox Talaia refused to sign the *Henoticon*, whereas politically astute Mongos said he would. Zeno ordered Talaia expelled from Alexandria and replaced him with Peter Mongos.

A religious tit for tat

Talaia now fled to Rome and made his case to Pope Felix, who defended his rights to Acacius and refused to accept Mongos. Stubborn Acacius refused to accede to the pope's demands, and at a synod held in Rome in 484 Felix had the patriarch excommunicated. So the story goes, there was no orthodox ecclesiastic courageous enough to read out the papal proclamation, so instead it was written out on a scrap of parchment and pinned to the back of the patriarch's cope when he was not looking, during a service in St Sophia. When he discovered it a few minutes later, the fuming Acacius instantly excommunicated Felix in turn.

This action declared that Constantinople now stood at the same hierarchical level as Rome, and the open schism between the two Churches was to last for thirty-five years. It was not the outcome that fumbling Zeno had hoped for.

Dying without further issue in April 491, Zeno was succeeded by a native of Dyrrachium by the name of Flavius Anastasius and by virtue of his immediate marriage to Zeno's widow, Ariadne. In his early sixties, Anastasius was a well-respected courtier notorious for his piety and for his meanness with money. During his reign, Constantinople became a dull place to live, but unfortunately not peaceful. He faced a four-year war with Persia, which arguably the Sassanians won by settling for an indemnity payment, a series of raids into Thrace by encroaching Bulgars, and the rebellion of a disaffected Gothic army officer named Vitalian. Leading several amphibious raids on Constantinople, Vitalian actually managed to briefly besiege Constantinople itself, before his forces were scattered through the efforts of a young Thracian officer of the *excubitorii* (imperial guard) named Justin.

However, the worst threat to Anastasius came from inside the capital itself in 510–11, when he was almost deposed by the rioting factions of Greens and Blues (*see pages 34-5*). In the event, the emperor managed to calm the situation, and died peacefully in his bed at the age of 87. Having already passed over his three nephews, he handed the empire to the tough officer of the excubitors, now their Count, the Thracian Justin.

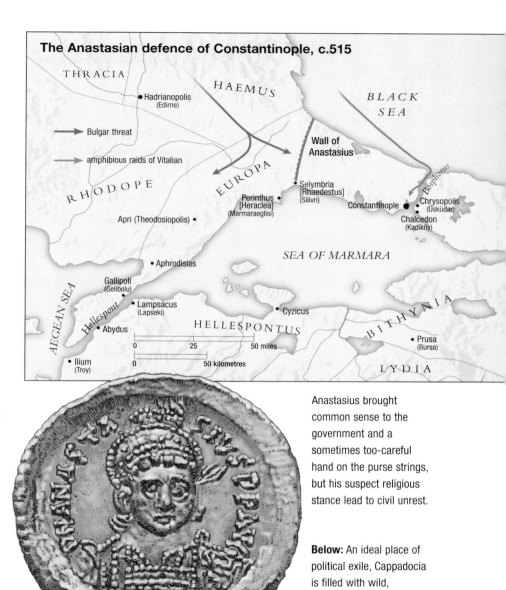

The Anastasian defence of Constantinople, c.515

Anastasius brought common sense to the government and a sometimes too-careful hand on the purse strings, but his suspect religious stance lead to civil unrest.

Below: An ideal place of political exile, Cappadocia is filled with wild, inhospitable landscapes.

Reconciliation: Justin and Justinian

Unlettered, Latin-speaking, the rough soldier from Thrace brought a solid spirit of Catholic orthodoxy to Constantinople. But it was Justin's clever, educated nephew Justinian who would bring a new golden age to the empire, and a final return to ancient Roman ways before the East slipped firmly into the Byzantine era.

Right: Justin, an illiterate Latin speaker from Thrace, was the right man in the right place at the right time, but it was his nephew Justinian who returned true stability to Byzantium.

The man who stepped into Anastasius's shoes was hardly imperial material. Justin (r.518–27) never learned to read or write, and like Theodoric – the great Ostrogothic king who Leo I had dispatched in 493 to Italy to seize it from Odoacer the Herulian – required the use of a stencil to make his signature. But Justin cherished a noble ambition: to heal the schism and reconcile the Latin and Eastern Churches.

The credit for this most important achievement must go to his clever nephew Justinian, who guided his uncle in all things. Born in 482 in the small hamlet of Tauresium, close to the birthplace of his uncle, Justinian came to Constantinople as a child, where he received a classical and legal education. In the year of his uncle's accession, the new regime moved swiftly to re-establish orthodoxy. On 1 August Justin wrote to Pope Hormisdas informing him of his wishes for reconciliation. The letter was drafted by Justinian, who at thirty-six was maturing his talent for theological disputation.

Hormisdas declined the invitation to go to Constantinople in person, but he sent a delegation to set out Rome's non-negotiable position. The papal legates were provided with an *indiculus*, instructions on how far they were to go

Above: The Herulian king Odoacer, who had ousted Romulus Augustulus and founded a barbarian kingdom of Italy under the nominal sovereignty of Constantinople, was in turn defeated by the Ostrogothic Theodoric (**right**) under Leo I's orders. Under King Theodoric Italy enjoyed a peace and prosperity that few imperial Romans had managed for almost a hundred years.

in negotiation (hardly anywhere, since they had been forbidden to enter into debate), and a *libellus*, or formula of submission to be signed by all who wished reunion with the see of Rome.

Predictably, John II, the new patriarch, was a bit sniffy about being seen to bow to pressure from Rome, but when on 26 March 519 the impatient emperor demanded he accede, John reluctantly agreed, and the *libellus* was signed by all parties. The *Henoticon* was repudiated, and Acacius, Timothy the Weasel, Paul the Stammerer, and the emperors Zeno and Anastasius were posthumously excommunicated. Some saw the accord as an unconditional surrender for

In a public relations exercise, Justinian, on the right, is seen in tandem with Constantine I in a mosaic that emphasises his status as co-equal of the great emperor and founder of Constantinople. While Constantine holds out to the Virgin and Christ a model of the city he built, Justinian offers a symbol of his massive church-building programme.

Constantinople, but it was a price Justin was willing to pay for a reunited Church.

In the following year Justinian met his future empress – one of late antiquity's most infamous women. Theodora, the daughter of a common bear-keeper employed at the hippodrome, was an accomplished mime and player of low comedy. She was also one of the capital's most notorious courtesans. They met during a race at the hippodrome, and now in her thirties, she immediately captivated him.

Taxes for churches

However, there were obstacles in their path to marriage. One was the law that forbade senators to marry actresses; another was the opposition of the empress. Justin's low-born wife Euphemia had retained her peasant attitude to one of baser extraction than herself, even though she was fond of her nephew, and supported him in most of his wishes. Against Theodora, however, she was implacable, and the marriage was impossible while she lived.

But after her death in 524, Justin was willing to clear the way. He had the law changed to allow an actress who abandoned her profession to marry whosoever she chose. With the way clear, Justinian and Theodora were wed in due pomp in St Sophia. Two years later, on 4 April 527, they were crowned jointly as co-Augustus and Augusta, and when Justin died on the first day of August in the same year, they found themselves the sole rulers of the Roman Empire.

For all that Justinian (r.527–65) achieved much

during his reign, he was not a popular ruler. His reforms of taxation in order to produce the funds necessary for his lavish church-building programme were partly to blame. In part it was because of his court's aloofness from the people, although this was much more due to the empress than the generally affable Justinian. Theodora's monophysite tendencies were distrusted, she was extravagant, lazy in life though ruthless with courtiers, cruel and surrounded herself with unapproachable magnificence. But Justinian must be blamed for the political unrest that almost ended his reign in 532 following his abandonment of the Blues once he no longer required their political support (*see pages 34–5*).

Much dislike in the provinces stemmed from the actions of Justinian's tax administrator, John of Cappadocia, who centralised the bureaucracy and reduced the powers of provincial officials. His morals matched his methods when he thought someone was hiding wealth from him. Suspects were frequently subjected to torture; he was a glutton and a drunkard who, in his travels through the provinces 'left behind not a single vessel of any kind; neither was there any wife, any virgin or any youth free of defilement'.†

However, it is for his magnificent legal *Codex* and for his attempt to recover and reunite again the ancient Roman Empire that Justinian is most remembered.

Empress Theodora, seen here from a contemporary Byzantine mosaic.

Left: Theodoric's mausoleum in Ravenna is a masterpiece of late Roman architecture. Its massive domed roof weighs 304.8 tonnes (300 tons).

† Procopius, *Annecdota*

New Laws, New Silk

In his long and sometimes muddled reign, Justinian achieved two great triumphs: a codification of laws that have guided the jurisprudence of nations ever since and the breaking of the Chinese monopoly over the most precious commodity of all – silk

Almost a century had passed since Theodosius II's recodification of the law in 438, but that had been a relatively simple exercise of compiling imperial edicts. Justinian's ambition was a total overhaul, an entirely new code that would substitute clarity for confusion. To head the commission he appointed a leading jurist named Tribonian, a completely corrupt judge for whom the outcome of a court case was for sale to the highest bidder.

However, Tribonian was also charming, an expert on the law and erudite. He was efficient, too, and set about the task with unbelievable speed. By 8 April 529, in less than 14 months, he produced the new *Codex*. It became the supreme authority for every court in the empire one week later. In 530 a codification of the writings of all the ancient Roman jurists was begun, in which

some three million clauses were condensed into 150,000. Collectively known as the *Digest* or *Pandects*, it was completed within three years. In 533 the *Institutes* were published, extracts from the two main books intended for use by law students.

In everything that was done in the recodification, Justinian ensured that there was nothing incompatible with Christian teaching, and he continued working on legal reforms up to his death: his last law fixed the official date of Christmas. The text in all these works was in Latin, but that was an exception; in almost all cases the language of Constantinople and the empire was now Greek.

Justinian's legislation makes it clear that the old worship had not yet been entirely eradicated. Pagans were barred from the civil service, and Christians who became apostate were condemned to death, as was any person discovered making a secret sacrifice to the old gods. As had occurred previously, classical scholars were expected to demonstrate their faith through baptism or be denied payment for their work and face banishment.

Map inset: Silk worms were the great Chinese secret, but when some Christian monks were able to steal a consignment of eggs from contacts beyond the River Oxus the most precious commodity of the time fell into Justinian's hands.

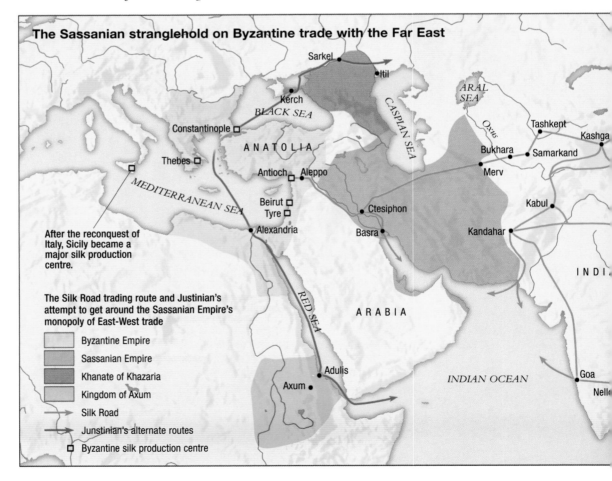

The Sassanian stranglehold on Byzantine trade with the Far East

After the reconquest of Italy, Sicily became a major silk production centre.

The Silk Road trading route and Justinian's attempt to get around the Sassanian Empire's monopoly of East-West trade

- Byzantine Empire
- Sassanian Empire
- Khanate of Khazaria
- Kingdom of Axum
- Silk Road
- Junstinian's alternate routes
- Byzantine silk production centre

A new industry

By the mid-sixth century Constantinople sat at the centre of trade between Europe and Asia, straddling the route between the Mediterranean and the Orient. With the decline of the impoverished West, the distant markets of China and the Indies became far more important, for spices, precious gems and – above all – silk. But for Byzantine merchants there was the perennial problem of Persia which sat smack in between. Once caravans coming from the East reached the Oxus river, they entered the Sassanian Empire, and the king levied heavy taxes, forbade at whim the trade in some goods at different times, and even suspended trade when there was a war – which was most of the time.

Since Persia would not allow Byzantine merchants to trade directly, even when relations between the two powers were going smoothly, the Persian middlemen took huge commissions. Justinian, determined to break this stranglehold, opened up two new routes. The northern one bypassed Persia by going via the Crimea and the Caucasus, where Byzantine traders were already doing good business, while the southern went through Egypt, the Red Sea and the Christian

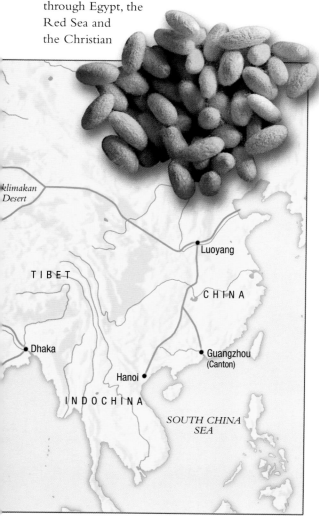

kingdom of Axum. Due to the vagaries of weather and the uncertain temper of local tribes, the first was not particularly successful; the second failed because the Persians had too strong a grip on the Indian ports.

When some orthodox monks approached the emperor to tell him that they could obtain some silkworm eggs from contacts beyond the Oxus, Justinian jumped at the opportunity. It was one of China's most closely guarded secrets, but the monks managed to get hold of not only a quantity of eggs, but also the technical knowledge to create a silk industry. By the end of the 530s silk factories had been set up around Constantinople, at Antioch, Tyre, Beirut and at Thebes in Greece.

Justinian ensured that the factories were under imperial control and silk-making remained a nationalised industry, becoming the most profitable in the empire, and a valuable source of imperial income for centuries.

Justinian with his senior advisors. The man standing to the left of the emperor is Belisarius, the greatest general of his time (*see the following page*). Justinian is seen standing on Belisarius's foot. This is probably intended to symbolise that Justinian can rely on (stand on) his right-hand man. The mosaic in Constantinople has been lost, but this contemporary version from the church of San Vitale, Ravenna is undoubtedly an accurate copy of the original.

Restoring the Empire

Having reconciled the papacy and the patriarchy, Justin's next dream was to recover the lost provinces of Africa, Italy and Spain, but its realisation fell to Justinian. In this huge enterprise he was blessed in the talented general, Belisarius, who went much of the way to accomplish this mission.

Belisarius, a young Thracian soldier, came to prominence in 530 when he won a spectacular victory against superior Persian forces at Daras in Mesopotamia. Two years later he was instrumental in helping to put down the terrible Nikā Revolt of Greens and Blues (*see pages 34-5*). Justinian picked him as the man to retake Africa from the Vandals. The pretext was the overthrow of King Hilderic, Gaiseric's grandson, by his cousin Gelimer. Since Hilderic was a Catholic (his mother Eudocia was Valentinian III's daughter, seized during the Vandal sack of Rome in 455) and Gelimer was typically an Arian, it became Justinian's sacred duty to invade and restore Hilderic.

The fleet of 500 transports manned by 20,000 sailors, and accompanied by 92 *dromones* (the Byzantine navy's speedy attack ship), set out in the summer of 533. On board were 10,000 infantry and 5,000 cavalry, composed of regular soldiers and a larger portion of barbarian auxiliaries. After a brief pause in Ostrogothic Sicily, technically still friendly to Constantinople, the fleet landed on the North African coast, disembarked the troops and

then shadowed their 50-mile northward march along the coast to Carthage.

As soon as Gelimer heard of the invasion, he had Hilderic and his family murdered, and prepared to meet the Byzantine army. But Belisarius had good intelligence provided by the provincials, who still regarded themselves as Romans, and on 13 September when the two forces met at *Ad Decimum* (the tenth milestone from Carthage), the Byzantines inflicted a resounding defeat on the Vandals. Gelimer fled with the remnant of his forces westwards into the desert, and two days later Belisarius victoriously entered Carthage.

But Gelimer was not finished. From his temporary base at Bulla Rego (Regia) in Numidia, he recruited from among the local Berber tribes, offering a bounty for every Roman head taken. And so by mid-December he was ready to go back on the offensive. Belisarius marched towards the approaching enemy and they clashed on 15 December at Tricamarum, and again Belisarius was victorious. Gelimer was later captured and taken to Constantinople in chains to feature in a triumph for Belisarius.

The struggle for Italy

The pacification of Africa took a further seven years, but Belisarius was recalled in the summer of 533 to collect his orders for the invasion of Ostrogothic Italy. For this much larger undertaking, Belisarius set out in 535 with an

Portraits depicting Belisarius are rare, but this coin shows the mounted Belisarius on the reverse of a coin of Justinian. The general is being guided by an angel in his holy mission of reconquest.

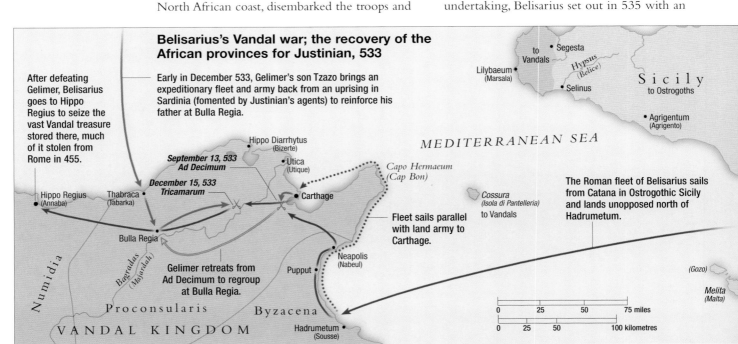

Belisarius's Vandal war; the recovery of the African provinces for Justinian, 533

After defeating Gelimer, Belisarius goes to Hippo Regius to seize the vast Vandal treasure stored there, much of it stolen from Rome in 455.

Early in December 533, Gelimer's son Tzazo brings an expeditionary fleet and army back from an uprising in Sardinia (fomented by Justinian's agents) to reinforce his father at Bulla Regia.

The Roman fleet of Belisarius sails from Catana in Ostrogothic Sicily and lands unopposed north of Hadrumetum.

Fleet sails parallel with land army to Carthage.

Gelimer retreats from Ad Decimum to regroup at Bulla Regia.

September 13, 533 Ad Decimum

December 15, 533 Tricamarum

Hippo Diarrhytus (Bizerte)
Utica (Utique)
Carthage
Capo Hermaeum (Cap Bon)
Neapolis (Nabeul)
Puppet
Hadrumetum (Sousse)
Hippo Regius (Annaba)
Thabraca (Tabarka)
Bulla Regia

Numidia

Bagradas (Majardah)

Proconsularis

Byzacena

VANDAL KINGDOM

MEDITERRANEAN SEA

Segesta
to Vandals
Lilybaeum (Marsala)
Selinus
Hypsus (Belice)
Agrigentum (Agrigento)

Sicily
to Ostrogoths

Cossura (Isola di Pantelleria)
to Vandals

(Gozo)

Melita (Malta)

0   25   50   75 miles
0   25   50   100 kilometres

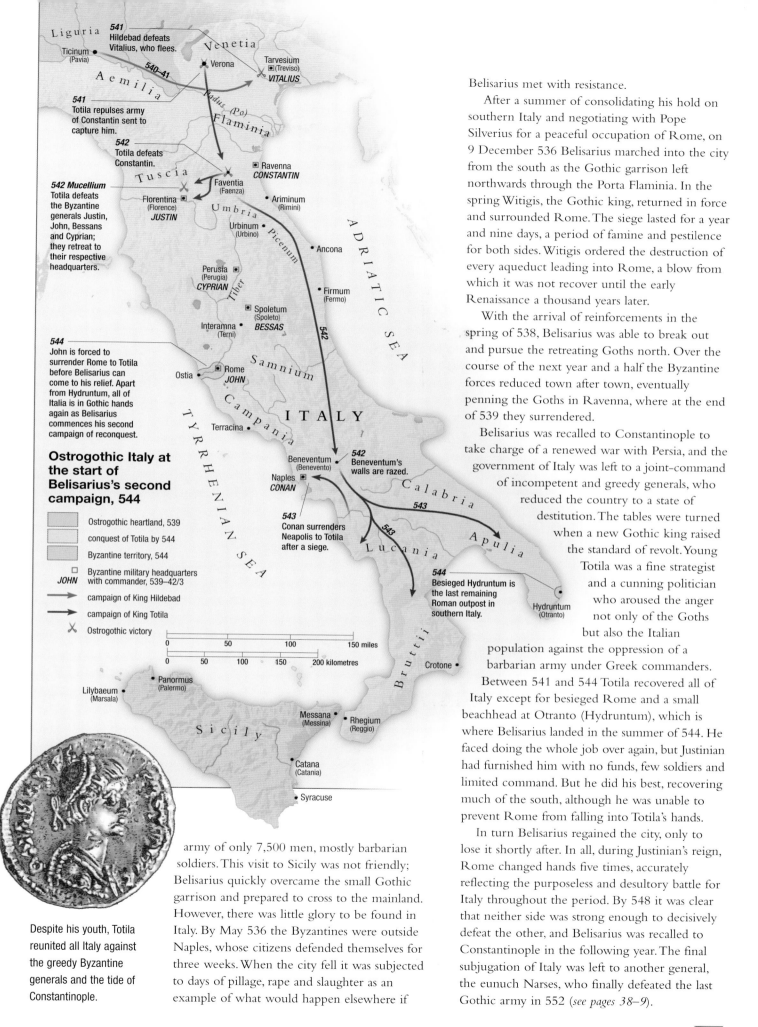

541
Hildebad defeats Vitalius, who flees.

Liguria

Venetia

Ticinum (Pavia)

Verona

Tarvesium (Treviso)
VITALIUS

Aemilia

Radus (Po)

Flaminia

541
Totila repulses army of Constantin sent to capture him.

542
Totila defeats Constantin.

Tuscia

Ravenna
CONSTANTIN

Faventia (Faenza)

542 Mucellium
Totila defeats the Byzantine generals Justin, John, Bessans and Cyprian; they retreat to their respective headquarters.

Florentina (Florence)
JUSTIN

Umbria

Ariminum (Rimini)

Urbinum (Urbino)

Picenum

Ancona

ADRIATIC SEA

Perusia (Perugia)
CYPRIAN

Firmum (Fermo)

Tiber

Spoletum (Spoleto)
BESSAS

Interamna (Terni)

544
John is forced to surrender Rome to Totila before Belisarius can come to his relief. Apart from Hydruntum, all of Italia is in Gothic hands again as Belisarius commences his second campaign of reconquest.

Samnium

Rome
JOHN

Ostia

ITALY

TYRRHENIAN SEA

Campania

Terracina

542

Ostrogothic Italy at the start of Belisarius's second campaign, 544

Beneventum (Benevento)

542
Beneventum's walls are razed.

Naples
CONAN

Calabria

543
Conan surrenders Neapolis to Totila after a siege.

543

543

Lucania

Apulia

Ostrogothic heartland, 539

conquest of Totila by 544

Byzantine territory, 544

□ Byzantine military headquarters with commander, 539–42/3

JOHN

campaign of King Hildebad

campaign of King Totila

✕ Ostrogothic victory

544
Besieged Hydruntum is the last remaining Roman outpost in southern Italy.

Hydruntum (Otranto)

| 0 | 50 | 100 | 150 miles |
| 0 | 50 | 100 | 150 | 200 kilometres |

Bruttii

Crotone

Panormus (Palermo)

Lilybaeum (Marsala)

Sicily

Messana (Messina)

Rhegium (Reggio)

Catana (Catania)

Syracuse

Despite his youth, Totila reunited all Italy against the greedy Byzantine generals and the tide of Constantinople.

army of only 7,500 men, mostly barbarian soldiers. This visit to Sicily was not friendly; Belisarius quickly overcame the small Gothic garrison and prepared to cross to the mainland. However, there was little glory to be found in Italy. By May 536 the Byzantines were outside Naples, whose citizens defended themselves for three weeks. When the city fell it was subjected to days of pillage, rape and slaughter as an example of what would happen elsewhere if

Belisarius met with resistance.

After a summer of consolidating his hold on southern Italy and negotiating with Pope Silverius for a peaceful occupation of Rome, on 9 December 536 Belisarius marched into the city from the south as the Gothic garrison left northwards through the Porta Flaminia. In the spring Witigis, the Gothic king, returned in force and surrounded Rome. The siege lasted for a year and nine days, a period of famine and pestilence for both sides. Witigis ordered the destruction of every aqueduct leading into Rome, a blow from which it was not recover until the early Renaissance a thousand years later.

With the arrival of reinforcements in the spring of 538, Belisarius was able to break out and pursue the retreating Goths north. Over the course of the next year and a half the Byzantine forces reduced town after town, eventually penning the Goths in Ravenna, where at the end of 539 they surrendered.

Belisarius was recalled to Constantinople to take charge of a renewed war with Persia, and the government of Italy was left to a joint-command of incompetent and greedy generals, who reduced the country to a state of destitution. The tables were turned when a new Gothic king raised the standard of revolt. Young Totila was a fine strategist and a cunning politician who aroused the anger not only of the Goths but also the Italian population against the oppression of a barbarian army under Greek commanders.

Between 541 and 544 Totila recovered all of Italy except for besieged Rome and a small beachhead at Otranto (Hydruntum), which is where Belisarius landed in the summer of 544. He faced doing the whole job over again, but Justinian had furnished him with no funds, few soldiers and limited command. But he did his best, recovering much of the south, although he was unable to prevent Rome from falling into Totila's hands.

In turn Belisarius regained the city, only to lose it shortly after. In all, during Justinian's reign, Rome changed hands five times, accurately reflecting the purposeless and desultory battle for Italy throughout the period. By 548 it was clear that neither side was strong enough to decisively defeat the other, and Belisarius was recalled to Constantinople in the following year. The final subjugation of Italy was left to another general, the eunuch Narses, who finally defeated the last Gothic army in 552 (*see pages 38–9*).

Green and Blue Politics

Chariot racing had evolved as a sport long before the Romans adopted it from the Etruscans and the Greeks before them. The Romans commercialised the sport and so created a vast fan base in the population. When Constantine outlawed gladiatorial combat for its pagan associations, the circus races became even more important in Byzantine society.

Scene of so much factional violence, the hippodrome of Constantinople seen today at the heart of Istanbul, with the obelisk of Theodosius I in the background.

In the early Republican era there were several racing factions, but the increasing costs of running a team had reduced them to four by the imperial period, known by their colours: red, white, green and blue. As with any modern commercial team sport, the administration was huge: directors, managers, secretaries, accountants, grooms and stable hands, carpenters and mechanics, not to mention the trainers and super-star charioteers. There were also poets, musicians and conductors, whose duty was to direct the audience in applause, chanting against the opposition and – most significantly – engage in discussions with the emperor.

During the fifth century, particularly in Constantinople, the costs of management had reduced the factions, or *demes*, to just the Greens and Blues, and an important shift of emphasis occurred. A logical extension of the fanatical following combined with the power of suggestion inherent in running a large fan base

had led the two *demes* to expand beyond the confines of the hippodrome and evolve into political parties. Their power and influence were even able to threaten the Augustus. In 456, Emperor Marcian heavily censured the Greens throughout the East for railing at his patronage of the Blues. When the Greens refused to desist in their jeering Marcian banned the *deme*'s managers from holding any administrative or public posts for three years.

The political affiliation of the Blues tended towards the big landowners, therefore Catholic orthodoxy, while the Greens were on the side of tradesmen and the civil service. Since many of the latter came from the eastern provinces where monophysite sympathies were more widespread, the Greens gradually became associated with the heretical creed. Anastasius, whose economic policies favoured manufacturing industries over agrarian and whose religious sympathies were monophysite, was drawn to the Greens – a support that had disastrous consequences.

In 511 the religious rivalry boiled over. To the important refrain in the Byzantine liturgy of 'Holy God, Holy and Mighty, Holy and Immortal' (the *trisagion*), the Greens added: '…who was crucified for us', emphasising their monophysite belief that it was not the *man* Jesus but God himself who died on the cross. The Blues reacted violently to this provocation, but when Anastasius blamed them for causing the disturbance, fighting boiled over into the city and continued unabated for two full days. In desperation Anastasius returned to the hippodrome and there, before 20,000 of his angry subjects, offered to lay aside the imperial diadem and let them choose his successor; or, if they preferred, he would continue in office and solemnly promise to sin no more. The ploy worked; quiet returned.

The Nikā Riot

Justin and Justinian, with their staunch orthodoxy, were open Blues supporters. However, once Justinian had established his rule, he abandoned his patronage in 532 and made it clear that he intended to suppress the political activities of both parties. He limited their privileges and handed out harsh punishments for any excesses. After a disturbance on 10 January seven ringleaders were condemned to death, although two, half-dead, were rescued and placed in sanctuary. One a Blue, the other a Green, they joined in a common cause. Three days later as Justinian took his place in the hippodrome he was greeted by jeers aimed at him from both Blues and Greens. For the first time ever, the factions were united in their common anger. The mob shouted 'Nikā! Nikā!' – 'Victory! Victory!' the usual cry of support for their team – in menacing unison at the emperor instead of at each other.

Justinian cancelled the races and beat a hasty retreat to the palace as the mob went wild. Public buildings were fired and guards killed, and by the end of the day much of Constantinople was in flames. The situation was so bad that Justinian prepared to escape the city by sea but was prevented by the scornful Empress Theodora. She called on Belisarius to deal with the mob. He was present in the palace in company with an Illyrian soldier named Mundus, and although neither commanded a large force they did have surprise on their side. The hand-picked troops went by separate routes to surround the hippodrome and block the exits, and then they fell on the screaming mob without mercy. The two generals

did their work relentlessly, slaughtering everyone, whether Green or Blue. By the evening as many as 50,000 lay dead.

It was to be the last factional riot, and while chariot racing continued as a popular spectator sport, the power of the Greens and Blues was for the time being broken.

A victorious charioteer rides in a *quadriga* with his stable hands.

Theodosius I watches a chariot race in the hippodrome; from the base of his obelisk.

The Monastic Revolution

The monastic movement was opposed to the worldly alliance of the Christian Church to the Roman State, for in the eyes of the monks of whatever creed, it was incompatible with the teachings of the Gospel. Justinian's ecclesiastical and legal reforms made it possible for the monastic movement to come out of isolation and eventually to penetrate into the life of the Christian Church in a way that was to complete the transformation of late antiquity into a Byzantine civilisation.

Theology was alien to the eremitic life; where churchmen ornamented the Gospel and debated the most infinitesimal definitions of the nature of divinity, the hermits simply prayed and directed their striving towards things beyond this world.

In the early fourth century, as Church and State were making their alliance, the anchorite Saint Pachomius (d.c.346) founded the first cenobitic mission, a commune of anchorites separated from society but governed by monastic regulations. In his previous life Pachomius had been a soldier, and his regulations echoed military organisation. Each monk had his own open cell and all the monks did the same manual work, taking it in turns to plait mats, weave, mend shoes and make clothes.

St Basil (c.329–79), the Bishop of Caesarea known as 'the father of Oriental monasticism', remodelled the rules of Pachomius to lay the foundations of monastic life in the Byzantine Empire, as did the founder of western monasticism, St Benedict of Nursia (c.480–543). But there are strict differences between their attitudes to monasticism. Basil's Rule reconciled the eremitic and cenobitic ways of life, the monk living in a monastic community but as an anchorite, his work being the pursuit of asceticism, whereas the Benedictine monk lived in an exclusively cenobitic house and placed work for others above work for himself. The Benedictine motto was *'Ora et labora'*, 'Pray and work', each as important as the other.

The West, therefore, was unlikely to promote the anchorite excesses of solitary contemplation that were to be found all over the East, most notably in the *stylites*. This form of penitential asceticism involved the anchorite living on top of a column. Constantinople had its own *stylite* named Daniel (409–93). Inspired by a visit to St Simeon Stylites in Antioch, Daniel erected his own pillar of modest height and lived on its top for some time. Emperor Leo I was so impressed by Daniel's piety that he had a much taller double-pillar erected for him. In order not to break his vow of touching the ground, Daniel

'Pray and Work', but relax too. Benedict set the pattern for monasticism in the West. *St Benedict with his monks at the refectory*, a late 15th-century painting by Sodoma.

The origins of monasticism go back to the early Christian era. The ascete Antony pointed the way in the middle of the third century when he withdrew from society into the solitude of the Egyptian desert. Gradually a number of disciples established themselves nearby and a colony of anchorites (hermits) was formed.

crossed from one to the other over a makeshift bridge of planks. Apart from his one visit to the ground to berate Basiliscus (*see page 26*) he remained aloft for a total of thirty-three years and three months.

Taking over education

The pressure of monastic disapproval of the Church in the late fifth and early sixth centuries was in direct proportion to the increasing number of monasteries. Early clashes occurred when the orthodox monks challenged the monophysite bishops at Alexandria and Antioch; monastic support for John Talaia (*see page 26*) was one cause of the schism between Rome and Constantinople in 484.

Byzantine monasticism demanded of the Church clerical celibacy and the renouncing of simony (the intentional selling of spiritual services for money). For instance, it was common practice for newly ordained clerics to pay considerable sums to a priest of the church as an admission fee. Some churches had rights of monopoly over an industry and were exempt from taxation. It was these kinds of abuses that Justinian was concerned to reform in his *Codex*, and it followed that – with imperial support – the best reformers would come from monasteries.

From the second half of the sixth century monks secured a firm place at the top of the

ecclesiastical hierarchy, gradually replacing those popes and patriarchs who had been classically educated in rhetoric in the antique universities. And the universities themselves, largely imperial preserves, became staffed by monks as the pagan classical teachers were replaced. The characteristic, then, of Byzantine education from the late sixth century was an emphasis on ecclesiastic law and theology rather than on rhetoric, the classics or the sciences.

Feeding the eremitic monk – a carved relief of the 5th century shows St Simon Stylites on his pillar. The ascete founded a highly limited sect of followers who displayed their piety by spending their lives on columns. His example inspired Constantinople's Daniel, who benefited from a pillar specially erected for him by Emperor Leo I.

Monasteries sprang up all over Byzantine Asia, especially in the wastelands of Cappadocia. This rock-cut monastery was carved into a pinnacle of eroded rock.

End of an Era

Justinian accomplished his dream of recovering the Roman Empire, but at great cost. For his attempt to recreate the glory of ancient Rome, and because he spoke Latin not Greek, Justinian is regarded as the last of the Roman emperors, and the story of his nephew Justin II belongs to that of the Byzantine Empire.

Narses' destruction of the Italian Gothic nation, 552

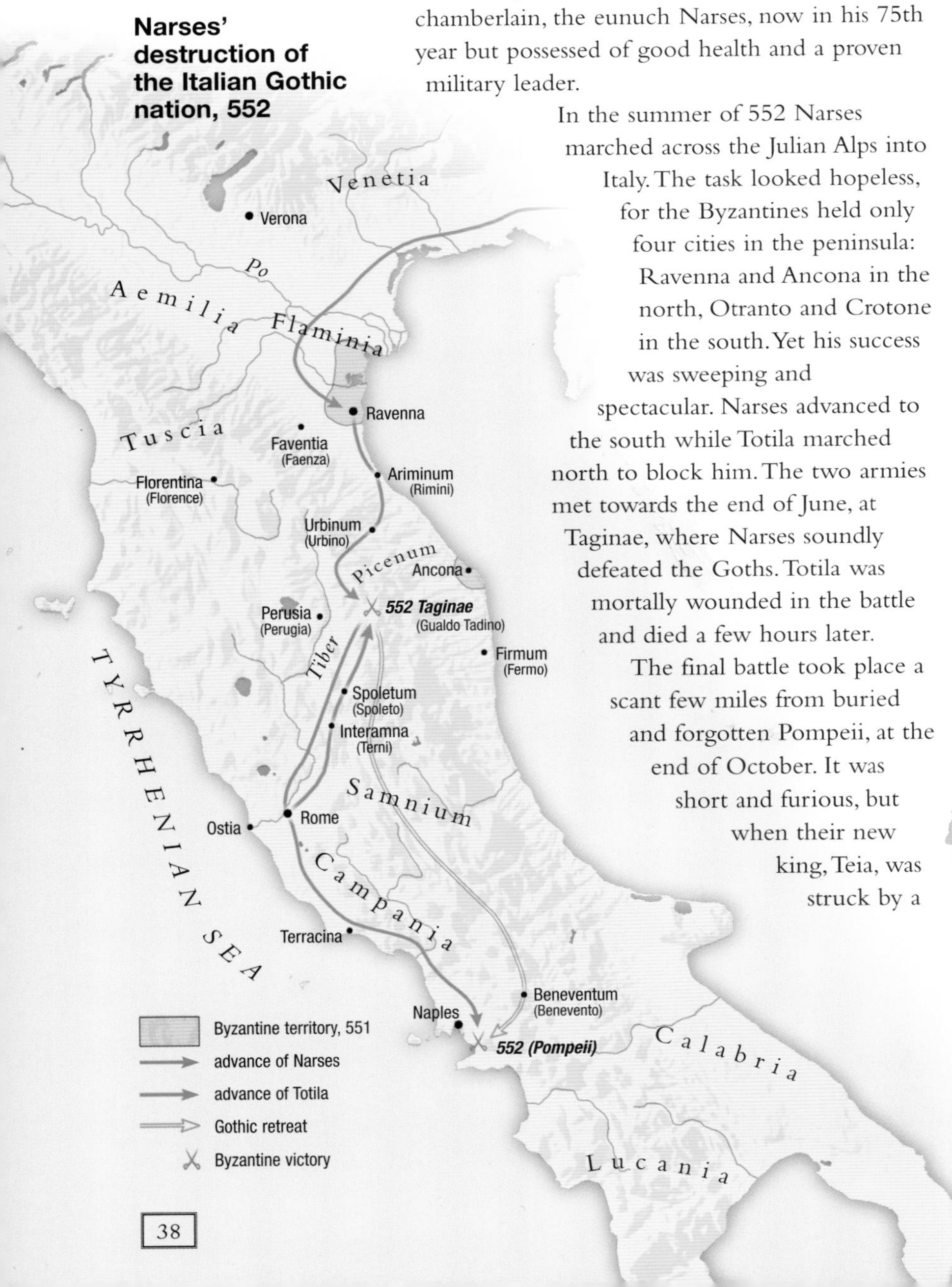

Since Belisarius had left Italy for the final time in 549, Totila had lost Rome to the Byzantines, only to regain it again in January 550. In response, Justinian appointed his first cousin Germanus to command a large army of relief. The soldiers had marched across Illyricum as far as Sofia, where Germanus was stricken by a fever and died. Justinian then turned to his chamberlain, the eunuch Narses, now in his 75th year but possessed of good health and a proven military leader.

In the summer of 552 Narses marched across the Julian Alps into Italy. The task looked hopeless, for the Byzantines held only four cities in the peninsula: Ravenna and Ancona in the north, Otranto and Crotone in the south. Yet his success was sweeping and spectacular. Narses advanced to the south while Totila marched north to block him. The two armies met towards the end of June, at Taginae, where Narses soundly defeated the Goths. Totila was mortally wounded in the battle and died a few hours later.

The final battle took place a scant few miles from buried and forgotten Pompeii, at the end of October. It was short and furious, but when their new king, Teia, was struck by a javelin and died on the spot, the remaining Goths agreed to leave Italy and never again make war on the empire.

The remaining pockets of resistance in the north were soon driven out (although Verona resisted for another nine years). Narses then reorganised the government of the Byzantine Italian state in 554 by a *Pragmatica Sanctio* (Pragmatic Sanction). But what was this new Italy? Years of warfare had reduced the once-prosperous peninsula to a smoking wasteland. Its greatest cities, formerly the pride of a powerful empire, had either been razed or left in such ruin as to be almost uninhabitable. Pestilence and famine stalked the hills and valleys, and the devastated populace had been left with no means of defending themselves from future raiders – and the many Lombards recently dismissed from imperial service by Narses were just waiting to return.

By his new social order, Narses obliterated the

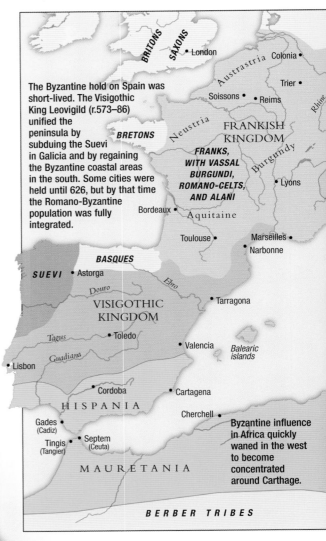

The Byzantine hold on Spain was short-lived. The Visigothic King Leovigild (r.573–86) unified the peninsula by subduing the Suevi in Galicia and by regaining the Byzantine coastal areas in the south. Some cities were held until 626, but by that time the Romano-Byzantine population was fully integrated.

Byzantine influence in Africa quickly waned in the west to become concentrated around Carthage.

Map labels (left map):
Venetia
Verona
Po
Aemilia
Flaminia
Tuscia
Faventia (Faenza)
Florentina (Florence)
Ravenna
Ariminum (Rimini)
Urbinum (Urbino)
Picenum
Perusia (Perugia)
Ancona
552 Taginae (Gualdo Tadino)
Firmum (Fermo)
Tiber
Spoletum (Spoleto)
Interamna (Terni)
Samnium
Ostia
Rome
Campania
TYRRHENIAN SEA
Terracina
Naples
Beneventum (Benevento)
552 (Pompeii)
Calabria
Lucania

Byzantine territory, 551
advance of Narses
advance of Totila
Gothic retreat
Byzantine victory

Map labels (right map):
BRITONS
SAXONS
London
Colonia
Austrastria
Trier
Soissons
Reims
Rhine
Neustria
FRANKISH KINGDOM
BRETONS
FRANKS, WITH VASSAL BURGUNDI, ROMANO-CELTS, AND ALANI
Burgundy
Lyons
Bordeaux
Aquitaine
Toulouse
Marseilles
Narbonne
BASQUES
SUEVI
Astorga
Ebro
Douro
Tagus
VISIGOTHIC KINGDOM
Toledo
Tarragona
Valencia
Balearic islands
Lisbon
Guadiana
Cordoba
Cartagena
HISPANIA
Cherchell
Gades (Cadiz)
Tingis (Tangier)
Septem (Ceuta)
MAURETANIA
BERBER TRIBES

senatorial class of Rome, which had survived the fifth-century barbarian invasions, even to flourish under the Ostrogoth Theodoric. The new government made Ravenna a resplendent Byzantine capital, but it had been done at the price of the impoverishment of Italy and Rome.

Beset by enemies

In his last years Justinian was the effective ruler of more Roman territory than any of his predecessors since the early fifth century, but at the cost of the empire's defences along the Danube and the eastern frontier, where they were most needed. Already the Slavs had begun their relentless penetration of the Balkans, in 548 and again in 550; and in 559 a Hunnish tribe known as the Kotrigurs had defeated the Danube forts and swept down into Thessaly and Thrace. On this occasion, the redoubtable Belisarius had again been called on to repulse the barbarians, which he managed in a brilliant guerrilla campaign. He might even have wiped out the tribe had he not been called off while the emperor's ambassadors negotiated a pay-off. It was his last victory.

Belisarius died at the age of about sixty in March 565, barely eight months before Justinian.

Justinian died suddenly on 14 November 565, leaving the throne to Justin, the son of his sister Vigilantia, and his wife Sophia, Theodora's niece. Justin II's accession went entirely smoothly, but his reign would be judged by how he handled the threats on every frontier. Immediately, he reversed his uncle's last decade of foreign policy – buying off would-be invaders. The Avars, a race of probably Mongolian origin that had first appeared in the West a few years earlier, were pressing on the frontier. His uncle had agreed to pay them an annual subsidy to remain outside the empire and keep other hostile tribes at bay, but in 562 they invaded Thrace, and now their ambassadors wanted a renewed subsidy from Justin. He flatly refused them.

In the following year he took a similar line with the Sassanian Great King Chosroes. These refusals made a popular policy for it seemed to hint at reduced taxes for the populace, but it soon transpired that Justinian's subsidies to perennial and potential enemies had not been for nothing.

Byzantium in the Crimea
During Justinian's reign Byzantine influence was extended to the Crimea. Inhabited by Goths and Alans who had entered the region earlier, they were hostile to the empire, but in the mid-6th century became allies. Kherson became the main bridgehead of the Byzantine ideological and political presence in the Crimea. The second point of operation was Kerch on the Cimmerian Bosphorus, which guarded the access to the Russian river network and the Eastern trade routes avoiding the Sassanian Empire.

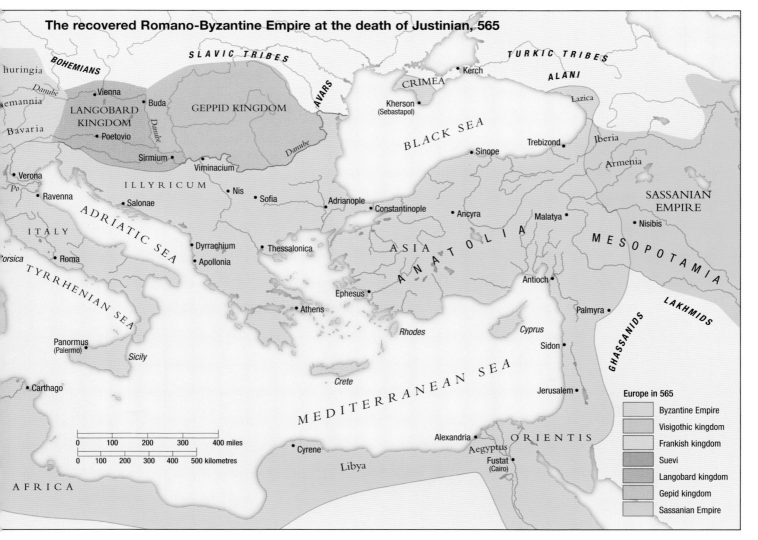

The recovered Romano-Byzantine Empire at the death of Justinian, 565

Europe in 565

- Byzantine Empire
- Visigothic kingdom
- Frankish kingdom
- Suevi
- Langobard kingdom
- Gepid kingdom
- Sassanian Empire

Lombards, Avars, Slavs and Persians

Within only 16 years of Gothic Italy finally falling to the Byzantine Empire, and within three years of Justin II's accession, the peninsula was in barbarian hands again. Ironically, the Lombards had never been recipients of Byzantine protection money, but they dealt Justin the worst blow of the many his reign was to suffer.

The Germanic Lombards (Langobardi, or 'Long Beards') originated from the region around the River Elbe and gradually migrated into Noricum. In 567, allied with the Avars, they annihilated the tribe of Gepids who had occupied the region for about 100 years. In the following year the Lombards crossed the Julian Alps into northern Italy, their chieftains already familiar with the terrain from service under Belisarius and, principally, Narses.

The country still lay largely in ruins, and the demoralised population was no match for the invaders. Faced with little resistance, the Lombards under King Albion rapidly overran northern Italy and Tuscany – but avoided well-defended Byzantine Ravenna. Independent duchies were established further south centred on Spoleto and Benevento. In general, this was less a conquest than a migration. The Lombards intermarried with the Italians, adopted Latin in a fashion as their language, and absorbed the late Roman culture. Along with Ravenna, they ignored Naples, and left Calabria and Sicily in imperial hands.

For all his tough talk, Justin's hands were tied when it came to sending an army to expel the Lombards from Italy. He had inherited a sadly depleted army from Justinian, who in his last years had preferred ecclesiastical rumination to managing military affairs. The army he left to Justin had fallen in numbers from 645,000 to only 150,000, much of it concentrated in mobile units while the fortresses of the frontier were left to decay. The empire's defence was the ring-fence of protection payments, which Justin had rashly thrown out. The Avars now occupied the former lands of the Gepids and, after they left for Italy, those of the Lombards. In 568 they attacked Dalmatia in revenge for Justin's refusal to continue their subsidy.

As large a force as could be mustered was sent under the command of Tiberius, Count of the Excubitors – northern and central Italy, too far away, was abandoned to the Lombards. After three years of exhausting warfare Tiberius was forced to a truce, and Justin paid out a sum to the Avars far greater than their original demands had been.

The Avar question was barely settled when Armenian Christians, obliged by the political division of their country to live under the Persian yoke, rebelled against King Chosroes in 571 and appealed to Constantinople for help, a request Justin could hardly ignore. Chosroes now had two contentions: interference within his realm and Justin's refusal to honour his uncle's tribute payments. In the spring of 572 the Persian army swept across the Tigris, seizing the important Christian see of Daras, and across the Euphrates into Syria where they took as many as 290,000 captives. Many of these were intended as a gift to the Khan of the Turks, another newly arrived Mongolian race that posed a threat to both Byzantium and Sassanid Persia, in hopes of a Turkish-Persian alliance. The Persian War was to continue, with brief interruptions, for 20 years.

A joint emperorship

One such interruption was the year's truce of 574, arranged by Empress Sophia. From about the beginning of the war, Justin began a decline into insanity that left him unfit to rule, and Sophia had to take over the empire's government. Finding the burden too heavy, she arranged for Count Tiberius to be raised to the rank of caesar and act as joint-regent with herself. But it was an unhappy arrangement. Theodora's niece was unaccustomed to sharing the trappings of authority, and thwarted Tiberius over financial matters – he was famously liberal with the treasury.

Justin died in October 578 and – adding Constantine to his name – Tiberius was his uncontested successor. In his barely four-year reign Tiberius accomplished much despite losing a stronghold in the Crimea to invading Turkish

Khazars and failing to prevent a mass migration of Slavs into Thrace and Illyricum. Having deprived Sophia of her position at court, he ended the persecution of monophysites that she and Justin had enthusiastically pursued. This roused the ire of the Latin Church, but pragmatic Tiberius recognised that unity within the Greek sphere would be more important than an accord between the two Churches. He revived the moribund Senate and encouraged healthy political activity again by lifting the ban on the Green and Blue *demes* suppressed by Justinian.

In 581 he established a new corps of 15,000 elite soldiers, raised from among the barbarian confederates, which would later evolve into the Varangian Guard. Most useful for Byzantium, he appointed as his successor a young Cappadocian named Maurice and married his daughter Constantina to him. 'Make your reign my finest epitaph,' were the last words of Tiberius, who died on 13 August 582.

The Byzantine Empire at the death of Justin II, 578

Byzantine Empire
Lombard kingdom
Lombard duchies
Sassanian Empire
Avar khanate
Khazaria

→ Khazarian advance
→ Slavs' advance
■ fortified Byzantine city
■ Byzantine enclave

KHAZAR KHANATE

Caspian Sea

SLAVS

KHAZARS

KHAZARS

Kerch

AVAR KHANATE

Kherson (Sebastopol)

Lazica

Sirmium

Belgrade

Danube

Nicopolis

Zara

Split

Nis

SLAVS

Mesembria

BLACK SEA

Sinope

Trebizond (Trabzon)

ARMENIA

Theodosiopolis

Lake Van

Iberia

Aghtamar

Lake Urmia

ILLYRICUM

Philippopolis

Adrianople

THRACE

Thessalonica

Constantinople

Nicaea

Ancyra

ANATOLIA

Melitene

Tigris

Daras

MESOPOTAMIA

ADRIATIC SEA

Dyrrachium (Durrazo)

Bari

Benevento

Amalfi

Thessalonica

AEGEAN SEA

Dorylaeum (Ekishir)

Caesarea (Kayseri)

Tyana

Iconium (Konya)

Tarsus

Aleppo

Euphrates

Syria

LAKHMIDS

Otranto

Nicopolis

IONIAN SEA

Thebes

Athens

Ephesus

Laodicea (Denizili)

Attaleia

Antioch

Seleucia

Calabria

Rhodes

Myra

Cyprus

Beirut

GHASSANIDS

Sicily

Syracuse

Rhodes

Mistra

Damascus

Tyre

Crete

Gortyn

Bostra (Busra)

MEDITERRANEAN SEA

Palestine

Cyrene

Alexandria

Egypt

Leptis Magna

Libya

Heliopolis

Red Sea

Maurice, the Firm Hand

Maurice came to the throne as a successful general, having inflicted a severe defeat on the Persians in 581. As an emperor, Maurice was good and wise in his vision but poor in his judgement of character. His nepotism was blind to the failings of the relatives he appointed to high command, and such decisions led to his downfall, but not before he had instituted governmental reforms that would shape the future of the Byzantine Empire.

A gold *solidus* of Maurice depicts the emperor proudly clad in armour, testimony to his warrior status.

Sassanian influence spread far and wide. This silver coin of King Hormisdas (Hormizd) IV (r.579–90) was found in the mouth of a person buried in the Astana cemetery, near Tufan, northwestern China. The king's son, Chosroes II, was to become a firm ally of Maurice after Hormisdas was murdered in a palace coup.

In his establishment of Byzantine government at Ravenna in 524, Narses had in principle created the first Exarchate. Maurice (r.582–602) now formalised the concept to control the far-flung parts of his empire that were cut off from the East by land or sea. The exarch, the title given to the proconsul or viceroy of a province at some remove from the central authority, wielded absolute power over the civilian and military administration. Ravenna was already existing in this relationship to Constantinople, and Maurice created a similar system for Africa, the Exarchate of Carthage. To Carthage, Corsica and Sardinia were attached, while Sicily formed a separate government. The Exarchates were to remain the principal western outposts of imperial authority for several centuries.

In his foreign policy, Maurice proved adept. The hostilities with Persia had been dragging on for more than a decade, with neither side gaining much advantage other than Maurice's victory in 581 over King Hormisdas IV, who had succeeded Chosroes in 579. When a Persian coup resulted in the death of Hormisdas, his son Chosroes II fled into Byzantine territory. Maurice seized the chance to form a treaty with the prince. In return for assisting him to regain his throne, Persia was to conclude a permanent peace and restore to Byzantium the great cities on the Tigris that his grandfather had captured. In 591 the plan was successfully executed, and Chosroes kept his word. The resulting peace in the East finally allowed Maurice to concentrate on his other great enemy, the Avars.

Failings outweigh achievements

Through such measures, his clear-sightedness, sheer hard work and because of his improvement of the empire's finances, Maurice left Byzantium in a much stronger position than he found it. Unfortunately, his parsimony – which helped fill the treasury – made him unpopular with the

people and the army. Thanks to his predecessors' extravagance, he inherited a bankrupt state, and ferocious savings were the only way to raise money to pay his potential enemies. Public entertainment was slashed and the army deprived of rations. In 588 he reduced all army rations by a quarter, which led to a mutiny in the East.

He refused to pay the Avars a ransom in 599 for 12,000 prisoners, who were promptly put to death by their captors. In 602 he decreed that the army should not return to winter quarters, but sit

rebels' demands, Maurice accused the two of treason. Theodosius fled the city and Germanus ran to sanctuary in St Sophia.

Having lost any military affection, Maurice turned to the revived Blue and Green *demes* to man the Theodosian Walls, but their uncertain loyalties turned against him and he was forced to flee with his family across the Bosphorus into Asia. Germanus now made his move and sought the backing of the more numerous Greens to make him emperor, but they suspected the

it out on the frontier. This was a false economy. The soldiers traditionally returned to their homes and families for the winter, and all the booty they had collected was worthless unless they could sell it in the markets of Constantinople.

The Danube army's commander was Peter, Maurice's incompetent brother, and when the troops mutinied he was lucky to escape with his life. The soldiers immediately proclaimed one of their number, a certain Phocas, to be their leader. The rebels began a march on the capital, not to make Phocas emperor, but to depose Maurice in favour of either his son Theodosius or his father-in-law Germanus. On hearing the

intentions of a lifelong Blues supporter, and instead proclaimed the approaching Phocas.

In his first act as ruler, Phocas dispatched soldiers to hunt down and murder Maurice and his family. When they soon discovered the imperial family's hiding place the dispirited and worn out emperor made no attempt to flee or defend himself. He was made to watch while the soldiers butchered his four younger sons before being executed himself. Their heads were sent to be displayed in Constantinople, a reminder to the citizens of the emperor they had helped murder to place the imperial diadem on the head of Phocas. It was a bad transaction.

The Danube had long been the border between civilised Rome and the barbarian hordes beyond. It was, however, rarely an effective barrier to tribes determined to cross it, and for the Byzantine Empire the river would not long be the frontier. This view shows the Iron Gate gorge, which separates Serbia from Romania.

The Folly of Phocas

The Byzantine historian George of Pisidia avoided mentioning the name of Phocas, indicating him only by phrases like 'that terrestrial leviathan' or 'the Gorgon-faced'. Other writers called him a barbarian half-breed who was the origin of all of the calamities that plagued the empire. Certainly, his eight-year reign brought Byzantium to the nadir of its fortunes.

Below: Coins of Phocas and his mortal enemy, the Sassanid king Chosroes II. The murder by Phocas of Chosroes' friend, Emperor Maurice, led to a war that brought Byzantium to her knees in a few short years.

Little is known about the early life of Phocas (r.602–10), except that he was probably of Thracian origin. By 600 he was a non-commissioned officer in the Balkan army. Despite this lowly rank, his fellow soldiers evidently considered him to be a leader because he was chosen to head a deputation sent to Constantinople in that year to lay the grievances about the commander before the

Facing: Smargadus, exarch of Ravenna, dedicated the statue of Phocas in 608 that topped this 13.4m (44ft) high column in Rome, the last monument to be built in the Forum. Like much associated with Phocas it was stolen from earlier buildings – the marble plinth originally supported the honorary column to Diocletian. It was Phocas who gave Pope Boniface IV the Pantheon in the same year to become the church of Santa Maria ad Martyres.

government. The plea was rejected, and Phocas suffered mistreatment at the hands of prominent courtiers.

Phocas was described as having an unprepossessing countenance, a bush of red hair over a single beetling eyebrow and a huge scar across his face. His behaviour on a good day was debauched, drunken and cruel. For his love of spilling blood, he introduced public gallows, hangings and torture to the East which had been rare before.

The murders of Maurice and his sons were but the start of a reign of terror and the executed included the deceased emperor's brother Peter and his son Theodosius (although rumours persisted that he escaped to Persia). For a while Germanus was spared after swearing loyalty to Phocas, but any other who had been connected

to Maurice died in various dreadful ways.

Young Chosroes II needed little encouragement to use the death of his benefactor as an excuse to attack, and the Persians invaded in 603. Phocas had few military commanders of quality left to him, and the best, Narses (no connection to Narses of Ravenna) loathed the upstart emperor and refused to fight against the Persians. Instead he raised the standard of rebellion and seized Edessa, appealing to Chosroes to help.

Phocas rapidly concluded a very expensive treaty with the Avars to free up the paltry western garrisons and march them to the East.

On the pretext of making his peace, Phocas lured Narses to the capital, where he was taken and burned alive. Having destroyed his most capable general, Phocas cast the next best into prison on a charge of treason, and the last of any note was killed in a skirmish. Command of the war now fell to one of the emperor's nephews, Dommentziolus, but his youth and inexperience were no match for his adversaries.

Within four years the Sassanian army had overrun western Mesopotamia, Syria, Armenia and cut deeply into the heartland of Anatolia: Cappadocia, Paphlagonia and Galatia. By 608 Persians were encamped at Chalcedon on the Bosphorus, staring greedily at the walls of Constantinople. Behind the city, uncaring of their subsidies, the Avars had encroached through the Balkans and were raiding on occasion up to the Theodosian Walls.

Civil war engulfs the empire

As if he did not have enough on his imperial plate, Phocas set out to forcibly convert the Jews within his realm. Since the majority lived in the eastern provinces and were therefore in war's front line, this had the entirely predictable result of raising rebellion. In Antioch the Jews rose up and massacred the local Christians. Others fled to the Persians, who welcomed them in. The picture was repeated in Palestine where a factional battle between Blues and Greens escalated into all out civil war, again involving the Jews in the middle.

Meanwhile in Constantinople a succession of plots against the emperor was uncovered and the ringleaders executed, among whom were Germanus and the ex-Empress Constantina. And then to make an already appalling situation even worse Heraclius, the exarchate of Carthage, cut off the grain supply on which Constantinople depended. News soon followed that he had sent his son, also Heraclius, with a fleet to attack Constantinople, while his nephew Nicetas was marching overland to Egypt. Nicetas defeated the peculant governor-general Bonosos and secured Alexandria towards the end of 608. He then began preparations to continue along the coast towards Antioch.

Young Heraclius sailed at a leisurely pace to Thessalonica, where he was received as a hero, and more men flocked to his banner. Meanwhile he was in secret correspondence with the emperor's son-in-law Priscus, who happened to be one of Maurice's old commanders, as indeed was Exarchate Heraclius. Priscus, who had himself faced execution and narrowly escaped, organised men loyal to his cause, and when the Carthaginian fleet approached the Sea of Marmara they took Phocas, bound him up and rowed the fuming emperor out to meet Heraclius. One story claims he had Phocas chopped up into little bits, another that he delivered him into the hands of the Blues and Greens and that the end result was much the same.

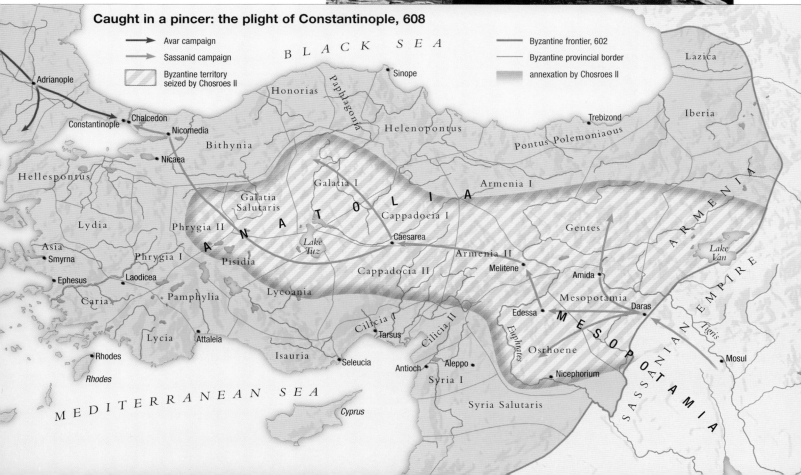

Caught in a pincer: the plight of Constantinople, 608

The Failure of Byzantine Government

Modern as well as Byzantine commentators have excoriated Phocas, so he was, and remains, one of the most maligned of all Byzantine emperors. However, histories always reveal a common theme – the damnation of the previous dynasty in order to heighten the virtues of the following. To the victor go the spoils, and the honour of rewriting history. Phocas was hardly a good ruler, but it is worth considering whether he really stood a chance.

From the time of Constantine the Great, the lot of the ordinary citizens of the empire had been little considered. Most were effectively labour slaves of the state, sons condemned to follow their father's trades with little hope of advancement. The couple pictured here from an altar symbolises piety, but their expressions are in keeping with most Byzantines' feelings.

Only 37 years separate the reign of Phocas from that of Justinian I, in which time the Byzantine Empire had been transformed from a state almost as large as the old Roman Empire from which it sprang into a string of beleaguered strongholds. Inevitably, the blame for this fragmentation was bound to fall on the man sitting on the throne at the end of this period. But structurally, the rot set in with Justinian's ambition and with the nature of his court which most of his successors accepted without significant change.

Justinian presented his successors with the burden of administering an over-extended empire whose resources he had drained for his conquests and whose infrastructure proved too weak to meet the task at hand. Instead of conceding territory he had no real way of protecting, Justin I hung on to what Justinian had gathered up, but in refusing to pay subsidies, almost guaranteed the forcible loss of provinces to the disgruntled barbarian tribes. Like his uncle, Justin also failed to provide the distant provinces with adequate protection, preferring instead a futile and costly expansionist war against Persia. As a result the Visigoths attacked Byzantine Spain, Moors began raids on Africa, and Lombards annexed most of Italy. There was to be some diplomatic success in Italy, where Emperor Tiberius prevented the Lombards from consolidating their power by bribing local chiefs to block the election of a new high king when Albion died.

The net effect of this desultory policy of half-hearted defence and paying protection money was to stretch the empire's resources to the limit without providing any added security. A terrible plague which struck all around the Mediterranean during Maurice's reign further reduced the pool of labour, and consequently tax revenues. However, the Avars also suffered and Maurice was finally able to push them back beyond the Danube, but at a cost he could not afford. Accordingly he ordered the soldiers to cross the river and live off the Slavic land for the winter, the fateful decision that ultimately cost him his life.

The quality of advice

The Byzantine court quickly became incapable of advising the emperor sensibly. Roman emperors from Augustus up to the end of the fourth century held the courtly ceremony of Orientals in contempt. Diocletian and even more so Constantine adopted the flummery as a means of enhancing their majesty in the eyes of the people, but soon enough the appearance had become the substance. A powerful Senate, that should have acted as a counterbalance to autocracy, was absent in Constantinople, Antioch and Alexandria. The powerful land-owning aristocracy of the West had not developed in the East, and their wealth never matched that of old Rome.

As a result the senators of Constantinople were not power-brokers as their western counterparts had been and the real elite was primarily made up of imperial appointees, often family and almost always entirely dependent on the emperor's patronage. Naturally enough, this spoils system in which either nepotism or purchased loyalty counted more than capability, induced a form of administrative and political torpor – his advisors only told the emperor what they thought he wanted (or sometimes needed) to hear. It also promoted a furious race for favour and position, a further waste of imperial energy. With a man of calibre like Constantine at the helm the worst excesses of the numerous chamberlains was mitigated, and no other emperor had the courage or desire to sweep it all out as Julian Apostate had done.

This, then was the situation Phocas contrived to inherit: an over-stretched empire, low on resources, poor in administrative capability, rife with conspiracy, surrounded by enemies. He was soon plagued with the same sorts of crises that had brought down his predecessor while having to rely on the same weak institutions that had already proven inadequate for the tasks at hand. It only took a man lacking in imagination – as he undoubtedly was – to bring the entire edifice crumbling down.

Amid this insecurity, Constantinople's immense and to date impregnable walls must have seemed like the only safe place in the world. It should come as no surprise that imperial isolationism was to become a major

Left: Detail of a fisherman from a floor mosaic. Desultory financial and political policies combined with the effect of plague had reduced the labour pool to a dangerously low level by the end of Phocas's reign.

characteristic of the Byzantine state from this date on. All too often the emperor's prime concern would not be with the wide realm but only with the ever-more elaborate court at the heart of Constantine's great city.

Below: With enemies pressing on all sides of the capital, it was easy for an emperor to ignore the outside while hiding safely behind Constantinople's impregnable Wall of Theodosius.

Eunuchs and Dignitaries

One of the characteristics of Byzantine administration was the army of eunuchs that filled posts from the most menial to the highest offices. They are usually portrayed as overweight, epicene characters, but the given image is misleading: it is conceivable that without eunuchs, Byzantine administration would have ground to a halt long before it did.

The glory of the court was reflected in the brilliance of holy objects, such as this crucifix of precious metals and gems.

Eunuchs were nothing new in the Byzantine Empire, and indeed they had been around at the edges of Roman government for centuries. Neither were eunuchs the mincing male sopranos, castrated before puberty to preserve their boyish treble singing voices, of later Western Europe nor the fat, greasy harem-keepers of the oriental tradition. The Romans tended to look down on eunuchs, although the example of Gannys from the early third century might be thought to disprove the prejudice. Gannys helped the teenaged Elegabalus's elevation to the purple, and fought bravely against the usurper Macrinus. Even Gibbon, who had little time for the morally perverted young emperor or his counsellor offers: *'Antoninus [Elegabalus], who, in the rest of his life, never acted like a man, in this important crisis of his fate approved himself a hero… whilst the eunuch Gannys, whose occupations had been confined to female cares and the soft luxury of Asia, displayed the talents of an able and experienced general.'*

He was not alone; for Justinian I his chamberlain Narses, despite his castration, proved to be one of the greatest generals in imperial history. For centuries eunuchs had been respected members of society in the Eastern Roman Empire and Byzantium, holders of many of the most distinguished offices of Church and State. Posts they were denied were only Prefect of the City, Quaestor, Domestic of the four imperial regiments and the throne itself. This last was because the emperor, as God's Vice-Gerent on Earth, had to be physically perfect. Castration, then, was a useful means of denying male imperial relatives any possible claim on the throne, and explains why so many sons, nephews and cousins ended up under the surgeon's knife – or were blinded or had their noses slit.

Castration in the Byzantine Empire was not the punishment or misfortune it is thought of being today. By the tenth century to be a eunuch was a virtual guarantee of advancement for a promising youth about to enter imperial service. Ambitious parents would willingly have a younger son castrated as a matter of course. This sometimes backfired if the older brothers died or were killed in action, but the risks usually paid dividends.

Eunuchs, with no wives and families of their own to support, tended to be far more industrious than their endowed colleagues. And having no sons prevented certain high offices from becoming hereditary, a process which had often hindered good government in earlier times, and frequently caused dynastic havoc in the West. By the same token, eunuchs hindered the advance of feudalism, which fostered the hereditary patrimony of land, and which was to cause the empire more and more trouble, particularly in Anatolia.

Most importantly, from the imperial family's point of view, eunuchs were politically safe. While they might – and frequently did – intrigue on the behalf of a brother or nephew, no eunuch, however powerful, could make a bid for the throne.

The pecking order

The empire's complex system of aristocracy and bureaucracy, inherited from Rome, changed greatly over the centuries as different titles were

450	455	468	475	477	484	511	512
Marcian succeeds Theodosius II and marries Theodosius's sister, Aelia Pulcheria	Gaiseric the Vandal sacks Rome, kidnapping Valentinian's wife and daughter	Emperor Leo's brother-in-law Basiliscus leads a disastrous invasion of Vandal Africa	Leo's son-in-law and successor, Zeno, is deposed by Basiliscus	Zeno is returned to power and Basiliscus banished to Cappadocia, where he dies	In Rome Pope Felix III excommunicates Patriarch Acacius; Acacius responds in kind	Religious tensions between the Green and Blue hippodrome factions lead to riots	The first invasion of the empire by Bulgars begins as they overrun Thrace

adopted and discarded, and many lost or gained in prestige. By the time of the seventh-century crisis many titles had become obsolete, and Heraclius revised the honorific system (*see page 63*); Alexius I Comnenus made further sweeping changes at the end of the 11th century, from which point titles remained essentially the same to the fall of the empire in 1453.

Unlike in the West, Byzantine titles were nonhereditary, but they were often bestowed through nepotism. From the 11th century onward the system of dignities depended greatly

dignities, called *Taktika* (the most famous being the *Kletorologion of Philotheos* of 899), ordered the degrees of favour in minute detail; from the ceremonial robing and undressing of the emperor and higher dignities to who could dine at the emperor's table, and in what seating order. These books also covered a wide variety of other questions of prestige and primacy.

Before the end of the 11th century, titles were given out broadly (sometimes even on merit), but the Comneni emperors began awarding dignities primarily for reasons of loyalty and kinship. As a

on the relationship of the office-holder to the emperor, with closer relations tending to hold higher positions. The Byzantine court was comprised of a bewildering array of offices, military and civil, organised into a complex, intertwined pecking order.

Little was left to chance in outlining the relative positions of the ranks. Several books of

military dynasty, this inflated the status of the military aristocracy above that of the civil bureaucracy – the so-called military or bureaucratic parties, which effectively replaced the Blues and Greens as the organising principle of the proletariat polity. Some of the many Byzantine titles of the 12th century are described in the Glossary.

Byzantine courtly pomp and circumstance are shown in this mosaic of Justinian I's Empress Theodora and her retinue of ladies, eunuchs and advisors. The elaboration only grew with the years.

518	527	533	536–39	554	565	568	608
Justin I ascends the throne; his nephew Justinian is architect of East-West religious reconciliation	Justinian I succeeds Justin; in 530 Julian's *Pandects* are published, a detailed digest of Roman law	Julian's general Belisarius invades Africa and expels the Vandals	Belisarius invades Ostrogothic Italy and brings the peninsula back into the empire	Narses effectively creates the Exarchate of Ravenna by Pragmatic Sanction	Death of Justinian I; Justin II succeeds, but his foreign policies damage the empire	Lombards overrun north and central Italy, setting up a kingdom and duchies	Under weak Phocas, Byzantine arms fail against the Persians, who sweep up to the Bosphorus

The Heraclian Dynasty

The end of Phocas marks a change in the fortunes of the Byzantine Empire, entirely due to the man who had deposed him. Heraclius was to stamp his authority on a seemingly hopeless situation with the shrewd flair of a Roman emperor of old. His reign also witnessed the emergence of a new force far more terrifying than any barbarian race, Islam.

In his mid-thirties and the prime of life, Heraclius swept into the Great Palace on 5 October 610 and went to the Chapel of St Stephen where two ceremonies took place. In the first he married his betrothed, a lady named Fabia, who changed her name to the time-honoured Byzantine one of Eudocia. In the second he was crowned Emperor of the Romans.

So much for the joy of his cheering subjects, happy to be released for the terror of Phocas, there was little else to smile about. Across the

The situation inherited by Heraclius, 610–20

→	campaign routes of Heraclius and Nicetas, 610
	Byzantine territory, 622
	region of skirmishes with Avar alliance
	region of skirmish with Sassanians
	Byzantine territory seized by Avars
	Byzantine territory seized by Sassanians
	Lombard kingdom and duchies
	Frankish kingdoms
	Visigothic kingdom
○	Byzantine enclave

Bosphorus glimmered the campfires of the Persians, unable without ships to cross over the heavily patrolled narrows but too close for comfort. To the west the Balkans swarmed with Slavs and Avars and the provinces were effectively lost, while the Persian forces of Chosroes II were pressing all along the eastern Mediterranean coast. In the following year Antioch fell, in 613 Damascus was in Persian hands and Jerusalem was sacked with a staggering loss of life in 614.

In Constantinople the news of Jerusalem's destruction was greeted with horror – the Persians had destroyed the shrines and carried off the True Cross, the Holy Lance and Sponge, and many other of the sacred relics that Empress Helena had made so famous. In 617 the Persians attacked Egypt and annexed the province, along with the imperial corn supply. With the Avars controlling the Thracian wheat fields, famine returned to Constantinople.

By 622 Heraclius had been emperor for 12 years, in which time the young ruler had taken no decisive action against his enemies. Energetic Heraclius may have been, but unlike so many of his predecessors he was not rash and at this time of unprecedented crisis there was no institution capable of taking the offensive. The treasury was exhausted, the civil administration corrupt, the army demoralised and badly led – victory would be beyond the empire's grasp until after he had turned the state into a fighting machine.

A plea to stay

But how was this to be accomplished? To remove himself from the destructive influence of the Byzantine aristocracy and the defeatist Senate, and to cut the ruinous cost of running the vast imperial palaces in Constantinople, Heraclius proposed a radical solution. The capital was to be abandoned and left – temporarily – to the mercies of the Avars and Persians. The plan was to retreat to Africa from where among his own people he would raise a new army and prepare a major amphibious offensive to retake all the territories of the empire.

The horror this suggestion roused among the people can hardly be imagined. However, Heraclius gave into the imprecations of Patriarch Sergius I and the terrified citizens' pleas. In return for remaining and sharing their privations, the emperor demanded that they must accept whatever sacrifices he asked of them. He then went to St Sophia and, in the presence of the Patriarch, pledged to remain and never desert the city. He may have feared a revolt had he stood by the decision to leave, which would have made the removal to Carthage difficult, if not impossible, but in any event by remaining he earned the gratitude of Sergius. This was to prove of inestimable value in the years to come.

And so the massive task of reorganisation continued. By the time the Roman army finally marched out of beleaguered Constantinople in 622, Heraclius had overhauled every aspect of the civilian and military administration.

Gold solidus of Heraclius minted in Constantinople, c.610–12.

The Creation of Themes

The early years of his life spent living in the Exarchate of Carthage had convinced Heraclius of the necessity of running the outlying provinces on disciplined military lines. He immediately set about creating designated regions called themes, a system so useful it would be expanded by his successors into a complex form of government.

T he Roman emperors Septimius Severus at the start of the third century and Diocletian a hundred years later had faced the difficulties associated with running a vast and widespread empire by sub-dividing the little more than 30 Augustan provinces into many smaller, more manageable regions. In time, there were over 200 distinct provincial divisions. Two hundred years on, Heraclius determined to do something similar. The designation was itself significant: *thema* was the Greek word that described a division of troops, so the new emperor's warlike intentions were emphasised from the start.

Heraclius also understood that the typical Byzantine method of raising an army – that of recruiting large numbers of barbarian or other foreign mercenaries, the *foederati* – had to change. For one, it was a hit-and-miss system that failed to guarantee the quality of the troops, for another, the mercenaries all too often betrayed their paymasters. A professional standing Byzantine army was now required to guard the whole empire. Each theme, therefore, was placed under the command of a *strategos* (military governor), and large numbers of soldiers were stationed in each theme.

In another move that would have been familiar to his ancient Roman predecessors, Heraclius settled the troops on land inalienably granted to them on the condition that they provided hereditary military service. The new arrangement would prove to be of immense value for the defence of the empire in the years to come. It laid the foundations for a disciplined, well-trained native army. Moreover, because of the land grants, the soldiers were defending their own property and so were much more assiduous in carrying out their duties.

Detail from The Battle of Heraclius Against Chosroes II by Piero della Francesca. For the first time since the fall of Rome, the Byzantines were possessed of a reliable and professional native army.

Genc

Corsica

Balearic
Islands

Sardinia

AFRICA Carthage

Exarchate of
Carthage

Byzantine Empire, 610
Byzantine Empire, 867
Byzantine Empire, 1025
border of Byzantine themes by 1025
Calabria name of theme

The Byzantine Empire, 610–1025, showing the European and Asian themes

A new yeomanry

In short order, Heraclius created a reliable army spread in sufficient numbers throughout the four Anatolian themes. These were the Opsikion in the northwest, the Armeniakon to the northeast, Carabisian, which covered most of the southern coast and its hinterland, and in the centre the Anatolikon. These initial four were soon supplemented (the Carabisian was further divided into Chios, Samos, Thracesion, and Cibyrrhaeoton), and before his death, he had expanded this number to 13 themes, which grew to 40 by the end of the 11th century. The older provincial administration run under the Praetorian Prefectures of Diocletian soon fell into disuse, although the larger divisions of his dioceses remained – to some extent – enshrined as the religious bishoprics.

Heraclius's success was such that by the end of the seventh century there had grown up, all over Anatolia, a whole new class of soldier-farmers who maintained themselves on their own land and, for a small payment, were expected to turn up for duty, armed and mounted, when summoned. In the essence this structure of vassalage foreshadowed the feudal system of the West, which the Franks adapted from the defensive arrangements they discovered in those regions of Italy that lay between Byzantine and Lombard lands.

The rights of these new landholders, however, were in stark contrast to the vassalage system the Franks would adopt in which serfs would effectively become slaves, and in beneficial contrast to those of the peasants who had worked on Byzantine senatorial estates previously. So too, they were far more their own men than any had been under the drudgery of Constantine's constitution. As a new political force within the empire, they contributed a degree of stability in opposition to the heated faction politics of the big cities.

Heraclius also intended that the soldier-farmers would be well paid in comparison to the working-class of the civilian population, which in turn would benefit the Byzantine economy through the increased amount of money in circulation. Ultimately, even if Heraclius could ensure greater military security, it would be a hollow victory if the economy, so ruined by the events of recent years, was not to recover and yield the returns necessary for his administrative and military reforms.

An Urban Economy

The desperate state of the imperial finances was one of the primary problems facing Heraclius. While he made arrangements to transform the military administration of the empire's depleted territory, he needed to resurrect as much of the commercial economy as he could for the first required the resources of the second. The Byzantine economy was a complex, intertwined business, easily damaged by conflict.

Whereas the early Roman Empire's economy was almost wholly slave-based, the monopoly over Mediterranean industry held by Byzantium – while it also owed much to slave-power – was due in equal part of mercantile enterprise and the capacity of a large part of the populace to save money. The capital circulating in Constantinople and other large urban centres was mainly obtained from private sources. This came from the surplus of interest earned from savings,

and found its way into the market via *argyropratai* (bankers) who financed the industries.

The marketing of products – mainly luxury goods in the case of export – was in the hands of the Jewish communities of Constantinople and Thessalonica, who earned their fees by commission on the sales. These communities had their own quarters where they were permitted to settle, usually outside the city walls. At Constantinople this was the Blachernae region, and when it was brought within the fortifications, the quarter was separated off from the rest of the city. It was not a ghetto in the modern sense, however, there was freedom of movement, and other foreign merchants were similarly gathered in their own *mitata*.

One part of the mercantile operation the Jews did not handle was the revenue raised from customs duties. In healthy times, with all goods coming from the Orient to the West having to pass through the Byzantine Empire, this was enormous. All ships from Syria and Egypt were forced to call in at Attaleia, the great harbour in southwest Anatolia, where customs officials boarded them and entered the duty payable against the list of goods. The annual revenue of customs dues taken at Attaleia alone was sufficient to pay for the Byzantine fleet.

Essential and capital-intensive businesses were often underwritten by the emperor, who could enforce the acceptance of state credit in the form of bonds with a rate of return of up $16^2/_3\%$. Shipowners and shipbuilders fell into this category. State control was essential for the economy's regulation, and it was generally handled in an enlightened way that ensured greater proportional returns for the less well off, so encouraging saving even among the poorer elements of society.

The interest rate was not rigidly fixed but varied with the social standing of the lender. Loans made by high officials only earned an interest of $4^1/_6\%$ for their money, others, as long as they were not in trade, received $6^1/_4\%$, while those in trade enjoyed a return of $8^1/_3\%$ for their loans. The graduation of permitted interest was based on salary scales, and so high officials got a lower rate of interest because they were better paid.

A one-sided bronze balance for weighing gold and jewellery.

610	622–27	628	629	630	632	633	636
Heraclius becomes emperor; institutes measures to restore the empire's fortunes over 12 years	Heraclius drives the Persians from Anatolia, and defeats them in Mesopotamia	Jerusalem greets Heraclius and the return of the True Cross stolen by the Persians	Monoenergism aims to heal the breach between orthodoxy and monophysitism	In Arabia, Mecca submits to Mohammed and becomes the centre of Islam	Mohammed dies and his followers begin a war against Sassanian Persia	Islamic Arabs destroy the Sassanian Persians and strike into Byzantine Syria	Battle of Yarmuk; the Byzantine army is wiped out by Arabs and Palestine falls to them

54

Paying for the army

The military were generally better paid than civil servants; officers were very well off, and even the common soldier earned more than an artisan. Every soldier received an annual salary of one *nomisma*, about the same as an artisan. The *nomisma* (pl. *nomismata*, the Greek word for the Latin *solidus*) was struck at 72 to the Roman pound (4.48gm). But unlike a worker the soldier also benefited from maintenance payments for his equipment and for the duration of a campaign as well as his military grant of farm land within his theme, and so may never have needed to draw on his pay. And when a campaign was over, he could earn extra cash by the sale of his share of the booty.

The soldier's pay increased by one further *nomisma* for each year of service to a maximum payment at 12 years. Further, it was expedient for a new emperor to offer his troops a donative on his accession, so Leo I, Anstasius and Justin had given each of their troops five *nomismata* and a pound of silver – the equivalent of almost seven years' pay. By contrast officers were paid between 1 and 3 pounds of gold annually, equivalent to between 72 and 216 *nomismata*, while *strategi* of themes received between 5 and 40 pounds of gold (360 and 2,880 *nomismata*) per annum.

There was good reason for this extreme preference of officers – they led the armies that conducted the campaigns and slave raids which swelled the ranks of specialist workers and thus ensured the superiority of Byzantine industry over other Mediterranean countries.

At the time of his accession, this delicate balance in trade and economy had all but vanished, and so not only did Heraclius have to rebuild the army and the military administration but he also had to contend with a serious shortage of cash to pay for everything.

Now called Antalya, the harbour at Attaleia once thronged with ships from every trading nation along the coasts of the Mediterranean. The customs revenues from trade between the West and the Orient furnished the imperial treasury and made the Anatolian city one of the empire's most important in the 7th and 8th centuries.

The Church Pays for a Holy War

Restoration of the imperial finances could not be accomplished overnight. Heraclius tackled the problem in a number of ways. Although Attaleia was still under his control, its port revenues had fallen due to the loss of Egypt, much of Syria and the Persian trade blockade. So the emperor was forced to raise taxation, force loans upon merchants and impose huge fines on former members of Phocas's corrupt bureaucracy.

While these measures helped, and there was also income to be derived through subsidies from his family in the Exarchate of Carthage, it was not sufficient for his needs. The wealth thus produced paled into insignificance compared to the revenue available to him from – for the first time in its history – the orthodox Church. Patriarch Sergius recognised that the coming war was like no other before it. This was

to be a religious war, a battle for the final victory of Christ over the fire-worshipping pagans of Persia. In this Sergius was entirely correct, although in the final outcome weakening Sassanian Persia was to expose the empire to a new power in the Orient, one that Byzantium would find hard to resist.

Sergius and Heraclius had not seen eye to eye. When Empress Eudocia died in 612, probably of an epileptic seizure, after giving birth to her second child, Heraclius had married his niece Martina. Viewed by everyone as an incestuous relationship, Sergius had been particularly violent in his condemnation, but now he was prepared to overlook the irregularity in the national interest.

Accordingly, the patriarch gathered together accounts from every diocoese and parish under his authority and put all the monastic and

Heraclius's Sassanian campaign, 622–27

Byzantines →
Sassanians →

Map labels: Constantinople, Trebizond, Cappadocia, Armenia, Azerbaijan, Lake Van, Lake Urmia, Heraclius cuts off Persian army in Anatolia, defeats Shahr-Baraz, Rhodes, Rhodes, Bay of Issus, Antioch, Syria, Cyprus, Nineveh, Tigris, Euphrates, Ganzak (Taq-e Bostan), Ctesiphon, Babylonia

Left: The 6th-century church of Panagia Drosani, Naxos, Greece. Sergius drew on ecclesiastical wealth everywhere, especially the largely unaffected Greek islands.

Below left: Constantine III and Empress Martina.

Below: Detail of soldiers from *The Battle of Heraclius Against Chosroes II*, by Piero della Francesca.

ecclesiastical treasure at the disposal of the emperor. Heraclius was happy to accept, and the Church's wealth was more than sufficient to solve his immediate fiscal problems.

By 619 Heraclius, with a measure of financial stability and the first established themes holding their own against the enemy in western Anatolia, reckoned he was ready to face the Sassanian threat. He was also confident that his new army was a match for the Persians, but before he could safely commit his forces, he required some kind of settlement with the Avars. This was achieved by some means unrecorded in the contemporary chronicles in 622, and in spring of the same year the Byzantine Empire went to war against Persia.

Since the situation in Asia Minor was fluid,

Heraclius decided to outflank Persian contingents in Anatolia by sailing his army via the Aegean and Rhodes to land near Antioch in the Bay of Issus. The Persians, who were convinced the attack when it came would be from the Black Sea and Armenia, were taken by surprise. Heraclius – the first emperor since Theodosius the Great to personally lead his army into battle – established a large beachhead, and spent the summer months training his men and raising morale by convincing them of their Christian invincibility.

The Persians in disarray

Finally, in the autumn the Roman army began its advance to the north towards the Back Sea, aiming to cut off the Sassanid forces to the west in Anatolia. In the Cappadocian highlands the two armies came face to face, the Persians under the command of their most experienced general, Shahr-Baraz. Although he had never before commanded an army in the field, Heraclius was triumphant, and the battle ended with the flight of the Persians.

Continuing problems with the Avars called the emperor back to Constantinople, and he sailed from Trebizond, leaving his men to winter in Pontus. But there was no repeat of the discontent that had brought down Maurice. Despite being denied the company of their families for the winter months, fired with success and convinced of the rightness of their cause, the soldiers of the Cross were satisfied with their lot.

The second year's campaign was even more successful. Heraclius, accompanied by Empress Martina, rejoined the army at Trebizond and then marched southeastward through Armenia and over the Persian frontier into Azerbaijan, heartland of the Zoroastrian fire-worship. Belief that the holy relics stolen from Jerusalem were being held at the Great King's nearby palace at Ganzak drew the Romans on. Chosroes chose not the defend the position and fled to Nineveh. Finding no relics, Heraclius had the palace razed, and the army pressed on almost to the Persian capital of Ctesiphon, before retiring to the western shores of the Caspian for the winter. There was news also of his brother Theodore's crushing defeat of another Persian army in Mesopotamia.

In the following year, 627, Heraclius scored even greater victories over three Persian armies Chosroes sent against him and drove the Great King and his court to abandon the Tigris-Euphrates basin for Suzania to the east.

Persia Destroyed

For almost 12 centuries Greeks and Romans had been involved in Persian affairs, against the Achaemenids, the Parthians and Sassanians. In whichever form it took, Persia was a continually malign presence, always seeking advantage against the West. Now, in 627, after an astonishing turn-about of Byzantine fortunes, Heraclius was poised to deliver the deathblow.

Below right: A rock carving at Ganza (Taq-e-Bostan, Iran) shows Chosroes II on a hunt, surrounded by horsemen.

Below: Detail from *Heraclius Restoring the Cross to Jerusalem* by Piero della Francesca depicts the Patriarch of Jerusalem eagerly waiting.

Persian general Shahr-Baraz remained a thorn in the emperor's side. In 625 he had engineered an agreement with the khagan (khan) of the Avars to attack Constantinople in conjunction with his guerrilla forces campaigning in Anatolia. However, Patriarch Sergius and leader of the Senate, the Patrician Bonus, led a spirited defence of the city's walls, holding at bay a combined force of 80,000 Avars, Huns, Gepids, Bulgars and Slavs. Successful action by the Bosphorus fleet held in check the Persian advance guard on the other side, outside Chalcedon. And then in 627 Shahr-Baraz

received instructions from his panicked king to return with all speed to Ctesiphon. As the Persians began a retreat, the Avar host gave up and melted away into Thracia.

The message Shahr-Baraz received was not quite the one his king had sent him. The first messenger had fallen into the hands of Heraclius, who had the missive altered to persuade the Persian general that all was well and to remain where he was. By the time news reached him that convinced him the truth was otherwise, it was too late, all significant Persian arms had been destroyed, and Heraclius had begun a triumphant return home.

Chosroes, deeply hated by his own people for such a parade of failures and feared by the nobility for increasing cruelty, was deposed shortly after by his half-brother Kavadh-Siroes. Chosroes was flung into a dungeon to emerge only to witness the execution of all his many children before being slowly shot to death by

arrows himself. Siroes then concluded a treaty with Theodore, who had remained behind for the purpose, that returned all Roman territory to Constantinople, as well as the holy relics taken from Jerusalem.

There was great rejoicing in Constantinople on Whit Sunday, 15 May 628 when Sergius read the emperor's message to his people. Heraclius, however, did not enter the capital until mid-September, having waited for the return of the True Cross from Persia. Heraclius deserved his triumph. He had restored the eastern provinces to the empire, and – if not in absolute control of the Balkans – his resounding defeat of Persia had certainly frightened the Avars into a degree of compliancy.

A failed reconciliation

Heraclius remained only six months at Constantinople. He was well aware of the fragility of the eastern provinces, and set out to tour every region, establishing courts at Antioch, Damascus and Emesa. He visited Jerusalem to return to the holy city the True Cross, which he himself carried along the Via Dolorosa identified by Helena to the rebuilt Church of the Holy Sepulchre. In all, Heraclius was to remain in the East for seven years, reducing the power of local landowners and ensuring an efficient administration.

At the same time, he gave deep consideration to the religious differences that had plagued Byzantium since the Council of Chalcedon over two centuries before and championed a new argument developed by Sergius. The patriarch hoped to reconcile the rift between orthodoxy and the monophysite communities, which was again becoming dangerous with the return of more normal conditions. The new proposal stated that Christ possessed two natures – the human and divine accepted by orthodoxy – but that these natures possessed a single force. This monoenergism went a long way to placating the monophysites, especially when the monophysite Bishop Athanasius endorsed it in return for being appointed to the see of Antioch in 629. In Rome, Pope Honorius I – although he did not bother one way or the other – raised no objection.

However, among the monastic movement there was a deal of resentment, led by a monk named Sophronius, which came to a head in 634 with his unexpected election to the patriarchate of Jerusalem. Sophronius thundered from the pulpit that monoenergism was simply a bastard of the older heresy, and support fell away. The rift continued, but for a great while it

seemed of little importance; a far worse disaster had befallen the barely recovered empire.

In 633, from out of the unknown wastes of Arabia beyond the Syrian desert, came a wave of invaders fired by a new religion and inspired by the teachings of the Prophet Mohammed. In short order, these Islamic warriors wiped out the tottering Sassanian Empire, the Ghassanid allies of Byzantium, and struck into Syria.

Heraclius at the gates of Jerusalem with the True Cross (and the spirit of the empress, and saint, Helena, who first identified the Cross); from a 15th-century altarpiece by the Renaissance Spanish painter Martin Bernat.

The Rise of Islam

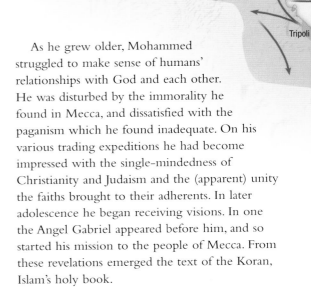

There are few parallels in history for so dramatic a story of rapid conquest than that of the Arabs. Even more astonishing is that they came from a land so inhospitable that a great part was known as the 'Empty Quarter'. Europeans knew little about Arabia and less about its barbarous inhabitants, but within 20 years the Persian Empire, Syria, Armenia, Palestine and Egypt were under the Arab caliphate.

Ruins of the Mosque of the Martyrs, erected in honour of the Arabs who died at Muta. In what was almost certainly little more than a skirmish over trading rights, a battle was fought at Muta between Arabs and the Byzantine garrison in 629. However, according to later Muslim tradition this was the first battle between the forces of Christianity and Islam, although it is unlikely that the governors of Palestine and Syria recognised the Arab raiders as the vanguard of a religious revolution.

Amid the vast distances of sun-parched land, Arabian nationalism seemed like an impossibility among the diverse and scattered tribes. Even their religious practices, a form of animistic polytheism, tended to separate rather than embrace the clans. And then, within an incredibly short space of time, everything changed; inspired by their first leader, the Prophet Mohammed, the Arabs were united by a great surge of religious fervour under a monotheist banner, and swept out of the Arabian peninsula.

Mohammed was born in about 570 and raised from infancy by the Banu S'ad tribe, the free and healthy air of the desert being regarded as better for a child than hot, dusty Mecca. With both parents dead before he was six, Mohammed went to live with his uncle, a relatively poor merchant with many children of his own. The orphan visited the Syrian frontier town of Bosra on two occasions, and there encountered a Christian monk, who was said to have greatly impressed him.

As he grew older, Mohammed struggled to make sense of humans' relationships with God and each other. He was disturbed by the immorality he found in Mecca, and dissatisfied with the paganism which he found inadequate. On his various trading expeditions he had become impressed with the single-mindedness of Christianity and Judaism and the (apparent) unity the faiths brought to their adherents. In later adolescence he began receiving visions. In one the Angel Gabriel appeared before him, and so started his mission to the people of Mecca. From these revelations emerged the text of the Koran, Islam's holy book.

Predictably, the inhabitants of Mecca rejected Mohammed, and he fled to Yathrib, which came to be known simply as 'the City', Medina in Arabic. There Mohammed was invited to take control and end the inter-clan quarrelling which had been tearing Yathrib apart. As a result Yathrib/Medina became the first Islamic state and remained the model for all subsequent Islamic governments.

Now the pagans of Mecca, fearing Mohammed's growing power, attacked him and his followers. The resulting struggle resulted in Mecca's submission in 630. Mohammed's skill was in presenting the unoriginal concept of total submission to God's will (*islam*) – Jews and Christians had maintained it for centuries – in a homespun way calculated to appeal to the desert tribes as though it were entirely new. In so doing he managed to identify his name with the doctrine, not by ascribing any divinity to himself but as the last and greatest of a long line of prophets which included Abraham, Isiah and Jesus.

The Islamic explosion

Mohammed exhibited all the traits of a statesman. Aware he would never part the people from polygamy, he embraced and regulated it. As early as 624 he decreed that the faithful should

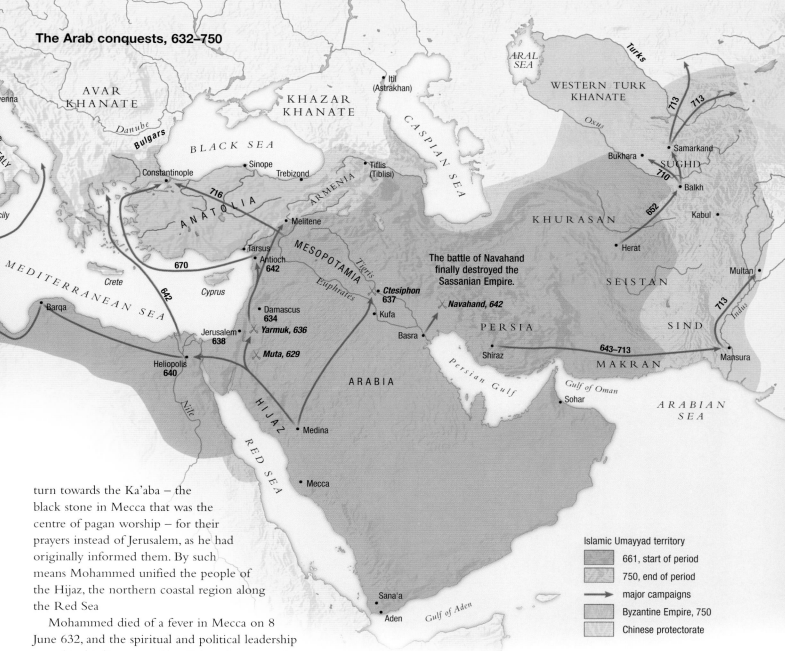

The Arab conquests, 632–750

AVAR KHANATE

KHAZAR KHANATE

WESTERN TURK KHANATE

Danube

Bulgars

BLACK SEA

Itil (Astrakhan)

ARAL SEA

Turks

713 713

ITALY

avenna

Sicily

MEDITERRANEAN SEA

Constantinople

Sinope

Trebizond

Tiflis (Tiblisi)

ANATOLIA

716

Melitene

ARMENIA

CASPIAN SEA

Samarkand

Bukhara

SUGHD

710

Balkh

652

Kabul

KHURASAN

670

642

Crete

Cyprus

Tarsus

Antioch
642

MESOPOTAMIA

Tigris

Euphrates

Herat

The battle of Navahand finally destroyed the Sassanian Empire.

Ctesiphon
637

✕ *Navahand, 642*

SEISTAN

Multan

Indus

Barqa

Damascus
634

✕ *Yarmuk, 636*

Jerusalem
638

✕ *Muta, 629*

Kufa

Basra

PERSIA

SIND

643–713

MAKRAN

Mansura

Heliopolis
640

Nile

HIJAZ

ARABIA

Shiraz

Persian Gulf

Gulf of Oman

ARABIAN SEA

Medina

Sohar

RED SEA

Mecca

Islamic Umayyad territory

661, start of period

750, end of period

major campaigns

Byzantine Empire, 750

Chinese protectorate

Sana'a

Aden

Gulf of Aden

turn towards the Ka'aba – the black stone in Mecca that was the centre of pagan worship – for their prayers instead of Jerusalem, as he had originally informed them. By such means Mohammed unified the people of the Hijaz, the northern coastal region along the Red Sea

Mohammed died of a fever in Mecca on 8 June 632, and the spiritual and political leadership passed to his lieutenant Abu-Bakr, who assumed the title of *khalifa* or caliph – literally 'he who follows behind'. Elderly Abu-Bakr died in the following year, and it was under the second caliph, Umar, that first historic victories were won. The first campaigns took place in Arabia (the Ridda Wars) and established Islamic control over most of the peninsula, but inevitably the Arab armies encountered the borders of the Sassanian and Byzantine empires.

Luck was on the Arabs' side. The recent war between Byzantium and Persia had left both sides exhausted. This fatal weakening was later presented as a result of Divine Will, but it permitted small Arab-Islamic armies to take control of richer territories where Islamic power could take root and grow stronger. For Byzantium, the situation was further aggravated by the fact that the peoples of Syria and Palestine felt no real loyalty to the Graeco-Roman culture whose lack of sympathy for their monophysite

traditions had often led to persecution. The Muslim armies were composed of Semites, like themselves, who professed a rigid monotheism not unlike their own and promising toleration for every variety of Christian belief and the Jews ('the People of the Book'). The invaders cannot have seemed much worse than the regime they swept away.

In 633 the invasion of Syria began, and by early the next year Damascus had fallen, Jerusalem by 638, Egypt by 640 and seven years later the exarch of Carthage was defeated in a battle (although it would not be until 698 that the Exarchate was actually conquered). By 711 all of North Africa was in Islamic hands, and by 732 they had invaded Spain, removing any last vestiges of Byzantine influence there, before crossing the Pyrenees and driving north to the banks of the Loire – where, after a ferocious battle against Frankish forces, they were checked at last.

Heraclius – the Last Years

The blow dealt Heraclius by Sophronius over the matter of monoenergism paled into insignificance when, in the same year, the armies of the Prophet first poured into Syria. News soon reached the emperor that his forces at Antioch had been annihilated, Muslims had occupied Damascus and Emesa and were laying siege to Jerusalem. Overnight, the campaigning of six hard years had been wiped out.

Heraclius applied himself to raising a full-scale army, and a year later 80,000 men were drawn up outside Antioch, although without the worn out emperor to lead them. The Muslims under their clever general Khalid reacted by

Monophysitism never died out. Although eradicated in the Middle East by Islam, it has continued to flourish in parts of Egypt as the Coptic Christian creed and as far south as Ethiopia, where this photograph was taken in Addis Ababa during the 1990s Marxist overthrow.

withdrawing their garrisons from Emesa and Damascus and fell back to the Yarmuk, a tributary of the Jordan. In May 636 the imperial army marched out to meet them but for some reason failed to take the initiative, which allowed Arab reinforcements to arrive. On 20 August a violent sandstorm blew up out of the desert from the south. Khalid seized his opportunity and charged the Byzantine troops, who, caught by surprise and with sand blowing into their eyes, were massacred almost to a man.

The war was effectively over before it had properly started. Emesa and Damascus were reoccupied and Jerusalem surrounded. Sophronius put up a stout defence, but with food running out and no Christian army nearer than

Egypt, he capitulated late in 637. In February 368, Caliph Umar himself rode into the city to visit the Temple of Solomon, where he believed his friend Mohammed had ascended to heaven.

Heraclius took no part in these struggles, beyond slipping into Jerusalem from Caesarea to save the True Cross and Holy Lance. He was already ill with the disease that was to kill him and spiritually tormented that he had been deserted by God. There were many who still could not forgive the emperor his incestuous union with Martina, herself a domineering and unpopular figure in Constantinople. Against his will, she ensured that he crowned her first-born Heraclonas as co-emperor with Constantine, his son by Eudocia. This took place in June 638, when the boys were 23 and 26 respectively.

A few weeks later, Heraclius tried one final time to reconcile the monophysites with orthodoxy through an infinitesimal alteration to the monoenergism promulgated by the Patriarch Sergius. He had dropped the notion of *energy*, and said that Christ possessed a single *will*. This monothelitism, or the doctrine of the Single Will, was proclaimed by Heraclius in what is known as the *Ekthesis*. All four eastern patriarchs assented to this, but disaster struck in 641 when the newly elected Pope John IV condemned the whole issue. A matter that had been largely one of indifference to the Latin Church, now flared up into open schism.

The end of Latin

And so morally and physically depleted, Heraclius died in misery on 11 February 641. His reign marks a cultural change and the beginning of a new era. Heraclius dealt the death-blow to the old Roman tradition. Until his day, Latin was still in regular use by the civil service, jurists and even the officer corps of the army – many of them coming from Thracian or romanised Gothic origin – despite that the language was incomprehensible to most of his Greek subjects. At such a time of crisis it was a ridiculous

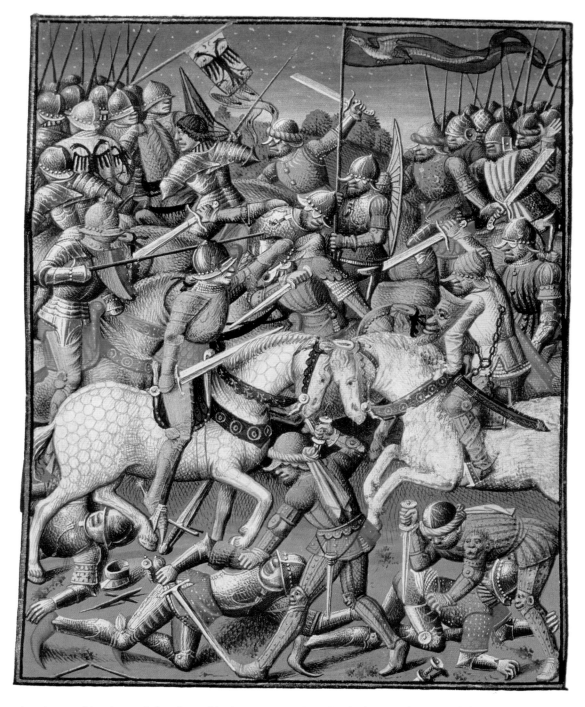

This 15th-century French manuscript illumination depicts *Heraclius Defeating the Saracens* from *Speculum Historiale* by Vincent of Beauvais. Its representation is clearly not contemporary with the time of Hercalius, and the arms and armour depicted are those of the late crusading period.

situation, and he decreed that from this time forwards Greek, the tongue of the Church and people, would be the official language of the empire. Within a generation, spoken Latin had become virtually extinct in the East.

Heraclius also abolished the ancient Roman imperial titles – *Imperator Caesar* and *Augustus* – and replaced them with the Greek word for king, *basileus*, which title was to remain in use to the end of the empire (although the Byzantines continued to emphasise that their *basileus* was Emperor of the Romans). As is so often the historical case when a strong-minded, powerful ruler dies, his sons prove to be a disappointment, and so it was with Heraclius. His ambitious wife

Martina had not only ensured the joint-succession of Heraclonas with the rightful heir Constantine III, but also that his will entrusted the empire not only to the sons but to herself as well. It was to cause outrage among the nobility and the people.

Despite his tragic last years, the reign of Heraclius was a glorious one. His leadership qualities had prevented the empire from falling to the Persians, in which case there would have been no bulwark to prevent the Muslims from overwhelming all of western Europe. Instead, he left Byzantium stronger than it had been for centuries, and the empire's survival for another 800 is in large part due to the efforts Heraclius made.

Constans the Uncaring

Through a series of tribulations that rocked the capital after the death of Heraclius, the short joint-reigns of Constantine III and Heraclonas left the empire in the hands of Constantine's young son Heraclius, renamed Constans to avoid confusion with his grandfather. Faced with the encroaching power of the Muslims, his was not an enviable task.

Pictured on the obverse of a gold solidus with his eldest son, Constantine IV, the long, luxurious beard that gave Constans II his nickname is proudly displayed. The coin's reverse depicts his other two sons, Heraclius and Tiberius.

Martina read out her husband's will and made it clear that she would rule over her sickly stepson and weak son. But her adherence to the hated monothelitism and her naked ambition made the Byzantines hate her. Fearing for his own safety, Constantine fled from the capital to Chalcedon, but soon succumbed to one of his illnesses and died on 25 May 641. Many suspected Martina's hand in his death – even her own son accused her of it.

During the years following the death of Justinian, the Senate had regained many of its earlier powers, serving as the supreme court of justice and the principal advisor to the sovereign. The august body now took matters into its own hands, and crowned Constans, Constantine's 11-year-old son, emperor, while at the same time deposing Martina and Heraclonas. Her tongue was cut out and his nose slit (or amputated, a recently revived oriental practice), then they were exiled to Rhodes. In his early years, Constans II 'Pogonatas' (nicknamed for the thick beard he grew in later life) was content to be guided by the Senate, but when he matured he proved to be an autocratic ruler.

In 642, the Byzantines surrendered Alexandria to the Saracen general Amr. When, two years after the death of Caliph Umar, his successor Uthman recalled Amr to Medina, a Byzantine fleet managed to recapture the city. But Amr hurried back and retook the city within the year.

Alexandria was razed to the ground and Amr made his capital at al-Fustat on the banks of the Nile (which in 969 would be rebuilt as al-Qahira, 'The Victorious' – or Cairo as it is known in the Western world).

Arab armies continued to expand across Africa, and under the leadership of Muawiya, the governor of Syria, began to push into Anatolia. Cappadocia and Phrygia were raided, and the city of Caesarea (Kayseri) occupied in 647. Muawiya began construction of a great fleet, which raided Cyprus in 649 and made successful assaults on the islands of Rhodes, Cos and Crete in 650–55. The celebrated Colossus of Rhodes, erected in 304 BC but brought down a century later by an earthquake, had lain where it fell for nine centuries. Now the Arab raiders cut it up for scrap and sold the metal to a Jewish merchant from Edessa. He required 900 camels to carry it away.

Constans – now in his 26th year – realised that left unstopped, this fearsome fleet would mop up all the Aegean islands and soon be standing outside Constantinople's harbours. So he gathered a fleet and attacked the Muslim navy off Phoenicus (Finike) in 655, but suffered a severe defeat and was forced to flee to Constantinople. Matters looked very grave, but the empire was spared by the outbreak of an Arab civil war, which lasted until 661, although it was a few more years yet before hostilities resumed with the West.

An imperial in Rome

Constans used the breathing space to deal with the continuing problems in the Church (*see pages 66–7*), matters of the succession and military campaigns in the West. In 654 he made his son Constantine IV co-emperor and five years later added his other two sons, Heraclius and Tiberius to the imperial roster. To alleviate any potential dynastic strife, he had his younger brother Theodosius murdered.

In 658 he invaded a region north of the Danube occupied by Slavs and forcibly resettled large numbers of them in Asia Minor. And then in 662 announced that he was moving the court from Constantinople to the West, as his grandfather Heraclius had once proposed. But where Heraclius had bowed to popular pressure, the opinions of his subjects were of supreme indifference to Constans. In truth he had good

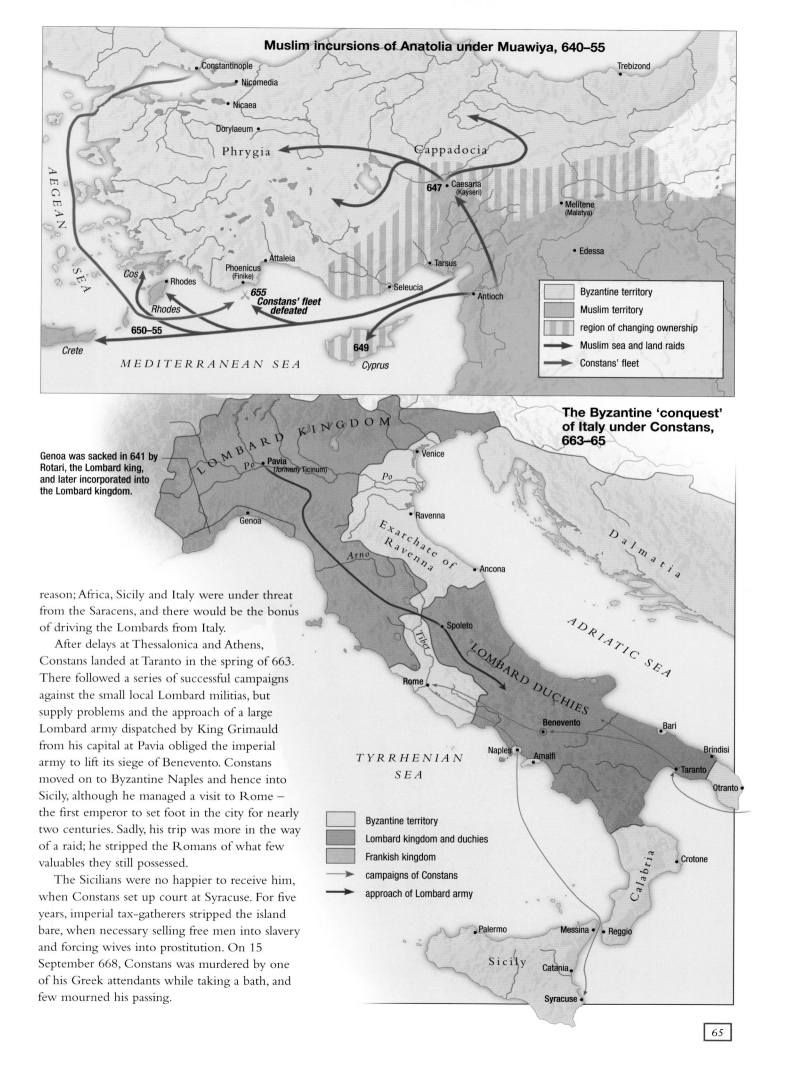

Muslim incursions of Anatolia under Muawiya, 640–55

Constantinople
Nicomedia
Nicaea
Dorylaeum
Trebizond
Phrygia
Cappadocia
647 Caesaria (Kayseri)
Melitene (Malatya)
Edessa
Attaleia
Phoenicus (Finike)
Tarsus
Cos
Rhodes
Seleucia
Antioch
655 Constans' fleet defeated
Rhodes
650–55
649
Crete
Cyprus
AEGEAN SEA
MEDITERRANEAN SEA

	Byzantine territory
	Muslim territory
	region of changing ownership
→	Muslim sea and land raids
→	Constans' fleet

The Byzantine 'conquest' of Italy under Constans, 663–65

LOMBARD KINGDOM
Po
Pavia (formerly Ticinum)
Venice
Po
Genoa
Ravenna
Exarchate of Ravenna
Ancona
Arno
Dalmatia
ADRIATIC SEA
Tiber
Spoleto
Rome
LOMBARD DUCHIES
Benevento
Bari
Naples
Amalfi
Brindisi
Taranto
Otranto
TYRRHENIAN SEA
Crotone
Calabria
Palermo
Messina
Reggio
Catania
Sicily
Syracuse

Genoa was sacked in 641 by Rotari, the Lombard king, and later incorporated into the Lombard kingdom.

	Byzantine territory
	Lombard kingdom and duchies
	Frankish kingdom
→	campaigns of Constans
→	approach of Lombard army

reason; Africa, Sicily and Italy were under threat from the Saracens, and there would be the bonus of driving the Lombards from Italy.

After delays at Thessalonica and Athens, Constans landed at Taranto in the spring of 663. There followed a series of successful campaigns against the small local Lombard militias, but supply problems and the approach of a large Lombard army dispatched by King Grimauld from his capital at Pavia obliged the imperial army to lift its siege of Benevento. Constans moved on to Byzantine Naples and hence into Sicily, although he managed a visit to Rome – the first emperor to set foot in the city for nearly two centuries. Sadly, his trip was more in the way of a raid; he stripped the Romans of what few valuables they still possessed.

The Sicilians were no happier to receive him, when Constans set up court at Syracuse. For five years, imperial tax-gatherers stripped the island bare, when necessary selling free men into slavery and forcing wives into prostitution. On 15 September 668, Constans was murdered by one of his Greek attendants while taking a bath, and few mourned his passing.

Way of the Single Will

Of the doctrine of the Single Will, Constans probably understood little, and cared less. He never had any time for theological debate, and his handling of such matters veered between indifference and heavy-handedness, neither of which did much to endear him to either his subjects or the clergy.

Right: A Byzantine painting of Christ Pantocrator (Christ, the creator of all). The nature of Christ and the divisibility of his human and divine natures had dogged the Eastern Church for almost three centuries – and was to continue to do so.

The Basilica of St John in Lateran and the Lateran Palace, home of the popes in Rome and of many councils, and the centre of Catholic opposition to Byzantine orthodoxy and the monothelitic heresy.

It made common sense to Constans II to forget the wretched doctrine of the Single Will business. Unfortunately, it would not go away. Monothelitism had a strong hold in Syria and Palestine, had been rejected by Africa and the Latin Church, but remained the religious official policy of Patriarch Paul II in Constantinople. In Africa, the most articulate critic of the Single Will was a monk known as Maximus the Confessor. In 646 Maximus arranged for a manifesto condemning the heresy to be endorsed by a synod of African bishops. This was then forwarded to Pope Theodore I. The pope wrote to Patriarch Paul, demanding a statement of his beliefs. When Paul responded by defending the Single Will, Theodore promptly excommunicated him.

The response from Carthage was as pronounced – Exarch Gregory proclaimed himself emperor in 647, but fortunately for Constans the rebellion was cut short in the following year by Gregory's death at the hands of Saracen raiders near Sufetula.

In 648, Patriarch Paul issued the *Typos* of Constans II in an attempt to bring about a compromise between the Christian factions. Constans' edict made no attempt to analyse the issue, it simply said that there was to be no further discussion of either the *Will* or the *Energy* of Christ. Of course, the *Typos* satisfied nobody. In the following year Theodore's successor, Pope Martin I summoned a council at the Lateran Palace which duly condemned it, and he wrote to Constans requiring the emperor to formally express his abhorrence of the monothelite dogma.

It was not calculated to please autocratic Constans, even had he agreed with the pope. He ordered the Exarch of Ravenna, Olympius, to march on Rome immediately and arrest Martin. Olympius, however, had other ideas, and counting on the widespread anti-Byzantine feeling and the pope's support, attempted to detach the entire province of Italy from the empire and seize secular power for himself. In this enterprise he failed, and retired with his army to Sicily, dying there three years later.

A brutal mercy

In June of 653 the new exarch, Theodore Calliopas, fulfilled Constans' orders by arresting Martin. Already a sick man, Martin was held for 90 days in a prison near Constantinople before

being brought before the Senate on the shaky charge that he had assumed the papacy without imperial consent and, more gravely, that he had conspired with Olympius against the emperor. In December of that year he was found guilty and condemned to death without being allowed to address the subject of the *Typos*.

But Patriarch Paul, himself on his deathbed, was moved by Martin's plight and begged Constans to spare his life. The emperor consented, but only after Martin had spent a further 85 days incarcerated with common criminals and suffered more brutalities. Then his sentence was commuted to exile at Kherson in the Crimea, where Martin, physically a ruin from his treatment, eventually died in 656. Maximus the Confessor was also eventually arrested and forced to stand trial. Found guilty, his tongue was removed along with his right hand and he was exiled to the fortress of Schemarion in the Caucasus, where he remained until his death in 662.

It was not Constans who solved the contentious matter, but his son, Constantine IV, who having secured a long peace on all his borders, was able to concentrate on the matter. At his insistence, Pope Agatho expressed his happiness to attend what would be the Sixth Ecumenical Council of the Church, held in the Domed Hall of the imperial palace in Ravenna. Delegates from all over the empire – 174 of them – poured into Ravenna during 680. The Italian

party were particularly honoured by being housed in the palace of Galla Placidia. Over ten months from November 680 to September 681, the council held 18 sessions, the first 11 being presided over by Constantine, who expressed no opinions of his own. At its conclusion the findings were unanimously endorsed and the doctrine of the Single Will consigned to history's waste bin. It dealt the monothelite heresy a blow from which it would never recover – and simultaneously ensured an even deeper split between orthodoxy and the monophysites.

Below: Engraving of a common image of the saint Pope Martin, chained in exile for thwarting the plans of Constans II.

The Fire of God

During Constans' long absence from Constantinople, the eastern provinces had been governed by the eldest of his three sons, Constantine IV (r.668–85), who at the age of 37 became emperor on his father's death. Constantine proved to be an able ruler, statesman and charismatic leader of men – he needed to be, Arab forces were about to besiege Constantinople.

Shown on this *solidus* appropriately armed and clad in armour, Constantine IV proved to be an adept strategist and military leader.

The reign began badly, when elements of the army demanded Constantine IV make his younger brothers Heraclius and Tiberius co-rulers with himself. It is not known whether or not they were guilty of conspiracy, but Constantine had them arrested and their noses were slit. It is hard to reconcile this cruel picture with the generally affable Constantine, but the painful indignity inflicted on his brothers publicly proclaimed their unfitness ever to rule, and so protected the succession of his own son.

He set out immediately in 669 for Sicily to bring back his father's body, but more importantly to establish his authority over the expeditionary army and bring it back to Constantinople. The emperor was only too well aware that the Arab world was once again on the move. In 661 Caliph Ali had been assassinated, and since then Muawiya had reigned supreme from his new capital of Damascus, where he had founded the Umayyad dynasty. Now he had resumed his successful naval tactics, capturing island after island: after Cos came Chios, then Smyrna was taken and finally in 672 Arab forces entered Marmara and occupied Cyzicus on the Bithynian shore, only 50 miles from Constantinople itself.

For a further two years the Arabs built their bridgehead at Cyzicus, and in 674 the assault began in earnest. As they had in the past, Constantinople's massive walls defeated the Arab's heavy siege engines and catapults. But it was a new secret Byzantine weapon that proved decisive. As the speedy, manoeuvrable *dromones* nipped in and out between the Arab war galleys, they hurled or sprayed Greek Fire onto the enemy. A chemist from Heliopolis (Baalbek) had invented this liquid fire some years previously and the composition of its ingredients was considered a state secret so zealously guarded that the essential elements remain unknown to this day.

The results were invariably catastrophic for the enemy, particularly since the oil-based flammable liquid floated on the water's surface, engulfing in flames any who jumped overboard to save themselves. Despite this setback, the Arabs continued their attacks for four years.

However, his failure to take Constantinople and news of a great Byzantine victory over Arab land forces in Anatolia in 678 brought Muawiya to the negotiating table; it seemed that the Byzantines were indeed under the protection of their powerful God. The peace terms were highly favourable to Byzantium: the Arabs evacuated the Aegean islands they had taken, and paid the emperor an annual tribute of 50 slaves, 50 horses and 3,000 pounds of gold. A year later Muawiya was dead.

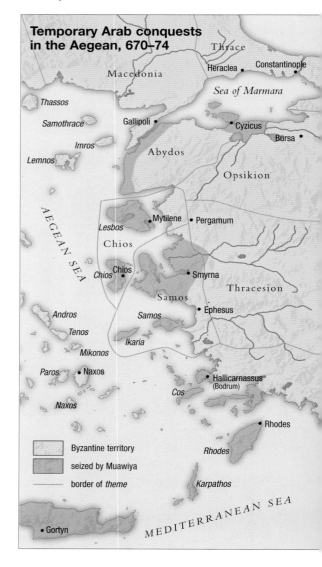

Temporary Arab conquests in the Aegean, 670–74

Thrace
Macedonia
Heraclea
Constantinople
Sea of Marmara
Thassos
Samothrace
Gallipoli
Cyzicus
Bursa
Imros
Abydos
Lemnos
Opsikion
Mytilene
Pergamum
AEGEAN SEA
Lesbos
Chios
Chios
Chios
Smyrna
Thracesion
Samos
Andros
Ephesus
Tenos
Samos
Ikaria
Mikonos
Paros
Naxos
Hallicarnassus
(Bodrum)
Cos
Naxos
Rhodes
Byzantine territory
Rhodes
seized by Muawiya
border of *theme*
Karpathos
MEDITERRANEAN SEA
Gortyn

A Western hero

By blocking their advance in Asia Minor, Constantine had forced the Arabs to travel the length of the Mediterranean along the North African coast before they could invade the European continent, and the extended lines of communication would render them unable to make permanent conquests beyond the Pyrenees. This overwhelming victory made Constantine the hero of the West, not only to his own subjects but also to those races that would have suffered at the hands of Islam – the Avars, Lombards and Frankish princes (the Slavs, however, remained sullen and fractious). The Avars now acknowledged Byzantine suzerainty, and the peace freed Constantine to turn his attention to a new irritant – the Bulgars.

This pagan race of Turkic origin had been wandering across the imperial frontier in the vicinity of the Danube delta in increasing numbers. A joint naval and land expedition under the emperor's personal command attempted to remove them from the area, but there had been poor reconnaissance of the swampy terrain, and the army was forced to retreat. In the following year Constantine agreed to a treaty that recognised the Bulgars' right to settle the disputed region. The Bulgars established their capital at Pliska, and soon were able to control Byzantine access to the lower Danube.

This setback was more a humiliation than a disaster, for given their numbers an accord with the Bulgars would have been made sooner or later, and at least this was a peaceful outcome. Constantine established the *theme* of Paristrion in what had been Roman Lower Moesia and settled many Avars there as a buffer against the Bulgars. And he scored a few more victories against the disorganised Arabs – raiding parties sacked Ascalon, Acre and Caesarea, and recaptured most of Cilicia.

With the Arabs in retreat and the Slav-Avar question satisfactorily settled, Constantine was able to tackle the stubborn doctrinal problem of the Single Will, with the outcome that was outlined on page 67. In 685, aged only 35, Constantine IV died from a dysenteric fever and was succeeded by his 17-year-old son, Justinian II.

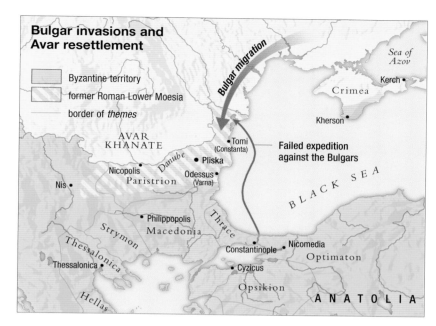

Bulgar invasions and Avar resettlement

Greek Fire – the most terrifying weapon of its time – came to the aid of the empire time and again. Its composition was the most closely guarded secret and even today no one is certain of the components or their relative mixture.

Emperor Cut-Nose

In the 56 years after Constantine's death, there was a succession of six desultory emperors, beginning with his monstrous son Justin II (who reigned twice), that plunged the empire into a state of restless anarchy. There were victories over Islam, but more due to Arab disunity than any real Byzantine ability. Byzantium needed a new strong man, and he was there – waiting in the background.

Justinian II (685–95, 705–11) suffered from a pathological suspicion of everyone and a lust for blood. He achieved two successes, the first being a renewal of the treaty concluded by his father with Muawiya. This resulted from successful military expeditions to Armenia, Georgia and Syria in 688, with the fifth caliph, Abdul-Malik, giving even more away. The agreed demilitarisation of Cyprus was a happy outcome for the Cypriots, who as a result gained an

A *solidus* of Justinian II shows the emperor in his first reign, and by far the most successful part of his rule.

enviable degree of autonomy they were to enjoy for almost three centuries. The second was his plan to repopulate Anatolia. The region had never quite recovered from the extreme taxation levied by his namesake, Justinian I, and the consequent migrations and falling birth rates.

In 688–9 he made a successful large-scale expedition into the Slav lands and then forcibly resettled vast numbers of villagers and peasants in the Theme of Opsikion. The Mardaites were transported from the Lebanon to the region around Attaleia with the willing agreement of Abdul-Malik – these wild tribesmen were a thorn in his side and he was pleased to be rid of them. Further transplantations were ordered from both East and West. In all, over the space of six

years a quarter of a million people were established in Asia Minor. The net result was a new class of peasant farmers independent of the old senatorial aristocracy but bound to their neighbours by the land held in common. More land came under cultivation, and improved living conditions led to a rise in the birth rate. Since Heraclius's institution of compulsory military service for the head or eldest son remained in force, this provided an ever-stronger local militia.

However, Justinian's uncontrolled passion for building soon led to increased rates of taxation, and in 691 some 20,000 resettled Slavs defected to the Arabs when hostilities were renewed. This ensured a defeat at Sebastopolis (Sebastea) for the empire and the loss of Armenia. Taxation fell worse on the aristocracy, and the methods of its collection were tyrannous; in a body they rose up and proclaimed an army officer named Leontius emperor. Justinian was seized and although his life was spared, he suffered the by now usual mutilation of the nose before his expulsion. For this disfigurement, he was known afterwards as *Rhinometus* – 'Cut-Nose'.

Justinian fled to Kherson, where the Khazar khagan Ibuzir welcomed him and gave his sister to Justinian as a bride. But he was later forced to abandon her when embassies from Leontius persuaded the khagan to accept the price for the exile – dead or alive.

The reign of Leontius (695–98) is notable only for the capture of Carthage by the Saracens and the eventual loss of the Exarchate of Africa in 698. He sent a fleet to the rescue, but its failure led its leaders to acclaim the vice-admiral, a German named Apsimar, who promptly changed his name to Tiberius. On their return to Constantinople, the Greens – who hated Blue-supporting Leontius – joined the rebels, and soon enough Leontius found himself with a slit nose and passage to a monastery.

Tiberius III (698–705) might have proved a worthy ruler – he secured Cilicia against the Arabs, and even inflicted heavy losses on them – but he was overthrown by Justinian. Having fled the Crimea, the exile had managed to secure the aid of the Bulgar king Tervel, and when avenging Justinian arrived before the walls of Constantinople with a barbarian horde of Bulgars and Slavs, the citizens wisely capitulated. Tiberius fled, but was captured and executed along with Leontius. By now Justinian was barely sane. The

reign of terror he instigated at Constantinople was echoed by senseless punitive expeditions sent against Ravenna and Kherson. The result at Ravenna was a series of insurrections, while the citizens of Kherson announced they no longer recognised Justinian. They acclaimed an Armenian exile named Bardanes, who adopted the Roman name of Philippicus.

End of the Heraclian line

With support of the local Khazar troops, Philippicus repulsed the Byzantine fleet, and in a repeat of the rebellion against Leontius, its commander bowed to Philippicus rather than report failure. The fleet sailed for Constantinople, whose citizens welcomed their new emperor. Justinian was captured outside the city and beheaded, his body flung unceremoniously into the Marmara, ending the dynasty of Heraclius.

Philippicus (r.711–13) was no sinecure for the ills besetting the empire. He was a hedonistic spendthrift with a penchant for theological debate that leaned in favour of re-establishing the hated monothelitism. Philippicus was also faced with an invasion by the Bulgars under Tervel in revenge for the killing of his friend Justinian, who probably trusting the Bulgar, had allowed the Thracian defences to dwindle. Philippicus summoned troops from the Opsikion Theme, but

they felt no loyalty to the upstart Armenian, and a group of their officers engineered a coup in which the emperor's eyes were put out.

The Senate now chose the emperor's chief secretary, a certain Artemius, who took the name Anastasius II (r.713–15). With the support of the Opsikians, the Bulgars were driven back, and Anastasius wisely rescinded the monothelitist edicts of Philippicus. Had he been given the chance, Anastasius might have proven a careful and wise ruler, but the Opsikian faction – probably peeved at being prevented by the Senate from making their own choice of emperor – selected a tax-gatherer named Theodosius and proclaimed him. After a few months of strife, Anastasius was deposed and Theodosius III (r.715–17) elevated in his place. Of his short, pointless and reluctant reign, little is recorded other than his willingness to stand down in favour of the most brilliant general of his time – Leo the Isaurian.

After his restoration to the throne, Justinian introduced an image of Christ on his coins – the first emperor to do so. This portrays Christ on the obverse (left) and Justinian II on the reverse, although the depictions suggest a similarity in the likenesses.

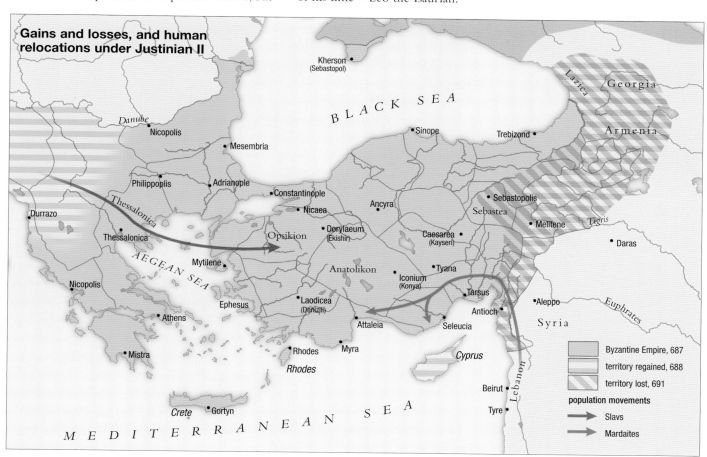

Gains and losses, and human relocations under Justinian II

Kherson (Sebastopol)

BLACK SEA

Danube

Nicopolis

Mesembria

Sinope

Trebizond

Lazica

Georgia

Armenia

Philippoplis

Adrianople

Constantinople

Nicaea

Ancyra

Sebastopolis

Sebastea

Durrazo

Thessalonica

Opsikion

Dorylaeum (Ekishir)

Caesarea (Kayseri)

Melitene

Tigris

Daras

Thessalonica

Mytilene

AEGEAN SEA

Anatolikon

Iconium (Konya)

Tyana

Tarsus

Euphrates

Nicopolis

Ephesus

Laodicea (Denizli)

Attaleia

Seleucia

Antioch

Aleppo

Syria

Athens

Rhodes

Myra

Cyprus

Mistra

Rhodes

Beirut

Lebanon

Crete

Gortyn

Tyre

MEDITERRANEAN SEA

Byzantine Empire, 687
territory regained, 688
territory lost, 691

population movements

Slavs

Mardaites

71

Two Empires Under God

The Isaurian dynasty founded by Leo III held the Arabs at bay but brought religious disunity to a new high. It was to be a period where the direst external threat lay to the West in the Balkans as the Bulgar nation expanded, and in which the Latin and Greek Churches became ever more estranged and Byzantine Italy turned its back on the East to bow before a new Emperor of the Romans – a barbarian king of the Franks.

The house that Leo III (r.717–41) founded is often known as Isaurian, but in fact he was not from Isauria, having probably been born in 675 in Comegene, a part of north Syria beyond the Taurus Mountains. What is certain is that his accession ended the anarchy into which the empire had fallen since the reign of Justinian II.

A victim of the huge population shifts during Justinian II's reign, as a child Leo had been resettled near Mesembria in Thrace. For a young man on the make, this was a happy move because it placed him in the proximity of Justinian's march on Constantinople in 705. The story is told that he offered the returning emperor 500 sheep for the army's supplies and in return was invited to join the imperial guard with the rank of *spatharius*. His abilities soon promoted him through the ranks and he held diplomatic posts in Syria and the Caucasus, where his fluency in Arabic was a great aid. In 715 Anastasius appointed Leo *strategos* of Anatolikon and it was here that his troops proclaimed him emperor.

Constantinople's defence in the face of a combined naval and land siege by the Arab generals Maslama and Suleiman was the first act of Leo's reign. Maslama crossed the Hellespont into Thrace and surrounded Constantinople on its landward side. From his diplomatic sessions, the emperor knew both generals well, and had even given them hints on how to take the city – advice that was purposely incorrect and which led them into a hopeless mess. In the ferocious winter of 717–18, the inadequately provisioned Arab troops suffered dreadfully, huddling in their

Map labels:
Celts
Saxons
York
London
Boulogne
Aachen
Frankfurt
Mainz
Bretons
Seine
Paris
Ponthion
Regensburg
Rhine
Loire
Orléans
Danube
Agri Decumates
Abandoned 275
FRANKISH KINGDOM
Lyons
Bordeaux
Milan
Pavia
Venice
Garonne
Rhône
Avignon
Genoa
Ravenna
Basques
Toulouse
Marseilles
Corsica
Rome
Ebro
Zaragoza
UMMAYAD EMIRATE
OF CORDOBA
Barcelona
Valencia
Balearic Islands
Sardinia
Cordoba
Seville
Cartagena
Saracen attacks
on Sardinia and
Sicily begin in 827.
Pale
Ceuta
Caesarea
(Cherchell)
Carthage
IDRISIDS

Legend:
frontier of Roman Empire, c.270
Eastern Roman Empire at death of Justinian I, 565
Byzantine Empire, 622
Byzantine Empire, 814 (barely nominal control of Italian territories)
empire of Charlemagne, 814
Arab territories by 800
Papal States, 756
titular border of Armenia

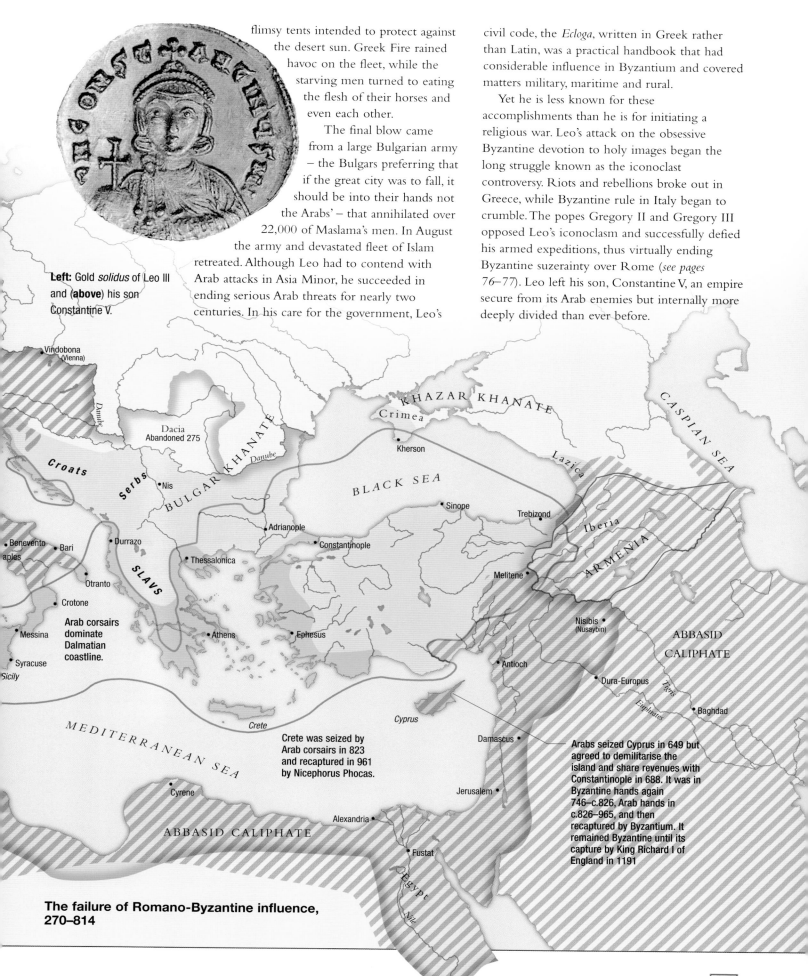

flimsy tents intended to protect against the desert sun. Greek Fire rained havoc on the fleet, while the starving men turned to eating the flesh of their horses and even each other.

The final blow came from a large Bulgarian army – the Bulgars preferring that if the great city was to fall, it should be into their hands not the Arabs' – that annihilated over 22,000 of Maslama's men. In August the army and devastated fleet of Islam retreated. Although Leo had to contend with Arab attacks in Asia Minor, he succeeded in ending serious Arab threats for nearly two centuries. In his care for the government, Leo's civil code, the *Ecloga*, written in Greek rather than Latin, was a practical handbook that had considerable influence in Byzantium and covered matters military, maritime and rural.

Yet he is less known for these accomplishments than he is for initiating a religious war. Leo's attack on the obsessive Byzantine devotion to holy images began the long struggle known as the iconoclast controversy. Riots and rebellions broke out in Greece, while Byzantine rule in Italy began to crumble. The popes Gregory II and Gregory III opposed Leo's iconoclasm and successfully defied his armed expeditions, thus virtually ending Byzantine suzerainty over Rome (*see pages 76–77*). Leo left his son, Constantine V, an empire secure from its Arab enemies but internally more deeply divided than ever before.

Left: Gold *solidus* of Leo III and (**above**) his son Constantine V.

Croats

Serbs

Nis

Dacia
Abandoned 275

Danube

BULGAR KHANATE

Danube

KHAZAR KHANATE

Crimea

Kherson

BLACK SEA

Sinope

Trebizond

Lazica

CASPIAN SEA

Iberia

ARMENIA

ABBASID
CALIPHATE

Benevento

Bari

aples

Durrazo

SLAVS

Thessalonica

Adrianople

Constantinople

Melitene

Otranto

Crotone

**Arab corsairs
dominate
Dalmatian
coastline.**

Athens

Ephesus

Nisibis
(Nusaybin)

Messina

Syracuse

Sicily

Antioch

Dura-Europus

Tigris

Euphrates

Baghdad

MEDITERRANEAN SEA

Crete

Cyprus

Damascus

**Crete was seized by
Arab corsairs in 823
and recaptured in 961
by Nicephorus Phocas.**

Jerusalem

**Arabs seized Cyprus in 649 but
agreed to demilitarise the
island and share revenues with
Constantinople in 688. It was in
Byzantine hands again
746–c.826, Arab hands in
c.826–965, and then
recaptured by Byzantium. It
remained Byzantine until its
capture by King Richard I of
England in 1191**

Cyrene

Alexandria

ABBASID CALIPHATE

Fustat

Egypt

Nile

**The failure of Romano-Byzantine influence,
270–814**

Destruction of the Icons

In the first quarter of the eighth century, there came about a great controversy. Its effects split the orthodox Church and threatened the very fabric of the Byzantine state.

The iconoclast controversy was the struggle between the iconophiles – those who worshipped icons – and the iconoclasts[†], who turned against the veneration of holy icons in churches. The word 'iconoclasm' literally means icon-smashing. The Latin Church's position had

Silver relief with Virgin and child. The Virgin Mary was among the most venerated of Byzantine icons.

been determined by the pronouncements of Pope Gregory I, who regarded icons in church as a useful form of Bible for the illiterate masses, but not as objects of veneration. The attitude in the East was very different. The spiritual leader of the

monastic movement, John of Damascus, had lifted icons to a higher spiritual plane, teaching that the grace of the represented figure passed over to the worshipper. 'I see the human form of God,' John said, 'and my soul is saved.' John, one of many Christian theologians formerly in Byzantine administration, who found themselves retained by the conquering Arabs in a similar capacity, became first minister to the Umayyad caliph Abdul-Malik.

The monastic movement had an enormous influence on the Byzantine governing class and the emperors (see pages 36–7). One particularly influential iconophile was Maximus, son of a distinguished family in Constantinople, whose spiritual home was Syria, from which the monastic movement received much of its stimulus. Maximus was secretary to the advisory council of Emperor Heraclius. So it is an irony that the two figures who closely advised their rulers – men facing each other across a gulf of enmity – shared exactly the same spiritual background.

Nevertheless, Islam, like Judaism, had never accepted the representation of God in images, a position similar to that of the monophysite Christians, who were prevalent in the east of Asia Minor and Syria, and who violently disagreed with the teachings of orthodox theologians like John of Damascus. And it was in the East that an iconoclastic manifesto appeared as a reaction to what many bishops considered as flagrant idolatry. With his Syrian background it is likely that Leo III had absorbed many of the practices of monophysitism and of Islam. He was horrified at the state to which icons had been raised in Constantinople. The cult had become uncontrolled; holy images proliferated and were openly worshipped in their own right.

Despite his personal feelings, however, Leo was not immediately persuaded to alter the state of affairs. He had himself employed the power of Constantinople's most popular wonder-icon, the Virgin Hodegetria, during the Arab siege of the city the year before. Two events changed his mind. In 723, Caliph Yazid, having been cured of a serious disease by a Jewish physician, was persuaded by his doctor to destroy all Christian images in homes and public places in his

717–18	726	727	741–75	750	754	756	771
The Arab siege of Constantinople is defeated by Bulgars and Leo III's diplomacy	Leo's destruction of the palace's principal gateway starts the iconoclast controversy	Ravenna revolts against Leo and the iconoclasts; founding of the Venetian republic	Reign of Constantine V, most vicious of the iconoclast emperors	Battle of the Greater Zab: Arabs of the Abbasid dynasty bring down the Umayyad Caliphate	Pope Stephen III crowns Pepin the Short as Emperor of the Frankish Western Empire	The Franks conquer Lombard Italy; the old Exarchate of Ravenna becomes the Papal State	Charlemagne the Great becomes sole ruler of the Frankish kingdom

[†] or iconodules

dominions. This, in itself, would hardly have affected Leo, except that there is evidence that the same Jewish doctor was at work in Constantinople a year later and put pressure on the emperor.

A religious programme

The second event was a mission of iconoclast bishops to the emperor in 725. It seems that the combination of Muslim and Jewish influences, together with the opinions of his own Christian subjects, swayed Leo into acting. First he preached several sermons pointing out the worst excesses of icon worship, which he held to be in open disobedience of the Law of Moses, as laid out in the Second Commandment. Then, in 726, he acted. As an example, he chose the destruction of the principal gateway – the Chalkē – to the imperial palace, in itself the most extraordinary icon in the whole city. Its tall central dome was decorated with a dazzling circlet of mosaics depicting the triumphs of Justinian and Belisarius, probably similar to those still surviving in San Vitale, Ravenna.

This act of destruction led to immediate rioting and almost civil war. But instead of retreating, Leo ordered the destruction of all holy images throughout the empire. Any who opposed him would be arrested and punished, and those who continued to cherish their icons could expect to be persecuted.

However, after Leo's death, it fell to his son

Constantine V (r.741–75) to increase the iconoclast pressure to the levels of a pogrom. By the last years of his reign, thousands of monks and nuns, abbots, and other clerics were put to death in defence of their chosen way of life. In the theme of Thracesion, the local governor, Michael Lachanodrakon, had a favourite way of dealing with recalcitrant iconophile monks. He had their beards smeared with a highly flammable mixture of oil and wax, and then set fire to them.

Ultimately, the iconoclast controversy split the orthodox Church and the empire, and greatly weakened the state by diverting energies that would have been better directed at its enemies gathering on all sides. Of course, it also destroyed countless priceless works of art.

Above: Triptych of Moses receiving the Ten Commandments, painted by monks of St Catherine's Monastery, Sinai. Remote places escaped the worst of the iconoclast controversy.

Below: Victims of the Iconoclasts are executed; an 11th-century illumination from the *Chronicle of John Skylitzes.*

The Loss of Italy

Leo's destruction of the icons in the principal gateway to the palace in Constantinople sent shudders of revulsion through every Catholic in the West. To them, iconoclasm represented sacrilege; inheritors of the old Graeco-Roman tradition of human representation, they revered their icons and were prepared to fight for them.

Facing: Despite Constantine V's persecution of monks, monasteries continued to flourish long after his death. Christ Pantocrator adorns the dome of Varlaam monastery, Greece, built in 1541, and unashamedly iconodule.

Pope Gregory II, irritated at the emperor's presumption in giving himself supreme doctrinal authority and disgusted at the destruction of the icons, gave his full support to the Italians in the Exarchate of Ravenna who rose in revolt in 727. The exarch was murdered, and his provincial governors went into hiding. The local garrisons chose the own commanders and declared their independence from the empire. Along the Venetian shore, the

Above: Charlemagne's father, Pepin the Short – son of Charles Martel, who turned the Arab invasion back at Poitiers in 732 – made an alliance with the papacy. In return, Pope Stephen III crowned him King of the Franks in 754, pictured here in a medieval French print.

communities chose an officer from Heraclea named Ursus, and gave him the old Roman title of *dux*. It was the birth of the Venetian Republic, and the *dux* (or *doge* in the Venetian dialect) was the first in a succession of 117 over more than a thousand years until the republic's end in 1797. Severely depleted of territory, a semblance of the exarchate was re-established around Ravenna, but it was a shaky state.

The pope publicly condemned iconoclasm and wrote to Leo III suggesting that he leave the task of defining Christian dogma to those best qualified to understand theology. Leo's response

was to order Gregory's arrest, but the ships sent foundered in a storm, and Gregory died before any further action could be taken. His successor, Gregory III, was equally adamant, and incensed when the emperor seized the Church revenues of Sicily and Calabria. Gregory summoned a synod in November 731, which threatened excommunication to any who laid hands on sacred objects. Leo struck back by transferring the Sicilian, Calabrian and several Balkan bishoprics to the see of Constantinople. The breach between the two Churches was now all but complete.

In the following year Leo's 14-year-old son Constantine was betrothed to the Khazar khagan's daughter, who became a Christian, and in 750 provided Constantine with his son and heir Leo IV, who was thus half-Khazar. At the age of 23 Constantine V (r.741–75) succeeded his father, only to be temporarily overthrown a year later. The short insurrection of his brother-in-law Artabasdus in 742, which interrupted Constantine V's reign, was notable only for his attempts to restore the icons, and the consequent enhancement of Constantine's hatred for the sacred images to the almost pathological degree outlined on the previous page.

Some historians have argued that Constantine's attacks on the monasteries (the monks were largely responsible for his nickname *Copronymus*, 'Dung-named') had a practical aspect – that they were promoting a no doubt beneficial piety but encouraging a sterile life in a time when a high birth rate was essential. During the seventh and eighth centuries their numbers had multiplied, and more and more of the population, rich and poor alike, were opting for a life in the cloisters. His solution, however, failed in the long term; monastic life continued to flourish after his death, draining the empire's life blood to the very end.

Lombardy wins… and loses

Constantine's military exploits were of a somewhat nobler level: he scored victories against the weakened Arabs in northern Syria, Armenia and Mesopotamia; Greek Fire helped to destroy an Alexandrian fleet. But in 750 at the battle of the Greater Zab the army of Abu al-Abbas al-Suffah destroyed that of Caliph Marwan II, and the Umayyad Caliphate of Damascus came to an end. Arab power passed to the Abbasid Caliphate of Baghdad, whose interest lay to the East, not in Africa, Asia Minor or Europe. Constantine could turn his attention to the Bulgars – he was to lead no less than nine campaigns against them, and it was on the last of them in 775 that he died on 14 September.

Had his care for the West been as great as for the East, Italy might have been saved, but he had antagonised his Italian subjects and the pope. The Lombards, who had been continually expanding, finally captured Ravenna in 751. Rome, abandoned by the emperor, turned to another power for security. This lay north of the Alps. In the same year that Ravenna fell, the Frankish leader Pepin the Short (r.741–68) secured his coronation. Pope Stephen III set out for France in 754 and met Pepin at Ponthion, and there anointed him, together with his two sons Carolus (Charles) and Carloman, as King of the Franks, and conferred on him the ancient Roman title of patrician.

Pepin returned the favour by promising to transfer to the pope all the territories that the

Lombards had captured from the empire.

In 756 the Franks swept into Italy and defeated the Lombards. Pepin formally handed over all the lands that had formerly been the imperial exarchate, and the Papal States came into being. Through much trial and tribulation, they would last for another 11 centuries.

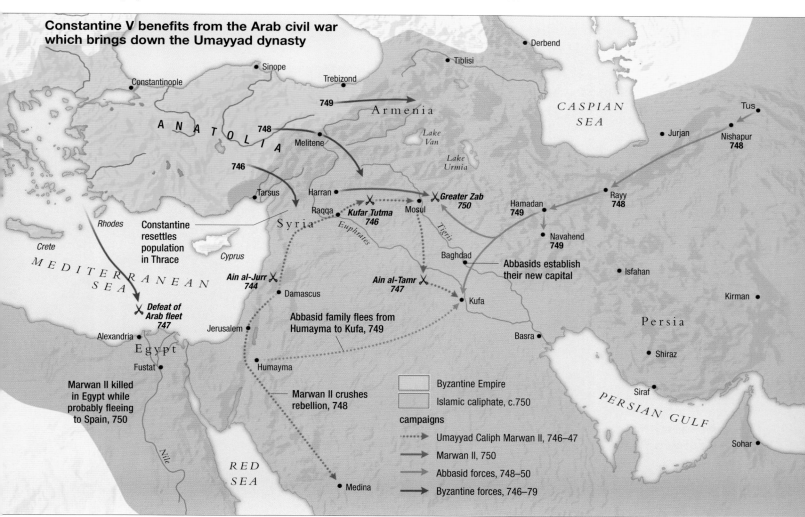

Constantine V benefits from the Arab civil war which brings down the Umayyad dynasty

Constantine resettles population in Thrace

Abbasids establish their new capital

Abbasid family flees from Humayma to Kufa, 749

Marwan II crushes rebellion, 748

Marwan II killed in Egypt while probably fleeing to Spain, 750

749 · 748 · 746 · Greater Zab 750 · Kufar Tutma 746 · Rayy 748 · Hamadan 749 · Navahend 749 · Nishapur 748 · Tus · Jurjan · Ain al-Jurr 744 · Ain al-Tamr 747 · Defeat of Arab fleet 747

| | Byzantine Empire |
| | Islamic caliphate, c.750 |

campaigns

- ······ Umayyad Caliph Marwan II, 746–47
- → Marwan II, 750
- → Abbasid forces, 748–50
- → Byzantine forces, 746–79

An Empress on the Throne

Despite his notorious preference for the company of young men, Constantine V fathered six sons and a daughter, the eldest of whom ascended the throne on his death as Leo IV. However, morally and physically weak, it was his scheming and ambitious wife Irene who ruled through him, and then in her own right when he succumbed to disease.

L eo IV (r.775–80) was an iconoclast like his father, albeit of somewhat milder temperament. His wife Irene, a native of Athens, took the opposite view and did everything in her power to defeat iconoclasm. Her effectiveness was limited while her husband lived, but when Leo died on 8 September 780, she became regent to their ten-year-old son, Constantine VI (r.780–97). He was never to be anything more than a cipher – everything he signed or decreed was done at her will, and a disastrous business it was to be.

She immediately faced a mutiny among the Anatolian military – iconoclasts to a man – which was put down ruthlessly, and the following army purge removed all her best officers. In consequence the Byzantine governor of Sicily declared independence and then made an alliance with the Saracens of North Africa, and the Armenian general Tatzates similarly defected with all his men to the Arabs when the caliph's son Harun al-Rashid crossed the border in 782. He was bought off by an expensive truce.

In 784 she dismissed the iconoclastic Patriarch Paul IV (his resignation was surely a push?) and replaced him with her former secretary Tarasius. It was he who brokered a reconciliation with Pope Hadrian I that led to the Seventh

Ecumenical Council, convened initially at Constantinople in 786 to debate the return to the see of Rome those bishoprics removed by Leo III and the restatement of iconophile orthodoxy. Frustrated by discontented elements of the military, it was later reconvened at Nicaea, and formally revived the supremacy of icons, though with the admonitory phrasing of 'veneration' rather than 'adoration'.

What is significant about the triumphant iconophile outcome of this council is that it emphasised Byzantine Christianity as belonging to the Graeco-Roman tradition and its rejection of the mystical, oriental side of Christianity as represented by the monophysite-iconoclasts. So it was rooting Byzantium in western theology at the very time the empire was losing political touch with the West. This would condemn the Byzantine Empire to a religiously obstinate isolation from which it could never emerge.

Murderer of her son

In 790 Irene's overarching ambition led her to insist that her name should always appear before her son's, which made the hapless emperor a magnet for the iconoclast malcontents fed up with her policies. When Irene got wind of the conspiracy, she had her son imprisoned and demanded an oath of loyalty from the entire army. Predictably, this was not forthcoming from Asia, and troops of the Armeniakon Theme mutinied. Soon there were shouts from every side acclaiming Constantine as the legitimate ruler.

Freed from his captivity, Constantine fled to Anatolia, and now the empress found herself

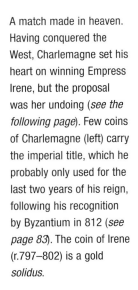

Facing: The Castle of the Seven Towers. The impregnable walls of Constantinople were proof against the many enemies of Byzantium, but internal strife frequently ended the reigns of emperors… and empresses.

A match made in heaven. Having conquered the West, Charlemagne set his heart on winning Empress Irene, but the proposal was her undoing (*see the following page*). Few coins of Charlemagne (left) carry the imperial title, which he probably only used for the last two years of his reign, following his recognition by Byzantium in 812 (*see page 83*). The coin of Irene (r.797–802) is a gold *solidus*.

incarcerated, although not for long. She had never trusted aristocrats in positions of eminence (most of them iconoclasts) and instead relied almost exclusively on eunuchs for ministers. Unfortunately, the incompetence and veniality of her appointees highlight her own inability to select competent and trustworthy staff, but collectively they were wily enough on her behalf on this occasion. Soon enough a deal was brokered, and Constantine VI returned to court and reinstated Irene.

The situation could not last long – while her son lived he was bound to become the focus for another mutiny – so when the time was right, she had him taken and brought before her in chains to the imperial palace. And there, on the afternoon of 15 August 797, Irene had her son's eyes stabbed out, a wound from which he died some time afterwards.

Irene now found herself the sole ruler, *basileus* – she rejected the feminine *basilissa* – but loathed by almost all of her subjects for her treatment of Constantine and feared by the numerically superior iconoclasts. Despite the empty imperial coffers, drained by the huge sums she was paying

in annual tribute to the Arabs, to curry popular support Irene announced massive tax cuts that the state could not possibly afford. But her subjects' affections were not so easily purchased, the axe had to fall soon. But when it did, it was none of the above that brought down Irene, it was the threat of her marriage to Charlemagne the Great.

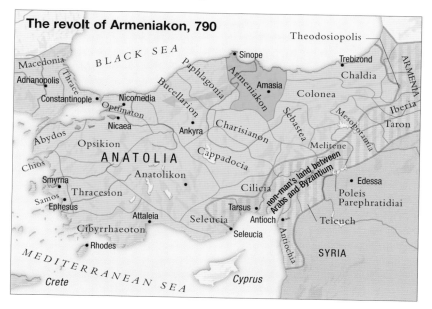

The revolt of Armeniakon, 790

Emperor of the Romans

King Charles (r.768–814), son of Pepin the Short, was 26 when he acquired half his father's realm. The other half went to his brother Carloman, but relations between them were strained until Carloman's death in 771, when Charles took control of the entire Frankish kingdom, becoming Carolus Magnus (Charlemagne, or Charles the Great).

Inset right: A Gothic reliquary bust of Charlemagne. Most 'portraits' of the great king are fanciful, partly based on the earliest known statue – at Metz – which itself is probably not an accurate likeness.

In 773 Charlemagne captured Pavia and proclaimed himself King of the Lombards, reconfirming the Papal States his father had helped to create. Two years later he began a ten-year crusade against the pagan Saxons which resulted in their subjugation and conversion to Christianity. In 778 he campaigned with only limited success against the Muslim Moors in Spain before annexing Bavaria. This was already a Christian state, but his cousin Duke Tassilo of Bavaria had revolted with the aid of the pagan Avars. Charlemagne moved on into Austria and Hungary and destroyed the Avar Khanate by 796 (the Avar remnant in the Balkans was then wiped out by the Bulgars soon after the turn of the century).

In little more than a generation, Charlemagne had raised the Frankish kingdom from just one more European tribal state to a single political entity unparalleled since the days of imperial Rome. In all this Charlemagne had enjoyed the papacy's support, a sustenance that should have been properly addressed to the emperor in Constantinople, had Constantine V been attentive to Italy's problems rather than obsessing over iconoclasm. Pope Hadrian had been disappointed that the reading of the Seventh Ecumenical Council's findings had omitted whole tracts his legates had agreed on, and the emperor had never returned to Rome the sees taken by Leo III. Charlemagne, then, was by far the more trustworthy partner for the future.

On Christmas Day 800 at St Peter's in Rome, Pope Leo III placed the imperial crown on Charlemagne's head and conferred on him the title Emperor of the Romans. Even so, this was not purely an action born of petulance. Leo had good reason to elevate the Frankish king to imperial status. Ever since his papal accession, Leo had been subjected to factional attacks, which culminated in his enemies fabricating charges against him of simony, perjury and adultery. In such a case, only the emperor could pass judgement on the Vicar of Christ, but as far as Leo – and indeed everyone in the West – was concerned the throne was vacant since Constantine V's murder.

According to Salic law, a female could not rule, and since Irene was undoubtedly a woman, there was no living emperor. Charlemagne, by virtue of his doctrinal orthodoxy, his reuniting Europe under the Latin Church, and his political and military might was clearly the man who should become emperor. But in crowning Charlemagne, Leo was also establishing the right for the first time of the pope to appoint and invest the Emperor of the Romans. He had completed the process of religious hegemony over temporal power in the West, begun so long ago when Ambrose of Milan humbled the great Theodosius.

The marriage proposal

In his new capacity, Charlemagne cleared Leo of all the charges laid against him, and then addressed the question of reuniting the western and eastern halves of the empire. The obvious solution would be to marry Irene. There had been a qualified indication that Irene might accept a proposal from him, for in 781 she had selected Charlemagne's daughter Rotrud

Saint Peter hands Charlemagne (right) the flag of Rome and Pope Leo III the holy stola – a symbol of the unity of Church and State. The deal that saw Charlemagne crowned Roman Emperor was a mutually advantageous one. In return for papal authority sanctifying the right of the monarch to rule, the papacy received the protection of a united Frankish empire, which rivalled Byzantium. The pope also enjoyed powerful support for the Latin doctrine against Byzantine orthodoxy.

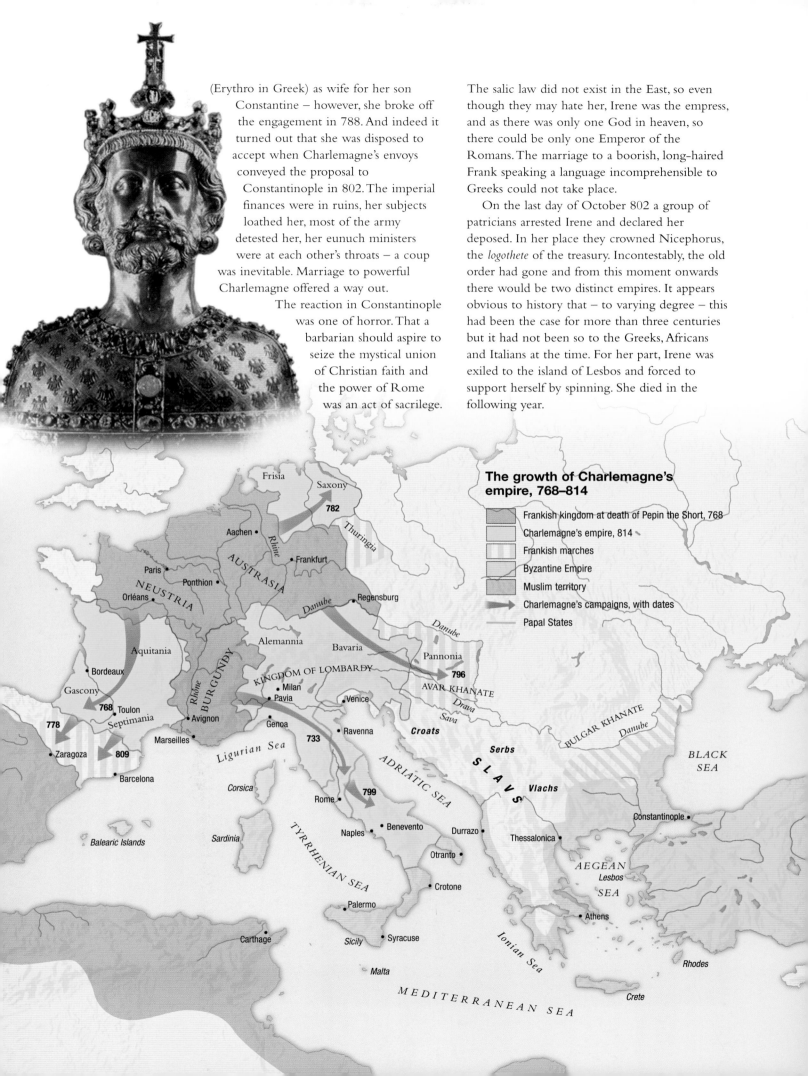

(Erythro in Greek) as wife for her son Constantine – however, she broke off the engagement in 788. And indeed it turned out that she was disposed to accept when Charlemagne's envoys conveyed the proposal to Constantinople in 802. The imperial finances were in ruins, her subjects loathed her, most of the army detested her, her eunuch ministers were at each other's throats – a coup was inevitable. Marriage to powerful Charlemagne offered a way out.

The reaction in Constantinople was one of horror. That a barbarian should aspire to seize the mystical union of Christian faith and the power of Rome was an act of sacrilege.

The salic law did not exist in the East, so even though they may hate her, Irene was the empress, and as there was only one God in heaven, so there could be only one Emperor of the Romans. The marriage to a boorish, long-haired Frank speaking a language incomprehensible to Greeks could not take place.

On the last day of October 802 a group of patricians arrested Irene and declared her deposed. In her place they crowned Nicephorus, the *logothete* of the treasury. Incontestably, the old order had gone and from this moment onwards there would be two distinct empires. It appears obvious to history that – to varying degree – this had been the case for more than three centuries but it had not been so to the Greeks, Africans and Italians at the time. For her part, Irene was exiled to the island of Lesbos and forced to support herself by spinning. She died in the following year.

The growth of Charlemagne's empire, 768–814

- Frankish kingdom at death of Pepin the Short, 768
- Charlemagne's empire, 814
- Frankish marches
- Byzantine Empire
- Muslim territory
- Charlemagne's campaigns, with dates
- Papal States

Pax Nicephori

Nicephorus I (r.802–11) was a native of Seleucia in Pisidia, though it was said he was of Arab extraction, a descendant of the Ghassanid King Jaballah. As a former logothete of the Treasury, no one better knew the empire's parlous financial state, and he determined to correct his predecessor's mistakes.

Irene's tax exemptions were rescinded, private loans to merchants forbidden, shipowners were only allowed to borrow from the state and at a ruinous 17% interest rate, better-off landowners had to pay for equipping destitute farmers who were compulsorily drafted into the army. Provincial administrators were authorised to sequester gold and silver plate from churches and

monasteries, and the latter had troops billeted on them, which they had to feed at their own expense. Of course, these arrangements made Nicephorus unpopular, especially with the monks, but he did refill the treasury.

He refused to pay Harun al-Rashid any further tribute agreed by Irene, which prompted an Arab invasion of Cappadocia in 803. The situation was worsened by the revolt of the Byzantine commander, an Armenian named Bardanes, who received support from other local officers, notably the later emperors Leo the Armenian and Michael the Amorian. Although the rebellion was quickly crushed, it allowed Harun to make deep inroads into Anatolia. Eventually, Nicephorus bought him off with 50,000 gold pieces, a subsidy that ended with Harun's death in 809. Freed of this pressure, Nicephorus concentrated on the Bulgars, who had been attacking cities in Thrace since 808.

They were now under the leadership of the formidable Krum. He had risen to prominence in the campaigns that wiped out the last of the Avars and then united the Bulgar tribes that lived in Pannonia and Transylvania with those of the Danube basin. Nicephorus led a campaign against Krum, but abandoned it at Adrianople because of a conspiracy among the officers. In the autumn of 808, Krum ambushed a large Byzantine army, before capturing Serdica and slaughtering the 6,000-strong garrison.

Unpopular as he was, Nicephorus now desperately needed a victory in order to hang onto the throne. His second campaign met with some success, and the Bulgar capital of Pliska was burnt down, but it had not defeated Krum. So in May of 811 he led another expedition to ravage Bulgarian territory, but without bringing Krum to battle. Towards the end of July, Nicephorus led his men through a narrow defile without adequate reconnaissance and the Bulgars trapped them in. Two days later, on the 26th, the Bulgars fell on the Byzantines without mercy. Hardly a single soldier escaped to tell the tale. Krum retrieved the emperor's body, cut off the head, and later had the skull mounted in silver to use for a drinking cup.

Stauracius, the emperor's son, was among the survivors, but he was too badly hurt to be effective, and in any case died of his agonising wounds six months later. This left another survivor – the emperor's son-in-law Michael

Rhangabe – as the only claimant standing, and on the second day of October he was acclaimed and crowned as *basileus*.

Because of the timing, the credit for the peace accord at this time between Byzantium and Aachen was taken by Michael, but it is with good reason known as the *Pax Nicephori*. In spite of having ignored Charlemagne's imperial claims for the better part of his reign, Nicephorus did send envoys north late in 810, and agreement on most issues was reached before his death. Michael's task was merely ratification of the treaty, which established the limits of the two empires. In 805 the Venetian doge, Obelerio degli Antenori, had paid homage to Charlemagne, but now the Franks relinquished all claims to Venice and the province of Venetia, together with the cities of Istria and the Dalmatian coast.

This treaty, however, was the highlight of an otherwise disastrous two-year reign. Handsome, strong and in his prime, Michael I was sadly lacking in intelligence and easily manipulated by those around him. As the tool of the ecclesiastic party, he was as diligent in his persecution of the iconoclasts as he and his wife Procopia were in

their prodigal spending on churches and monasteries, thus returning what Nicephorus had taken from them. Unfortunately he had little care for the empire's defence.

With poor leadership and through worse advice, Michael let Krum divest Byzantium of a string of Thracian strongholds throughout 812: fortified Develtus on the Black Sea fell first in the spring, followed by Anchialus (Pomorie), Beroe (Stara Zagora) and Philippopolis (Plovdiv). Finally, early in November, Mesembria (Nesebur), one the richest ports in the Balkans, fell after Michael refused to come to the besieged city's aid. As had his successor, Michael needed a victory to keep his throne.

In May 813, the Byzantine army marched out from Constantinople, and brought the Bulgars to battle on 22 June at Versinicia, 20 miles northeast of Adrianople. The Macedonian units charged, but astonishingly, their Anatolian comrades under Leo the Armenian fled the field. The brave Macedonians were slaughtered and by 17 July Krum was encamped beneath Constantinople's walls and Michael Rhangabe had abdicated in favour of perfidious Leo.

Facing: The Thracian hinterland, with its forested and rocky defiles was a treacherous place for unwary armies on the march – it suited the kind of warfare practised by the Bulgars and it hindered the Byzantine cavalry.

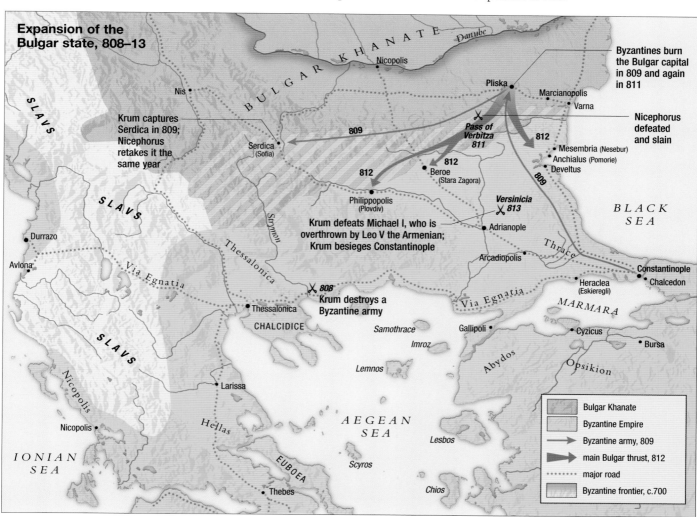

Peace and Civil War

The reigns of Leo V and his successors Michael II and Theophilus were marked by a return of iconoclasm in the periods of peace between bloodshed occasioned by both external and internal enemies.

Two scenes depicting the persecution of the monk and historian Theophanes, from the *Chronicle of John Skylitzes*. Theophanes (c.758–817), son of an imperial governor, was influential at the second General Council of Nicaea (787), and signed its decrees in defence of the sacred images. When Leo the Armenian resumed his iconoclastic warfare, he tried in vain to induce Theophanes to condemn what had been sanctioned by the council.
Theophanes was cast into prison and suffered cruelly for two years before being banished to the tiny island of Samothrace, where he died 17 days later.

All the evidence points to treachery on the field of Versinicia. The Bulgars were happiest fighting in their rocky landscape, not the open plains of southern Thrace in set battle. The Macedonian charge almost won the day, yet the experienced Anatolian troops abandoned the field without a fight. Leo V the Armenian (r.813–20) had won his throne through a deal with Krum, who had not expected to fight at all. Michael was allowed to retire to a monastery, Procopia to a convent, and their three sons were spared, other than being castrated to prevent their making any future bids for power.† For his part, Krum saw no necessity in supporting Leo once their pact was complete, and he quickly besieged Constantinople.

Leo almost justified his usurpation by his spirited defence of the city, although the Bulgars laid waste the surrounding towns and countryside. Byzantine ambassadors were sent to the court of Lewis the Pious, who had recently succeeded his father Charlemagne, but Lewis had enough problems of his own and was unable to offer any help. In the event it did not matter: on 13 April 814 Krum died and his young son Omortag – facing a revolt of the Bulgar aristocracy – concluded a treaty with Leo that was to last for 30 years. With a similar eruption in the Arab court preventing further hostilities in the East and the *Pax Nicephori* still holding with the Franks, an extraordinary peace descended on the empire.

But with peace came internal unrest in 815 as a swell of iconoclast anger manifested itself again, a reaction designed to damn Irene's memory. Leo, who had strong iconoclast leanings, supported and even led by the example of an edict a new rash of icon-smashing, condemning 'the unprofitable practice of making and adoring icons… preferring worship in spirit and in truth'. The wave of ruination was without precedent as every holy image, vestment or panel was destroyed.

Where in the past religious extremism had frequently led to imperial downfall, it was simple jealousy combined with ambition that felled Leo. His brother officer and friend Michael the Amorian (he came from the Phrygian city of Amorium), who had also been involved with the revolt of Bardanes in 803, was detected in a conspiracy against Leo, and thrown into a cell in December 820 to await his execution. However, Michael's partisans laid their plans carefully and struck down Leo while he was celebrating Christmas Mass. They then rescued Michael from his prison, and he was hastily crowned still wearing his leg-irons (no one could find the key, and a blacksmith struck them off afterwards).

† An emperor had to be perfect in body, hence the proliferation of nose slitting and castration that became common in the Byzantine Empire.

Gold *solidi* of Michael II the Amorian (left) and his son Theophilus.

The moderate iconoclast

The key events in the reign of Michael II (r.820-29) – who could not justify Leo's murder on religious grounds, since he was himself an iconoclast – were the virtual civil war caused by Thomas the Slav, the Moorish conquest of Crete in 823 and the start of Saracen attacks on Sicily in 827. Crete fell to a band of 10,000 Moors expelled from Andalusia after an unsuccessful insurrection against their emir. For more than a century, Crete was to be a corsair haven, and the pirates a scourge of the Mediterranean.

Thomas the Slav, another brother officer, simply aimed for the throne, successfully carrying a greater part of the Anatolian army with him. His siege of Constantinople was undone from an unexpected quarter. Omortag the Bulgar brought an army to the rescue and smashed Thomas's forces near Heraclea. Thomas and the remnant of his army fled, but desertions brought him down by 824. Michael placed his booted foot on the rebel's neck before having his hands and feet cut off and the living torso impaled on a stake.

In spite of his sympathies, Michael aimed to conciliate the iconophiles, but incurred the wrath of the monks by entering into a second marriage with the daughter of Constantine VI and the unspeakable Irene, Euphrosyne, who had previously taken the veil. Nevertheless, despite monastic imprecations against an emperor marrying for a second time – and a nun – the marriage was a happy one, and Euphrosyne was at his side when Michael II died in October 829 – the first emperor for half a century to do so while a reigning monarch.

To his son Theophilus, strong, healthy and in the prime of life, Michael left an empire secure in peace but financially exhausted from the civil war that had left tens of thousands of destitute peasants thronging the capital in search of welfare. However, Theophilus was to enjoy a stroke of luck that altered the empire's financial position.

Restoration of the Icons

The second of the Amorian (or sometimes Phrygian) dynasty, Theophilus was a more pronounced iconoclast than his father and strictly forbade the veneration of icons, but the doctrine was running out of steam and within another twenty years the iconophiles were to be triumphant.

In marked contrast to his barely literate father (his courtiers joked that in the time it took Michael to spell his name, one of them could read a whole book), Theophilus (r.829–42) was intellectually gifted, had a passion for theology and a love of Islamic culture. Nevertheless, he was to fight the Caliphate all of his reign in a series of costly campaigns. He also spent great sums of money in beautifying Constantinople, especially the Great Palace, on lavish entertainments for visiting dignitaries and in public largesse that went a long way to alleviate the penury of the citizens after the civil war.

Where did all this wealth come from? His father, after all, had left the treasury almost depleted. The answer has been a matter of speculation ever since – evidence of its source is lacking from any record.

Evidence does, however, point to the economy suffering a bout of severe inflation, suggesting that indeed there was a great deal of money in circulation. The answer would appear to be that towards the end of Michael's reign the opening of gold mines, probably in Armenia, created an almost inexhaustible supply of new wealth – but it remains a mystery.

The renewed Arab hostility was mainly his own fault for giving asylum to the Persian sect of Hurramites, who had been in revolt against Caliph Mamun for some time. To the caliph, this was an act of war and the Arab army was soon on the move. The Byzantine army was at first successful. Theophilus himself led an expedition in 830, sacking the city of Zapetra, and another in the following year that took back much of Muslim-held Cilicia. The Christian-Islam war now took a new turn. For the first time the caliph vowed never to make peace unless emperor and people forswore Christianity for Islam. Mamun's death in 833 while campaigning changed nothing; his brother-successor Mutasim

A weak and ineffectual ruler, Michael III earned the nickname 'the Sot' or 'the Drunkard'.

vowed that the *jihad* would continue.

Eager to avenge the sack of his birthplace Zapetra, Mutasim swore to destroy Amorium – home of the emperor's family – and assembled a vast army. One division defeated Theophilus at Dazimon (Tokat), while the other advanced against Amorium. After a brave resistance of 55 days, on 23 September 838 the city fell into Mutasim's hands through the treachery of a converted Muslim. The city was razed to the ground, 30,000 inhabitants were slain and the rest sold into slavery.

Theophilus, horrified at the destruction and now seriously alarmed at the power of Islam – and its newly avowed intention to destroy Christianity – appealed to Emperor Lewis, proposing a joint venture against Islam. Had he succeeded, the Crusades might have started 250 years before they did, but negotiations dragged on over four years. During this period the emperor's health gradually failed, and on 20 January 842 he died, following his bitter enemy Mutasim to the grave by 15 days.

Michael the Drunkard

Theophilus's widow, Empress Theodora, had (secretly) never shared his iconoclast adherence, and when she found herself acting as regent to their barely three-year old son Michael, she determined once and for all to end the heresy. But Theodora, from an aristocratic Paphlagonian family, was no Irene and she moved with caution. Recognising that the forces of iconoclasm were almost spent, she saw no reason to act vindictively towards those who espoused the doctrine. By such a manner, Theodora accomplished her aims by the end of 843 – iconoclasm was never again to rend the empire.

Theodora's piety – not to mention her success over iconoclasm – led her to perpetrate one of the worst crimes of the ninth century, the persecution of the Paulicians. This Armenian sect, which had arisen some 200 years previously and which might be described as eccentric but harmless, was an offence to orthodoxy. Following the heavily adapted teachings of third-century Paul of Samosat, they rejected almost all orthodox Christian values and ceremonies, including the holy images, but also baptism, marriage, the cross and marriage, as well as most of the Bible; and of course they were

monophysites. When they refused to renounce their faith, a vast military force was sent against them. In the resulting massacre, more than 100,000 lost their lives and the pitiful remnant fled across the border to seek asylum with the emir of Melitene (Malatya).

Much discredit for this virtual genocide must go to the *logothete* Theoctistus, who for almost 13 years had been the effective joint-ruler with Theodora. But his end was at hand. In 855 the actual emperor, Michael III, was 15 and fell under the sway of his uncle, Bardas. Theodora's brother resented the way Theoctistus had ousted him from control. Bardas now engineered the assassination of the *logothete* and the house arrest of Theodora.

Michael was to prove lucky that Bardas, now raised to the rank of caesar, was also a good administrator, for the young man was weak-willed and feckless, preferring debauchery and drinking (for which he earned the sobriquet the 'Sot') to government. In a period of ten years Bardas won a string of victories over the Arabs and Cretan corsairs, and presided over the conversion to Christianity of the Bulgars (*see pages 96–7*). But in his turn, his days were numbered. One of Michael's unwise habits was to raise his drinking cronies to high position and one of them, a groom named Basil, contrived to assassinate Bardas and persuade Michael to make him co-emperor. Sixteen months later Michael III lay dead at the feet of his friend.

The Great Palace

Much mention is made of 'the palace' or the 'imperial palace'. In fact the emperor had the use of several palaces in and about Constantinople, and these were in a constant state of evolution, just as the imperial residences on the Palatine in Rome had grown to eventually occupy the entire hill to the exclusion of any other houses.

There is almost nothing left to see today of the Great Palace (with the exception of St Sophia), but we can reconstruct it to some extent from the detailed contemporary accounts, such as the *Book of Ceremonies*.

The special position of the emperor as the Vice-Gerent of God was expressed in both the imperial palace buildings and in church architecture. In Constantine the Great's days church architecture had naturally adopted the same style of building as that used for civil functions and imperial audience halls, namely the basilica. In effect, the early church was a copy of the emperor's audience hall, except that where in a palace the apse at the end housed the throne, in a church it was where the altar was placed. This is emphasised in the story of Theodosius and Ambrose, where the emperor as a matter of custom attempted to take communion in the altar enclosure (*see page 17*).

The reverse became true by the time of Justinian, where churches built in the shape of a Greek cross – that is a cross with equal length arms – became the model for later palaces. An example is to be found in descriptions of the chrysotriklinos, or Golden Throne Room, built by Justin II, which copied the Greek cross ground plan of St Sergius in Constantinople and San Vitale in Ravenna. In the 10th century it was still the centre of the Great Palace and featured the astonishing *pentapyrgion*, a huge confection of gold shaped like a tree in which the imperial crowns and crown jewels were displayed. In the tree's branches, golden birds sang and warbled whenever an honoured visitor attended an audience. Constantinople became a city of palaces, each with a special significance. The palace of the Hebdomon had a ceremonial purpose associated with old Roman tradition. It sat in the Byzantine equivalent of the Campus Martius, the Field of Mars, and it was where the emperor reviewed the European troops before the start of a campaign, and where the patriarch and high ecclesiastics gathered to greet an emperor returning from campaign.

The Blachernae Palace owed its position to the annual imperial procession to the Blachernae church which, built by Marcian, was an exact copy of the Church of the Assumption built in Jerusalem by Empress Helena. At first outside the city walls, its incorporation in the defences by Leo V resulted in its expansion.

But these and many other fine palaces paled

into insignificance when compared to the Great Palace – an entire city within the city, it was not one structure but many interconnected buildings. It had its own water supply, cisterns, baths, sports arenas, gardens and churches. Founded by Constantine for ceremonial purposes – he did not live in it – every emperor since had built at least some addition. Even honoured visitors got to see little of its extent beyond a few state rooms.

Designed to inspire awe

The Great Palace was usually entered through the Chalkē, a large building taking its name from its bronze doors. By the end of iconoclasm the vestibule was only a museum containing statues of past generals, emperors, and Hellenistic sculptures. Beyond the vestibule was the tribunal room where legal sessions took place, and to the left and right were the rooms of the imperial guard. Through these rooms lay the Room of the Nineteen Divans where the emperor and his guests were served reclining, an ancient habit that fell out of fashion during the seventh century.

Behind this room there was a chapel and the assembly halls of the large and little *consistorium*, for the imperial counsellors. From here a corridor connected to the *sacellum*, the imperial treasury and the state archives. To one side stood the domed room used for the Church Council sessions in 691–2, and the *Delphax* where the emperor invested high officials.

A passage led from the front of the Room of Nineteen Divans to the oldest part of the complex, built by Constantine the Great. This comprised the Palace of Daphne, named after the statue of the nymph brought from Rome, and the Magnaura. There was a magnificent room for state receptions, next to which was the Octagon, a collection of private rooms and an imperial bedroom. The church of St Stephen was also connected to the Palace of Daphne, where coronations and imperial burials took place. To one side Theophilus built the throne-room called the Triconchus in 838, also used for receptions, and nearby stood the ramp from which the emperor reviewed the gold-caparisoned horse of the Greens and Blues.

Further to the east lay the pavilion-style buildings of Theophilus, including the Tzykanisterion, a pleasure palace that stood in front of the polo ground he constructed; this and the Triconchus were inspired by models in Samarra and Baghdad.

The Magnaura was a basilica with three aisles separated by pillars, like a Christian church of the fifth century. On a dais, six steps up from the end of the centre aisle, flanked by golden lions, sat the throne of Solomon from which the emperor presided at audiences. A great terrace surrounded the Magnaura on which stood statues of various emperors from the sixth and seventh centuries. The last statue erected was that of Phocas, after which the custom was discontinued. In the second half of the ninth century the Magnaura was assigned to the university, newly founded by Bardas.

The Great Palace was not intended to be a comfortable residence for the emperor. It was a statement of the power and glory of the empire, a gargantuan symbol of Byzantine achievement designed to overawe any who visited.

Today, only Hagia Sophia (St Sophia) remains to give the modern visitor to Istanbul a sense of the immensity of the Imperial Palace. The four minarets and several side chapels were added later, after the Ottoman conquest of 1453, when the great church was converted into a mosque.

The Apogee of Byzantium

As so often in Byzantine history, Basil's reign began with the bloodshed of his predecessor, and yet because of the great legislative work he undertook he is often called the 'second Justinian'. Basil inaugurated a new age, associated with the dynasty which he founded, the Macedonian. It was a period of territorial expansion, during which – once again – the empire became the strongest power in Europe.

Basil I (r.867–86) is misleadingly called 'the Macedonian', in fact he was an uneducated Armenian peasant. His family, along with many of their countrymen, had been resettled in Thrace and subsequently fell into the hands of Krum. They were transported beyond the Danube to the theme known as Macedonia – probably because of the number of genuine Macedonians who had suffered a similar fate. He spoke Greek badly with a strong Armenian accent and remained illiterate all his life. As a young man he had managed to escape his Bulgarian bondage and was lucky enough to enter the service of Theophilitzes, a relative of Bardas, as groom. He is said to have earned the notice of Michael III

The Mediterranean, c.878

SLAVS

Paris

Frankfurt

Rhine

Danube

FRANKISH KINGDOM

Lyons

Rhône

Milan

Po

Venice

Republic of Venice

CROATS

SERBS

BULGAR KHANATE

Danube

Avignon

Genoa

Ravenna

Zara

Split

Dalmatia

Nis

Marseilles

Elba

Corsica

PAPAL STATES

Rome

Duchy of Benevento

Bari

Benevento

Naples

Otranto

Adrianople

Thessalonica

SLAVS

from 714

Sardinia

from 711

from 800

Byzantines manage to hold onto Taormina.

Palermo

Sicily

Taormina

Sicily lost to Saracens, 878

Syracuse

Carthage

Athens

SLAVS

I f r i q y a

after 650

Malta

Crete

The Mediterranean in c.878

	nominal Byzantine suzerainty
	Byzantine Empire
	empire of Charlemagne
	Arab territories
	Bulgar Khanate
	Khazaria
	Armenian kingdom
→	Arab attacks, with date

Crete is lost again to control of Arab corsairs.

by winning a wrestling match, and soon became the emperor's closest companion.

Basil was obliged to divorce his wife Maria to marry the emperor's mistress Eudocia Ingerina. This unusual step may have been designed to introduce Eudocia into the Palace without causing a scandal for Michael. It must certainly have been the cause of a commonly held belief that the son, Leo, who arrived on 19 September 866, was not Basil's but Michael's – and therefore the dynasty known as Macedonian was in fact a

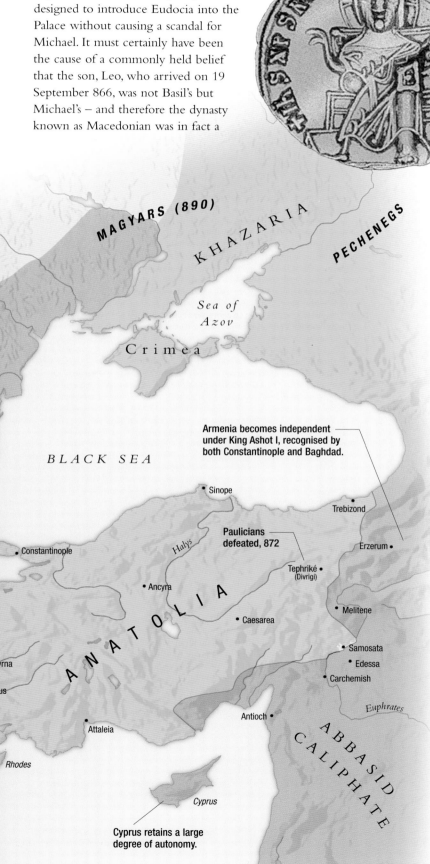

Gold *solidus* of Basil I.

continuation of the Amorian.

Basil's ecclesiastical policy was in marked contrast to that of his predecessors; he made immediate moves to establish good relations with Pope Nicholas I by dismissing Patriarch Photius and restoring his rival Ignatius, whose claims were supported by Nicholas, before he himself was deposed (*see pages 94–5*). Basil had a reason: his ambition was to recover the empire's western provinces, a task that would be made easier with papal support. However, the relationship was lukewarm at best – Nicholas's successor Hadrian II had mistakenly taken Basil's overture as an indication that Rome would be returned to its once supreme ecclesiastic position. When the newly converted Bulgars wanted a patriarchy of their own, Basil weighed the advantages of stronger ties with Bulgaria, and to papal fury the khan got his way (*see pages 96–7*). From this point on Roman Catholicism and Greek Orthodoxy were to go forward as very separate entities.

In the military sphere, Basil had many successes. In the East, the Paulician heretics who had fled to the Arabs were on the rise again and spreading back into Anatolia. In two campaigns Basil destroyed their fortified base of Tephriké (Divrigi) near the Euphrates in 872 and killed their leader Chrysocheirus. Over the next ten years Byzantine forces kept up the pressure on the Arabs, capturing several strongholds, including Zapetra and Samosata; only Melitene stubbornly refused to yield.

In the West, Basil failed to hold onto a brief recovery of Crete and was unable to dislodge the Saracens from Sicily, whose last city, Syracuse, fell in 878 (although the garrison of Taormina was to hold on until 902). But these upsets were far outweighed by the huge gains made in Italy and Dalmatia. The Saracens were expelled from the entire Dalmatian coast and it became an imperial theme. In 873 Benevento acknowledged his suzerainty and Otranto was recovered; in 876 Bari also recognised Byzantium. From these two strategic bridgeheads, virtually all of southern Italy was restored to the empire.

These victories would not have been possible without a strong navy, and Basil ensured that it was returned to its former state. Thanks to his efforts, it was to become the most powerful force in the Mediterranean and one of the best trained and most efficient that the world had seen. With control of the Mediterranean and the Adriatic, Byzantium was poised on the edge of the most glorious period of its existence.

MAGYARS (890)

KHAZARIA

PECHENEGS

Sea of Azov

Crimea

BLACK SEA

Armenia becomes independent under King Ashot I, recognised by both Constantinople and Baghdad.

• Sinope

Trebizond •

Paulicians defeated, 872

Erzerum •

• Constantinople

Halys

Tephriké (Divrigi)

• Ancyra

ANATOLIA

• Caesarea

• Melitene

ymyrna

• Samosata
• Edessa
• Carchemish

Antioch •

Euphrates

sus

• Attaleia

ABBASID CALIPHATE

Rhodes

Cyprus

Cyprus retains a large degree of autonomy.

Basil I and Leo VI, Law-Makers

Remarkable for the illiterate 'Macedonian' is the ambitious revision of Roman law that Basil began. But his resemblance to Justinian I lies not only in his attention to jurisprudence and the recovery of Italy but also in his lavish church-building programme.

Beneficiary of his older brother's fatal accident, Leo VI the Wise succeeded Basil as emperor.

A revision of the law on such a scale had not been attempted since the days of Justinian over three centuries before. Leo II had produced the *Ecloga*, but it was in effect only a handbook for judges; besides, it was now virtually obsolete. Basil's ambition – to produce a massive encyclopedia, what he described as an *anacatharis*, or purification, of the old laws – was never quite fulfilled. The extent of collection, collation and reconciliation of introduced contradictions was such that it was never completed in his lifetime, nor as he had conceived it. What did appear was a shorter work, the *Procheiron*, or Handbook. In this, a résumé of the most

important legislation in general use was grouped under 40 convenient headings.

Before his death Basil – with the names of his sons Leo and Alexander also appended – published the *Epanagogē*, or Summary. A rearrangement of the *Procheiron*, its greatest significance lay in the supplementary material on the rights and duties of the emperor, patriarch and other high prelates and administrators. It clearly laid out the structure of the Byzantine State – a single polity headed jointly by the emperor and patriarch, working together in parallel for the temporal and spiritual welfare of their subjects.

Constantinople had seen little building under the ninth-century iconoclasts; Theophilus had deliberately restricted his extensive work to domestic architecture. Basil now began a massive restoration and construction programme in which visual adornment dominated in the form of glittering mosaics. St Sophia, badly damaged in an earthquake of January 869, was repaired in the nick of time to prevent its total collapse. Constantine's Church of the Holy Apostles, rebuilt by Justinian but now in a sorry state, was also repaired and lavishly decorated.

But his greatest triumph was the new church he built within the Palace precincts. Dedicated to

St Michael, the Prophet Elijah, the Virgin Mary and St Nicholas, everyone knew it as the Nea, the 'New'. The Nea was probably inspired by the Triconchus of Theophilus, with its three half-domes over three apses. Basil provided the Great Palace with a new treasury, fabulous new baths and rebuilt the dilapidated Chalkē to restore it as the appropriate gateway to the world's most important residence.

In 869 Basil crowned Constantine, his eldest son by his first wife Maria, as co-emperor, but he died ten years later of unknown causes. Distraught, Basil never got over the tragedy, and had little affection for his three youngest, Leo, Alexander and Stephen. He particularly loathed 13-year-old Leo – another indication, perhaps, that Leo was not really his. However, seven years later when Basil died in 886 as the result of a hunting accident – which may have been a murder plot – it was Leo the Wise who became emperor.

Lucky in law, unlucky in love

'Wise' because Leo VI (886–912) possessed a fine academic mind; he read widely, thought deeply on theology and philosophy, and composed liturgical poems and hymns. He also completed the legal work begun by his father, published in the Greek language in a series of six huge volumes known as the *Basilica*. They were largely based on Justinian's *Codex* and *Digest*, but did include parts of the *Procheiron*. Having noted the latter's elevation of the patriarchy to that of almost equal status with the emperor, Leo had

the undoubted author of that inclusion, Patriarch Photius, replaced by his young brother Stephen.

The emperor was unfortunate in his domestic life. He had been forced by Basil to marry his first wife, the suffocatingly pious Thephano. When, to his relief, she died in 897, he married his former mistress Zoe, but she died in 899. He now faced a problem – an heir was desperately need but canon law forbade any after two marriages. In view of the need for stability, however, Leo received patriarchal dispensation an married a Phrygian named Eudocia. Alas, she died in childbirth in 901, and the baby boy followed her a few days later. Unable to get around canon law again, Leo took a mistress – another Zoe – and when she gave birth to his son Constantine VII in 905, he was allowed to marry on condition that she would not be legitimised as empress.

While contentment reigned in Constantinople, Leo was less fortunate abroad. In 894 the Bulgars routed Leo's army and again two years later (*see page 97*). In 907 Constantinople itself came under attack by the Kievan Rus, who were seeking favourable trading rights with the empire. Leo paid them off, but they attacked again in 911, and a trade treaty was finally signed. And in 912 a Muslim fleet all but wiped out that of Byzantium, which was returning from a failed attempt to wrest Crete from the Arabs. It was the last news Leo received. He died through ill health on 11 May, leaving his dissipated brother Alexander to rule for a mercifully short year and a few days.

Above: The fall of Syracuse, as portrayed in the *Chronicle of John Skylitzes*. The loss of Sicily robbed Constantinople of grain and silk supplies.

Facing: Also from the *Chronicle of John Skylitzes*, the marriage of Basil I and Empress Eudocia Ingerina.

Pope versus Patriarch

The iconoclast struggle had bitterly divided the religious community. With its end, iconoclasm effectively vanished, and the aristocratic clergy that had been its greatest supporters tended towards a new moderateness. Not so the victorious iconophiles, and so the echoes still sounded and found expression in another divide, one that came to be known as the Photian Schism.

The iconophiles had looked for their leaders among the monastic community, and in Ignatius found their most outspoken proponent. One of Michael I's castrated sons, he had never wavered in his devotion to the holy images, but like so many of his kind his mind was too narrow to encompass any but the simplest theological doctrines. When the moderate iconophile Patriarch Methodius I died in 847, Ignatius succeeded him. Ignatius, like many iconophiles, had always been a staunch supporter of the pope,

The emperors Basil I and Leo VI receiving presents; from the *Chronicle of John Skylitzes.*

and this stance plus his intransigent zealotry found little favour with Caesar Bardas.

Bardas looked to the moderate party, and found his man in Photius, an aristocratic civil servant, but a layman. Having engineered Ignatius's arrest on an implausible charge of treason, Bardas put Photius through an accelerated ordination: over six days starting on 20 December 858 Photius was tonsured, ordained lector, then subdeacon, deacon, priest and on Christmas Day he was consecrated bishop. A few days later and he was enthroned as patriarch.

No single person better exemplified the new age, nor indeed did any other play a larger part in the cultural rebirth and missionary activity among the Slavs, Bulgars and Russians, which mark the middle of the ninth century. However, the accession of Photius was not calculated to please Pope Nicholas, who deplored the uncanonical speed of his ordination and, as a supporter of the deposed patriarch, demanded the restoration of Ignatius. Photius refused to bow to the pressure, and went so far as to convince papal delegates at a council – summoned at Constantinople to investigate the matter – that he was indeed the lawful patriarch.

Nicholas now wrote to the patriarchs of Alexandria, Jerusalem and Antioch calling on them to do everything to restore Ignatius to his rightful throne – a waste of time, since all three sees were under Arab jurisdiction. And then in 863 Nicholas excommunicated Photius. This insult was greeted by patriarchal silence at first, but when western missionaries began spreading the dangerous heresy among the Bulgarians that, as the most recent, the Patriarchy of Constantinople was the least venerable of the five Christian sees, Photius acted.

In his plan to have Nicholas deposed he received support from an unexpected quarter, the Western emperor, Lewis II. The pope had refused his sanction for the emperor's younger brother King Lothair of Lorraine to divorce his wife and marry his mistress, and Lewis was determined he should be brought down. A council of 867 in Constantinople proclaimed Nicholas deposed, and Lewis sent a military force to Rome to physically remove him. In return, Byzantium officially recognised him as Emperor of the Franks. Michael III appears to have expressed no concern that his supremacy was compromised by this recognition, but he was probably too drunk

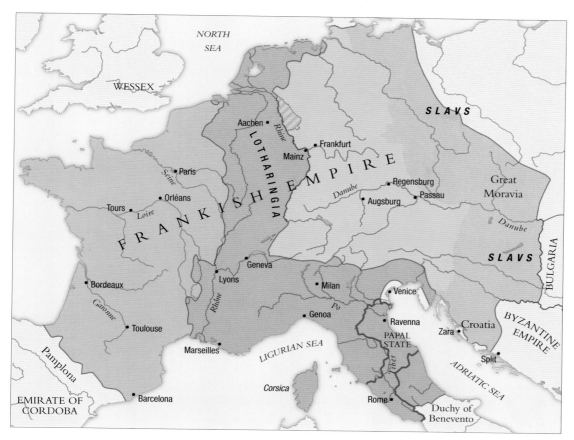

The division of the Frankish empire:
After his death in 814, Charlemagne's empire fell apart as his grandsons – Charles the Bald, Lothar (emperor) and Lewis (the German) – squabbled with each other. The partition was agreed on at the Treaty of Verdun (843). A further treaty of 870 (**below**) settled Italy on Lothar's surviving son, Lewis II, and so made him the ruler most in touch with the Byzantine Empire.

to notice, and his by then co-emperor Basil had his own plans – for papacy and patriarchy.

Removed, restored and removed

Michael was not even in his sarcophagus when Basil I dismissed Photius and replaced him with his old adversary Ignatius, for the purpose outlined on page 91. With his monastic zeal, the missionary work in the Balkans continued apace, not only in Bulgaria but throughout the Balkans. The Slav tribes embraced Christianity in Greece, Macedonia and Serbia, although Roman influence prevailed in Croatia and the northern Dalmatian coast.

However, Photius was not finished. Ignatius became a victim of his own missionary success. The exponential expansion of Orthodoxy he had sponsored created huge administrative problems, and the ill-educated patriarch was not up to the task. There was little he could do to prevent the new clerical positions being filled by key Photian supporters, and when he died aged 80 in October 877, Photius assumed the patriarchal throne for the second time. Three years later the schism ended when he received official recognition from Pope John VIII.

Photius was to enjoy a fruitful relationship with Basil during the rest of the the emperor's reign, despite their earlier falling out, helping him with framing the *Epanagogē* (*see page 92*). Ironically, it was his most notable contribution in this work that was his final undoing after Leo the Wise came to the throne. Perceiving – accurately enough, given the

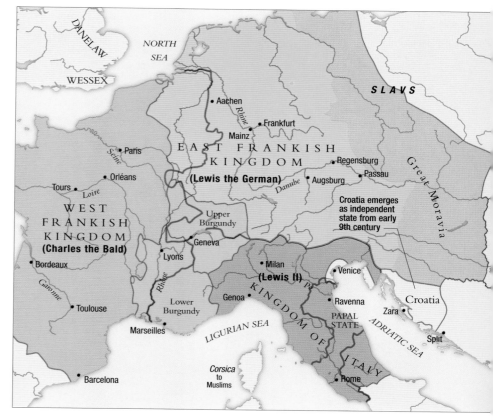

the protracted quarrel with Ignatius – the danger of allowing the Church too much freedom of action, and considering the patriarch's views on the relationship of the spiritual and temporal thrones as expressed in the *Epanagogē* to verge on treasonous, Leo obliged Photius to abdicate in 887. He was exiled to a monastery in the Armeniakon theme, where he died a few years later.

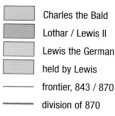

	Charles the Bald
	Lothar / Lewis II
	Lewis the German
	held by Lewis
	frontier, 843 / 870
	division of 870

The Orthodoxy of Bulgaria

When Khan Boris, grandson of Omortag, ascended the Bulgarian throne in 852 he inherited one of the largest states in Europe, bounded by the Dniepr in the northeast, the Carpathians in the north, almost to the Adriatic in the west and the central Thracian highlands in the south. Within its borders lived many Slavic tribes, the old romanised Thracians (Vlachs) and several Bulgar tribes. With a mix of different enthnicities, languages and religions, Boris welded them together through the adoption of Christianity.

The Bulgar state stretching across the top half of the Byzantine Empire connected to that of the Slavs, who had taken much of Greece. This pagan bulwark effectively cut the empire off from the West. But the religious ambitions of Boris created an opportunity for Byzantium to re-establish a measure of control over its former lands. But there was an obstacle in the way in that Pope Nicholas had insisted on newly converted pagans acknowledging the see of

Rome, and when Boris concluded a treaty with Emperor Lewis II (r.855–75) early in 862 it was obvious in which direction the khan would lean.

However, this same treaty panicked the Slavs of Moravia, who were under threats from both the Franks and the Bulgars, and Prince Rotislav sent a mission to Constantinople offering to convert his Moravian people to Orthodoxy in return for help. Photius sent him two monks from Thessalonica, Cyril and Methodius, and they began the process of conversion. Due to language difficulties, this proved a disappointment in Moravia, but their mission found more success across the borders among the Serbs and Bulgars.

At the same time, Photius persuaded the Caesar Bardas – Michael III now perpetually in a drunken state – that to allow Lewis a free hand in the Balkans would be disastrous. In 863, the Byzantine army took the field against Boris, and with the Bulgar army drawn up far to the north along the Moravian border and the south in the

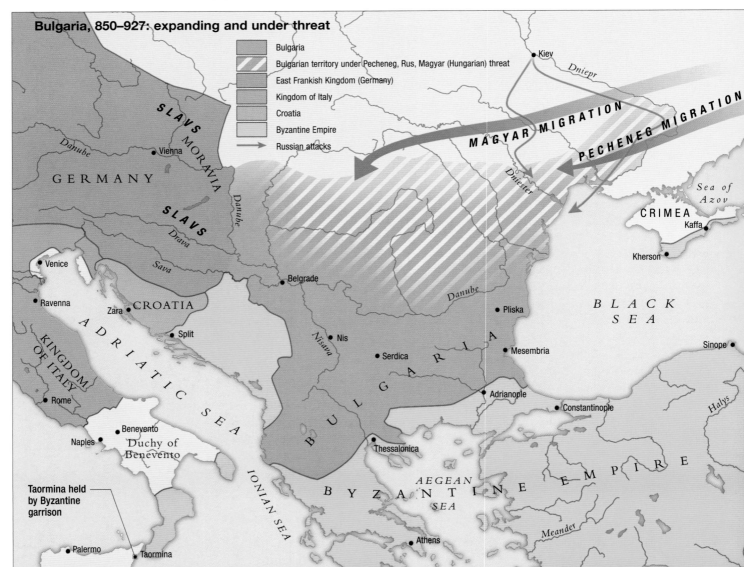

Bulgaria, 850–927: expanding and under threat

- Bulgaria
- Bulgarian territory under Pecheneg, Rus, Magyar (Hungarian) threat
- East Frankish Kingdom (Germany)
- Kingdom of Italy
- Croatia
- Byzantine Empire
- → Russian attacks

Taormina held by Byzantine garrison

grip of a severe famine, Boris asked for terms. These were that he should abandon the treaty with the Franks and adopt Orthodoxy. Accordingly, in September 865, he travelled to Constantinople and was there baptised and received the rank of caesar, which in the Bulgarian tongue became czar (or tzar).

Photius seemed to have achieved his aim, but when Boris requested an autonomous Patriarchy of Bulgaria, Photius – naturally wanting to keep Bulgaria within the Byzantine sphere – refused. So the infuriated czar played Constantinople off against Rome, and in 866 sent a delegation to Pope Nicholas with a list of the points Photius had dismissed. Nicholas responded favourably and Boris swore allegiance to Rome. The Greek missionaries who had swarmed over the land were promptly expelled. This state of affairs did not last, however, because neither Nicholas nor his successor Hadrian II would permit Bulgaria its own archbishop. By this time, as part of his new accord with Rome, Emperor Basil I had replaced Photius with the more amenable Ignatius, and when Boris appealed again to Constantinople he got his way. On 4 March 870, Bulgaria received an archbishop and several bishops, and returned to the Orthodox fold, in which it has remained to the present day.

The czar who would be emperor

Boris abdicated in 889, leaving the throne to his elder son Vladimir. He proved to be a poor choice, associating himself with the once-powerful boyar aristocracy, which detested Christianity, and encouraging a return to paganism. Boris left the seclusion of the monastery to which he had retired, and in a lightning campaign deposed Vladimir and acclaimed his younger son Symeon as czar in 893. This should have further cemented relations with Constantinople, for the 29-year-old had been educated there, possibly even with Leo VI. But the actions of Leo's *logothete*, Stylian Zautses, sparked a trade war.

In the wake of the Christian missionaries, a lucrative commercial route had opened up between Bulgaria and the empire, centred on the capital. The *logothete* now awarded this monopoly to two cronies in Thessalonica, at one stroke eliminating the short and easy route along the Black Sea and forcing Bulgar merchants to make the rough, sometimes impassable, and long land route across Thrace. The resulting war was a disaster for Leo, and proved that under Symeon the Bulgars were now a nation to be reckoned with.

A treaty brought hostilities to an end in 896, but they recommenced in 912 when Leo's useless brother Alexander and successor insulted Symeon's ambassadors. By the time Symeon's vast army was encamped outside the great walls in 913, Alexander was dead and Patriarch Nicholas Mysticus, acting on behalf of the infant Constantine VII, managed to appease him.

For the rest of his reign, Symeon pressed Constantinople to be acclaimed emperor, but through patience and diplomacy Romanus I Lecapenus (r.920–44) thwarted his ambition. Soon after his death in 927, Symeon's son Peter I made peace with the empire and married a granddaughter of Romanus. For the next 50 years, Bulgaria was to become effectively a Byzantine vassal, and when next a strong Bulgar leader arose, he was to be met by an opponent of steel – the greatest of all Byzantine emperors, Basil II the Bulgar Slayer.

Fresco painting of a czar in the Chapel of Saint Nicholas, Sofia, Bulgaria. With the acceptance of Greek orthodoxy came the Byzantine style of iconic representation that was to characterise Bulgarian art well into the Renaissance period.

A Wholly Byzantine Affair

The 90 years between the reigns of Basil the Macedonian and Basil II were to be a complex period of conflicting imperial politics, dominated by powerful and ambitious generals. Although there were military failures, in general the gains made by Basil were continued, and within the empire a degree of economic stability promoted a flowering of Byzantine culture.

The triumphal entry of Nicephorus Phocas in Constantinople; from the *Chronicle of John Skylitzes.* The illustration shows the Byzantine fleet returning to the Golden Horn after the successful recapture of Crete in 961 by Phocas, who two years later would be emperor.

Debauched and worn out, Alexander III (r.912–13) achieved nothing good and antagonised Czar Symeon into a war. But before it began, Alexander was dead, having named his nephew, Leo's infant son Constantine, as his successor and Patriarch Nicholas Mysticus as his regent (cutting out the boy's mother, Zoe). The reign of Constantine VII Porphyrogenitos ('Purple-born') is given as 913–59, but his nickname emphasised his legitimacy in the face of others who claimed the throne during his lifetime, and for the first 31 years he remained in the shadows.

When Patriarch Nicholas appeased Symeon by recognising him as Emperor of the Bulgars – which unfortunately gave the czar the idea that he was also being offered the throne of Byzantium through a betrothal of his daughter to the emperor – Constantine's mother Zoe had Nicholas deposed. Her regency goaded Symeon into activity, and her armies fared very badly. The admiral of the Danube fleet, Romanus Lecapenus, who had manoeuvred himself into the affections of the young Constantine, sailed for Constantinople in 919 and announced he was taking over the empire's government. Subsequently, Zoe's hair was shorn and she was exiled to a convent.

Romanus now married his daughter Helena to Constantine and was shortly afterwards crowned as co-emperor. During his reign, Romanus I elevated three of his sons to a superior position to Constantine, and constantly hoped the sickly boy would die, but – no Basil the Macedonian – he never laid a hand on him.

Romanus was extremely successful at outwitting Symeon through talk rather than arms. Finally, in 924, at an arranged meeting at which Romanus was supposed to sue for peace terms, he unremittingly sermonised the Bulgar into a state of impotence. Symeon retired, bewildered that from a position of strength he had been fooled into being the weaker party. In petty revenge, he proclaimed a Bulgarian patriarchate and removed Bulgaria from the see of Constantinople, naming himself Basileus of the Romans and Bulgars. Romanus is said to have replied that he could call himself the Caliph of Baghdad for all it mattered.

In the end the messy arrangement of having five emperors was terminated by his sons, who in 944 forcibly retired Romanus, now in his 70s, to a monastery on the island of Proti. But public enthusiasm for gentle Constantine curbed their ambitions, and they were reluctantly forced to acknowledge their brother-in-law as the senior emperor. His wife Helena, who had long supported her husband's interests against her family, urged Constantine to end the arrangement, and in the following year the sons joined their father Romanus on Proti.

Byzantium regains territory

Constantine VII is best remembered for his literary works *De Ceremoniis Aulae Byzantinae* – a suffocatingly detailed account of Byzantine court ritual for every conceivable occasion – and a textbook on the art of government, *De Administrando Imperio*. Two major events in his reign stand out: another failed attempt to seize Crete from the Arabs in 949, and the visit of Princess Olga of the Kievan Rus in 958, during which she was baptised, an event that marked the beginning of Russian Christianity – but not the end of Russian hostility.

Constantine was succeeded by his son Romanus II (r.959–63). A pleasure-loving sovereign, he nevertheless showed judgement in the selection of his ministers, notably the generals Nicephorus Phocas – who finally recovered Crete in 961 – and his nephew John Tzimisces. Romanus married a Peleponnesian inn-keeper's daughter named Theophano, who gave him two sons, Basil and Constantine. However, his judgement here was poor, for Theophano probably poisoned him and certainly married Nicephorus II Phocas (r.963–69).

True to his military upbringing, Nicephorus added to his Cretan success with victories over the Arabs in Cilicia and Syria. Matters in the West went less well: campaigns in Sicily failed and territory in Italy was lost to Frankish Emperor Otto I. The cost of these wars led to the severe financial retrenchment that cost him his life. With Constantinople slipping into riots, Theophano conspired with John Tzimisces and Niceophorus was assassinated.

The accession of John I Tzimisces (r.969–76) may have been a bloody one but he proceeded to justify his usurpation by his energy. In 970–73 he launched a series of campaigns against the newly established Russian power and drove the enemy out of Thrace, besieged Dorystolon on the Danube and so broke Russian strength that he was left master of eastern Bulgaria. In 975 he turned to the East and in a spectacular series of campaigns returned most of Palestine, Syria and the Lebanon to Byzantine control for the first time since Heraclius.

Before his death, Romanus had crowned his two sons co-emperors, but since Basil was five years old and Constantine only three, the boys remained in Theophano's care. When John died suddenly while returning from his second campaign against the Arabs in 976, Basil was able to take control of his own destiny. Constantine, a young man with not the slightest interest in government, was content to leave everything to his brother – the emperor they would call 'the Bulgar-Slayer'.

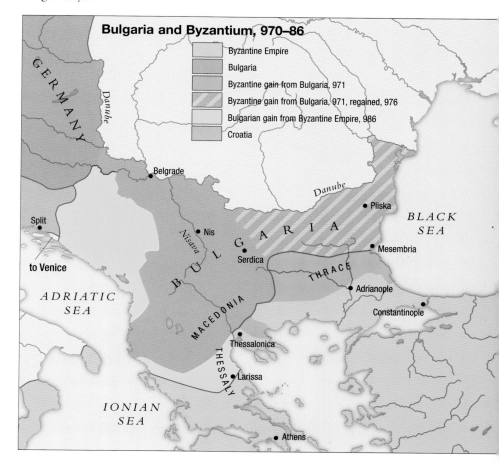

An Unbyzantine Emperor

Among the many emperors of Byzantium, a few stand out as great leaders, but none as magnificent as Basil II. Of the 65 years of his reign, the first 16 were overshadowed by Niceophorus Phocas and John Tzimisces. But with the latter's death, there were still hurdles in his way to absolute power – his great-uncle and the Anatolian military aristocracy.

For a further nine years after John Tzimsces' death Basil was to remain under the thumb of his formidable great-uncle, the eunuch Basil *parakoimomenos*, son of Romanus Lecapenus, who had been chamberlain under Romanus II, Nicephorus Phocas and John Tzimisces, and had little intention of relinquishing his powers. During those years it was the eunuch and not Basil who fought the rebellious Anatolians, led by by Bardas Sclerus, commander of the Eastern army, and Bardas Phocas, nephew of Emperor Nicephorus. These hoary soldiers had come to the conclusion that they were better suited to rule than a callow youth like Basil, and soon made their moves.

However, by clever manipulation the *parakoimomenos* persuaded Phocas to take on what became a civil war against Sclerus, which was fought to a stalemate by 979, although the contenders would arise again. In 985 Basil was ready to divest himself of the suffocating mantle of his great-uncle, whose notorious corruption provided him the ammunition. The *parakoimomenos* was arrested and exiled, and Basil was at last his own master… just in time to face a new enemy on his own…

Czar Samuel of the Bulgars had come to prominence shortly after the death of John Tzimisces. By 980 he had secured his position and began to encroach on Thessaly. In 986 he besieged Larissa and Basil responded by marching on Serdica (Sofia). Failing to bring the Bulgars to battle, he turned back and fell into a prepared trap at the pass known as Trajan's Gate. The vast majority of the Byzantine army was cut down, and it was a sobered Basil who returned to Constantinople vowing never to fail again – and to take revenge (*see the following pages*).

For a while, he was occupied against the Anatolian barons, who were on the march again.

Gold *solidus* of Basil II (left) and his brother and successor Constantine VIII.

Basil, showing the ruthlessness that would become his trademark, took the field himself in 988 and suppressed the rebellion. Over the past 60 years a few families had illegally acquired vast tracts of land that had once belonged to the farming communes, and this was the source of their power. Basil determined to break these feudal barons once and for all, and formulated laws that obliged them to restore to their former owners any land acquired since the reign of Romanus I Lepacenus. At one stroke, many wealthy families were beggared, but the Anatolian yeoman communes flourished and the revenues of taxation flowed again.

At this time Vladimir I, Prince of Kiev, offered Basil an alliance and 6,000 Varangian warriors in return for a marriage to Basil's younger sister Anna. Basil hesitated because Anna was horrified, but when Vladimir agreed to convert to Christianity and send away his four wives and

hundreds of concubines Anna became reconciled to her fate. Vladimir took his conversion seriously. After the wedding ceremony at Kherson, he returned the Crimean cities to Byzantium and began the wholesale conversion of his land that later earned him a sainthood.

Father of the army

In 995 Basil led an expedition to Syria to relieve Aleppo from the Fatimid forces of the Egyptian Caliph Aziz, and drove them back to Damascus, Between 989 and 1009, Basil was largely occupied with the war against Czar Samuel, but not exclusively. In 1000 Armenia was returned to Byzantium for the first time in two centuries. Byzantine forces restored much of southern Italy, lost to Norman adventurers who had begun infiltrating the region in 1017 and supporting Lombard separatists against Franks and Greeks. When Basil II died on 15 December 1025, he was ruler of an empire that stretched from the Adriatic to Azerbaijan, and planning a military expedition to recover the island of Sicily.

Although Basil remained unmarried and had no heir, the question of succession might have been answered in a strange manner but for the hand of fate. In 1001 Emperor Otto III had requested a marriage to one of Basil's nieces, and the middle girl, Zoe, was selected, apparently to her delight. In January 1002, she set out by ship for Bari, only to discover on her arrival that Otto had died of a fever on 24 January. If the couple had had a son, he might one day have come to inherit both empires and ruled over a territory extending from the borders of France to Persia.

Basil II was the opposite of any Byzantine emperor. Short and stocky, he cared nothing for court flummery, none of the pomp and ceremony, and usually held court dressed in military uniform, but he had a fine grasp of administration and legislation. The army worshipped him because he ate their field slops, buried their dead and took care of their widows and orphans. Typically he ordered his burial in the army training field and not the imperial mausoleum. The day he died, 15 December 1025, the long decline of Byzantium began – with the reign of his brother Constantine VIII.

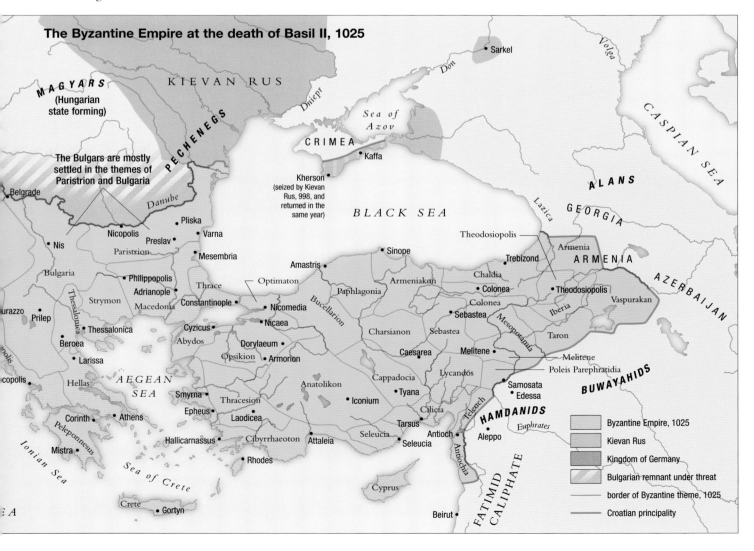

The Byzantine Empire at the death of Basil II, 1025

Basil the Bulgar-Slayer

The year 989 was a watershed in Basil's reign – having shaken off the shackles of internal dissent he was free to make good the vow he had made in 986 to avenge himself on Czar Samuel. He was ready to begin the task that earned him his nickname: the reduction of the Bulgar khanate.

The year could hardly have been worse for Byzantine fortunes. One of the hardest winters in living memory presaged a powerful earthquake that destroyed half of the buildings in Constantinople. Across the Black Sea came news of the capture of Kherson by the Russians, and only days later that of Beroea (Veroia) – a strategically important fortress town guarding the approaches to Thessalonica – to the Bulgars.

Basil's primary advantage was his highly trained and disciplined army; the Bulgars' that they were operating on home ground. All Czar Samuel had to do was keep to the hills and wait for Basil to be called away on other business – which happened frequently, leaving his European army in lesser hands. So that in 995, when he was urgently called to Syria to upset the designs Caliph Aziz had for Aleppo, the situation in Macedonia and northern Thessaly had hardly improved in Byzantine favour.

Samuel took full advantage of Basil's prolonged absence in Syria by killing the governor of Thessalonica and invading the defenceless theme of Hellas. The Bulgars sacked towns and cities as far south as Corinth. In 997 Samuel seized the important Adriatic harbour of Durazzo (Roman Dyrrachium) and began advancing north along the Dalmatian coast towards Bosnia.

Basil concluded a treaty with the Republic of Venice that would have long term consequences for Constantinople. In return for Venetian ships transporting his army by sea to tackle Samuel, Venice was granted generous commercial privileges in Constantinople and given the rule of Dalmatia under Byzantine suzerainty. For Doge Pietro Orseolo II, this gave Venice an enormous advantage over bitter mercantile rivals Genoa, and provided a vast supply of corn to feed Venice's expanding population, as well as an inexhaustible supply of timber for ship-building.

Ending the Bulgar khanate

Basil was now free to move men and materièl, and once again the slow, cautious Byzantine advance began. By almost continuous campaigning, Basil regained virtually all of the eastern half of the Balkan peninsula by 1004, from Thessalonica to the Iron Gates of the Danube. For his part, Samuel now faced an enemy that had learned the mountainous terrain and guerrilla tactics, refused him the opportunities of ambush and who had grown used to the bitter cold and searing heat of the region. With his advantages reduced, Samuel was forced to retreat continually. It was still to be a whole decade, however, before the climactic battle.

This occurred on 29 July 1014, in the narrow gorge of Cimbalongus, leading from Seres into the Upper Struma valley, near Balathista. Fearing that an ambush – which Samuel would certainly have considered in earlier years – would fail, the Bulgars occupied the narrow defile, blocking the emperor's way and forcing a long and dangerous detour. Basil seemed stymied until one of his generals, recalling the Persian defeat of the Spartans at Thermopylae, suggested leading a detachment of troops secretly up the wooded hillside to come down to attack the Bulgars' rear.

The tactic worked. Taken entirely by surprise, the Bulgars were unable to defend both ends of the gorge. Most panicked and fled, cut down as they ran from the defile's ends, and as many as 14,000 were captured. These unfortunates were then blinded in one eye at Basil's command and sent to Samuel's fortress of Prilapon (Prilep), to which the defeated czar had fled after being saved by the heroic actions of his son, who had remounted his father and taken him to safety.

Byzantine territory, 986

Bulgar territory, 1014

Bulgar losses, 1009–14

→ campaigns of Samuel

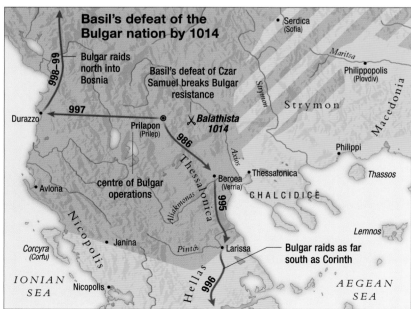

Basil's defeat of the Bulgar nation by 1014

986–99 Bulgar raids north into Bosnia

Basil's defeat of Czar Samuel breaks Bulgar resistance

• Serdica (Sofia)

Maritsa

Philippopolis (Plovdiv)

Strymon

Strymon

997

Durazzo •

Prilapon (Prilep) ⊙

986

✗ *Balathista* 1014

Macedonia

• Philippi

Axios

Avlona •

centre of Bulgar operations

Thessalonica

Aliakmonas

Beroea (Verria) •

• Thessalonica

Thassos

CHALCIDICE

995

Nicopolis

• Janina

Pintós

• Larissa

Bulgar raids as far south as Corinth

Lemnos

Corcyra (Corfu)

IONIAN SEA

Nicopolis •

Hellas 996

AEGEAN SEA

But Samuel was a broken man, and the sight of thousands of his blinded troops drove him to an apoplectic fit, from which he died.

The Bulgar threat was at an end. Although resistance to the Byzantines continued until 1018, it had little effect on the empire. Eventually, the Bulgars were swept into a narrow province and left to their own devices. After their final capture, the descendants of Samuel were kindly received by Basil, who took them all into his protection, and several prospered, one becoming the *strategos* of the important Brucellarian Theme. For the first time since the Slavs had first arrived, the whole of the Balkan peninsula was again in Byzantine hands.

As for the Bulgars themselves, the majority welcomed the peace, particularly since Basil set the levels of taxation low and allowed them to pay in kind rather than in gold. Most of the conquered territory was divided between the themes of Bulgaria and Paristrion, but western regions like Croatia and Bosnia continued to be ruled by their own native princes under imperial suzerainty. Basil could be happy to have finally settled the Bulgarian question 500 years after the Bulgar tribes first began attacking Thrace.

This frontispiece of a contemporary Psalter depicts Basil II standing triumphant over the conquered Bulgarian chiefs after Balathista. The righteousness of his actions is illustrated by Christ handing down a crown for an angel to place on his head. Basil is also flanked by the warrior saints of Byzantium.

The Coming of the Rus

In order to reach the wealthy trading markets of the Middle East, Viking adventurers set out from Baltic trade centres to explore Russia's extensive river networks. The rivers became avenues of trade, and Viking merchants provided trade links between the Caspian and Black Seas and Viking Scandinavia. It was not long before Viking and Byzantine interests clashed.

Swedish Vikings in central Europe; from left to right:
A 9th-century Viking merchant-venturer with his wares; a warrior with baggy pants typical of eastern Vikings; a Kievan Rus – one of many to harass the Byzantines.

Viking slaving expeditions ventured deep into central and eastern Europe along the river arteries at the end of the eighth century. The most important source of slaves was the Slavic heartland of eastern Europe; the term 'slave' is probably derived from Slav. Before long, they began to found settlements and integrated with the local Slavic population. These Vikings became known as the Rus (red-haired) from the Slavic derivative of the Finnish name for Swedish Vikings.

The Slavic settlement of Kiev was well positioned to exploit the trade, and in 850–911 the Rus annexed the city and rapidly expanded it to become the new capital of the Rus. Even as this process was taking place, the Rus were beginning to sail into the Black Sea, where they soon encountered the wealthy cities of the Byzantine Empire and – as Vikings did – they began raiding.

The first known Rus-Byzantine contact occurred as early as 838–9, when a small group of them had arrived on a diplomatic mission to the court of Theophilus. But perhaps it was more in the way of a reconnaissance mission, for in 860 Constantinople awoke to a terrifying sight. A fleet of some 200 longships entered the Bosphorus and slowly made its way towards the city, pillaging and burning every village, and plundering the wealthy monasteries that lined the shores. The great walls were impregnable to any means the Vikings possessed, and having exhausted the possibilities of extra-mural plunder, they sailed away after a few days.

A state of continual warfare

One consequence of this raid was a heightened fear of the Slavs – the Byzantines thought the Vikings were such – and the willingness of Michael III and Photius to embrace Prince Rotislav of Moravia when he offered to become a Christian. The advantages were obvious: Moravia would become a Christian ally to the north of the troublesome Bulgars, but also a bulwark against the Kievan Rus 'Slavs'. As related, this mission failed in its primary aims (*see page 96*).

(*see page 96*)

869	**870**	**886**	**907**	**913**	**919**	**924**	**927**
Basil I crowns his eldest son Constantine as co-emperor, but he dies in 879	The Bulgars, thwarted by Rome, return to the Orthodox Church, receiving the right to create sees	On Basil's death, his younger son becomes Leo VI the Wise	A Kievan Rus fleet enters the Bosphorus and assaults Constantinople; a treaty is made, 911	The Bulgars besiege Constantinople, but Patriarch Nicholas Mysticus persuades them to leave	Admiral Romanus Lepacenus seizes the government; becomes co-emperor in 920	Czar Symeon declares Bulgaria to be its own patriarchy, independent of Byzantium	Bulgar Czar Peter I signs a treaty and Bulgaria becomes a Byzantine vassal

For a period, relations with the Rus improved as trade between Kiev and Constantinople began to develop. In 911 Leo VI signed a treaty with Prince Oleg that gave Russian merchants certain rights in the city. But after Oleg died, his successor Igor began a campaign of rapid territorial expansion over the Bulgars and Khazars, and inevitably made war on Byzantium. In 941 a Russian fleet put at about a thousand vessels laid siege to Constantinople at a time when the armies of Romanus Lepecanus were engaged elsewhere. Fortunately, the Black Sea fleet was able to engage the Russians, and once again Greek Fire saved the day. The remnant retreated along the Bithynian coast, ravaging as they went, until in a second naval engagement, trapped between the shore and the Byzantine ships, they were destroyed in flames.

Three years later Igor tried again with a massive amphibious force, but this time Romanus bought him off to avoid further bloodshed, and a trade treaty was eventually agreed on. Relations between Russia and Byzantium were to remain peaceful for quarter of a century until Igor's son Svyatoslav took up arms. Deeming Constantinople impregnable from the sea, in 969–70 he marched his massive army comprised of Russians, Magyars and Pechenegs through Bulgaria and onto the Thracian plain. The attempt by John Tzimisces to negotiate came to naught, but Russian might was not to triumph. Outnumbered probably 5:1, the Byzantine army under the superb generalship of Nicephorus Phocas employed every tactic in the book and Svyatoslav's army was trounced.

John determined in the following year to take the war to Svyatoslav, and mounted a huge expedition ready to invade Bulgaria, but it was delayed by the need to deal with Bardas Phocas, who had returned from exile in the East and was already gathering an Anatolian army. The outcome went in John's favour, and in 972 the Byzantines with John at their head advanced into Bulgaria and fell on the unsuspecting Russians at the Bulgarian capital of Preslav. The result was a massacre, and a few months later Svyatoslav, trapped in the port of Dristra, sued for peace.

On his way back to Kiev he passed through Pecheneg territory, and furious at not receiving the spoils of war Svyatoslav had promised them, they slew him. He was succeeded by his son

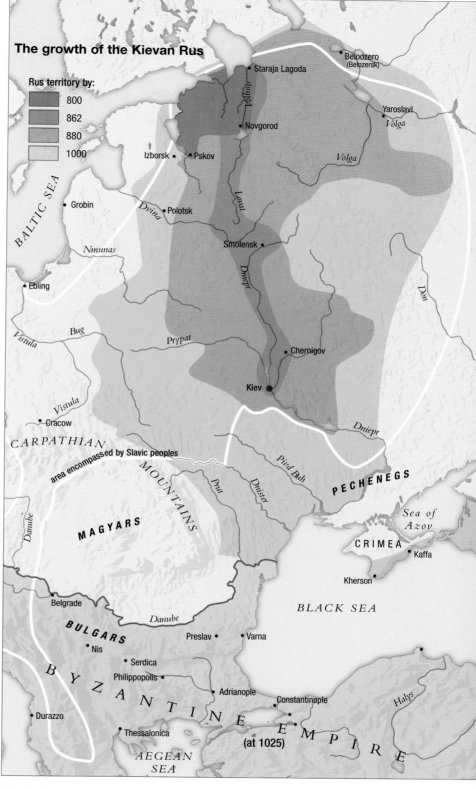

The growth of the Kievan Rus

Rus territory by:
- 800
- 862
- 880
- 1000

area encompassed by Slavic peoples

Vladimir, whose accord with Basil II has been related (*see page 100*). From this time on, through the offices of the Orthodox Church in both states, Russian-Byzantine affairs were – apart from one further abortive Russian raid in 1043 – to remain friendly.

Prelude to Catastrophe

The latter half of the 11th century was a precarious time for the Byzantine Empire. Ironically, at a time when Byzantine art and culture was flowering as never before, its envious enemies were gathering on all fronts and centralised military control was disintegrating. Byzantium desperately needed another Basil II, but none was forthcoming.

European and Muslim fragmentation in the later 11th century

DENMARK

BALTIC SEA

NORTH SEA

Danzig

Stettin

SLAVS

Bremen • Hamburg

ENGLAND
(to Denmark)

Magdeburg

POLAND

Vistula

Breslau

COUNTY OF FLANDERS

KINGDOM OF

Frankfurt

Prague •

Cracow •

Rouen

DUCHY OF NORMANDY

Reims •

Mainz •

GERMANY

Regensburg

Paris •

COUNTY OF CHAMPAGNE

Strasbourg •

Danube

Augsburg •

Vienna •

Pozsony

Esztergom

COUNTY OF BRITTANY

Orléans •

FRANCE

Rhine

Zurich •

Salzburg •

HUNGARY

Pest

ATLANTIC OCEAN

Nantes •

Tours •

Dijon •

KINGDOM OF BURGUNDY

Fehévár

Pécs •

Danube

Loire

Geneva •

Drava

Belgra

Bay of Biscay

DUCHY OF

Lyons •

Milan •

Venice •

Sava

CROATIA

Hungarian incursions

Bordeaux •

Rhône

Turin •

KINGDOM OF ITALY

REPUBLIC OF VENICE

Zara

AQUITAINE

Genoa •

Ravenna •

ADRIATIC SEA

Split

Corunna •

Avignon •

Nice •

Pisa •

Florence •

Bayonne •

Toulouse •

Marseilles •

León •

LEÓN

NAVARRE

Corsica
(to Pisa, 1017)

Aléria •

PAPAL STATE

Rome •

PRINCIPALITY OF BENEVENTO

COUNTY OF APULIA

Durazzo •

Oporto •

CATALAN COUNTIES
(to Aquitaine)

PRINCIPALITY OF CAPUA

Benevento •

Bari •

Tulaytulah
(Toledo)

Saraqustah
(Zaragoza)

Barcelona •

COUNTY OF AVERSA
(to Normans, c.1050, first Norman acquisition in Italy)

Naples •

Taranto •

Al Ushbunah
(Lisbon)

CALIPHATE OF CORDOBA

Balansiyah
(Valencia)

Sardinia
(to Pisa, 1017)

PRINCIPALITY OF SALERNO

Otranto •

UMAYYADS

Qurtubah
(Cordoba)

Balearic Islands
(to Cordoba)

Cagliari •

Crotone •

Ishbiliyah
(Seville)

Cartagena •

Messina •

Reggio •

Qadiz
(Cadiz)

Malaqah
(Málaga)

MEDITERRANEAN SEA

Palermo •

Catana •

Sicily
(to Zirids)

Syracuse •

Tunis •

Malta
(to Zirids)

IDRISIS

MIDRARIDS

Qayrawan •

ZIRIDS

FATIMIDS

Tripoli •

Benghazi

	duchy of Normandy	
	royal French demesne	Pisan republic
counties of France	kingdom of León	Hungary
duchy of Aquitaine	kingdom of Navarre	Kieven Rus
kingdom of Burgundy	kingdom of Germany	Byzantine Empire
county of Brittany	Venetian republic	fragmented Islamic states

The decline of the Byzantine Empire was not an isolated phenomenon. Events were evolving along similar lines in both East and West as older powers abdicated and new orders took their place. In Latin, Greek and Muslim spheres the forces of feudalism were preparing the way for new national states. The Abbasid Caliphate had already ceased to be any form of universal government in the first half of the ninth century and the peripheral emirates had become independent: Aghlabid North Africa, Umayyad Spain, Fatimid Egypt, the Hamdanids in eastern Syria.

In the West the German ('Roman') Empire also faced fragmentation within from a rash of semi-autonomous states, such as the Normans in the northwest and in Italy, and the newly formed Kingdom of France, itself a patchwork of incompatible duchies. In Byzantium those responsible for this feudal development were baronial magnates of Anatolia, the former commanders of military units and the officers of themes who became landed rulers: the Phocas, the Scleri, the Curcuas and the Maleini.

As a result the great themes of eastern Asia Minor, the Armeniakon and the Anatolikon were divided into smaller units: Chaldia with its centre at Trebizond; adjoining it was Colonea named after its main city, and similarly Charsianon and Seleucia. In the middle a separate Cappadocian theme was created. These divisions were made largely independently of the central authority, and the new feudal families looked to the supremacy of Byzantium in the East, almost completely disregarding the affairs of southern Italy and the Balkans.

In the Balkans, the Christian mission to the Slavs had widened the sphere of Byzantine civilisation, which might be seen as some compensation for the provinces lost to Islam. But cultural subjection is hardly military conquest, and although the empire consolidated its position, especially under Basil II, the peninsula was developing along lines that pointed to disintegration rather than expansion.

With the overthrow of Basil's legislation against the large landowners under his successor Constantine VIII, only the term 'theme' had retained any connection with the former Byzantine administration, which was by now a thin disguise for feudal structures. One serious consequence of Byzantine feudalism was a decline in military power, since the great armies were no longer the emperor's to command and were all too often found marching on Constantinople in support of one baron or another's claims on the throne. And all this was happening at a time when the Seljuk Turks were about to overrun Asia Minor and the Normans were poised to explode out of southern Italy and march right across the Balkan peninsula on Constantinople.

A Sorry Series of Rulers

For the next quarter of a century the empire's affairs were dominated by the whims and wiles of the one legitimate member of the imperial family, Zoe. After her, there was a seven-year period of virtual interregnum. It was, without question, a period of sudden decline after the glories of Basil II's reign.

In this wall mosaic Constantine IX Monomachus and Empress Zoe sit either side of Christ the Pantocrator.

When he came to the throne in 1025 after his brother's death, Constantine VIII (r.1025–28) had technically been an emperor for 49 years, but in that time he had been content to let Basil rule. Now 65, he was thrust onto the throne unprepared, and his reign of less than three years was an unmitigated disaster during which inexperienced but ambitious eunuchs lost control of the baronial Anatolian families while the emperor occupied himself – as he always had

– with personal pleasures.

A widower without sons, Constantine married his middle daughter Zoe to a sexegenarian senator named Romanus Argyrus, and when he died unlamented on 12 November the throne passed to his choice. Now nearing 50, Zoe must still have dreamt of what might have been when she set sail to marry Otto III in 1002. But if the empress was happy her husband was not. Romanus III (r.1028–34) had had to divorce the wife he loved to marry Zoe and he soon abandoned any pretence of liking her.

Romanus spent large sums on new buildings and in endowing monasteries, but in relieving the pressure of taxation he disorganised the finances. He was equally unsuccessful in war. In 1030, while personally leading an army against his nominal vassal, the obstreperous Emir of Aleppo,

he was surprised on the march from Antioch and sustained a serious defeat. Pride in Byzantine arms was only restored by the young *strategos* of Teluch theme, George Maniakes, who wiped out 800 Arabs a few days later; in 1032 he was to heroically recover Edessa for the first time since the days of Heraclius.

The chamberlain John the Orphanotrophus – prevented from ambitions on the throne because he was a eunuch – was ambitious for his young brother, the strikingly handsome young Michael the Paphlagonian, who he introduced to the empress. She was instantly besotted. For the disaster of Aleppo, Romanus had lost popularity, and frustrated Zoe replaced him in her affections by Michael. In only a short time she and John arranged for Romanus to be poisoned, and in April 1034 Zoe married her new lover.

The loss of southern Italy

Michael IV (r.1034–41) was of lowly birth and hardly deserved to be ruler of a great empire. He owed his elevation to the sexual longings of an ageing empress, which he had only reciprocated with deep reluctance. And yet he possessed wisdom, vision and courage, and might have reversed the empire's declining fortunes but for the fact that he was subject to violent epileptic seizures. These were to take their toll on his health and render him a bloated wreck by his early forties.

Fortunately, John the Orphanotrophus was a good partner in the government; his main weakness lay in promoting his family's interests, often beyond common sense. This included his sister Maria's husband, a humble ships' caulker of no intelligence named Stephen. In 1038 John arranged for him to take command of the transport fleet for a campaign to recover Sicily. Fresh from his triumph at Edessa, George Maniakes led the two-year expedition – which included in its number the legendary Norse hero

Harald Hadrada, still 28 years from his moment of destiny contesting the throne of England with King Harold and William the Conqueror. Maniakes almost drove the Saracens from the island, but they recovered when the army was rushed to the mainland to contend with the Normans (*see following pages*).

In the north the Serbs achieved a successful revolt in 1040, but an uprising of the Bulgarians was put down by a triumphant campaign which the decrepit emperor undertook in person shortly before his death on 10 December 1041.

Having anticipated his brother's imminent death, John had persuaded Zoe to adopt Stephen's son. Michael Calaphates ('caulker', after his father's profession), was a callow and mean-spirited youth. His utter obscurity aroused popular anger, and riots broke out when the treacherous snake banished his uncle John and his adoptive mother Zoe to monasteries. Michael V was dethroned after a brief reign of four months, blinded, and himself relegated to a monastery, where he died on 24 August 1042.

For two months Zoe shared the government with her spinster sister Theodora, but their joint-rule was divisive, so she married for a third time, choosing Constantine Monomachus, and they ruled together until Zoe's death in 1050. Constantine IX (r.1042–55) managed to do more damage to the empire than Romanus III, Michael IV and Michael V put together.

His treatment of George Maniakes led to the loss of Byzantine power in southern Italy (*see page 110*), and perhaps indirectly to an attack by a Kievan Rus fleet in 1043, which was repulsed thanks to Greek Fire. In 1046 the Byzantines came into contact for the first time with a new Islamic enemy, the Seljuk Turks, and instead of strengthening the eastern frontier Constantine actually reduced troop strength to help meet the costs of his profligate spending. And although he was hardly to blame for it, Constantine presided over the final and fatal separation of the Greek and Latin Churches in 1054 (*see pages 112–13*). When he died on 11 January 1055 his sister-in-law Theodora became the sole ruler of a wracked empire.

The portrait on this gold *solidus* of Constantine IX conveys the self-satisfied appearance of the emperor who did more than his three predecessors put together to damage the Byzantine Empire's fortunes.

The Normans in Italy

Norman knights, returning from pilgrimages to Jerusalem, passed through southern Italy. They saw a desirable land and wanted to possess it. During the 11th century Norman adventurers battled with Moors and Byzantines to create a new Norman kingdom in Sicily and the heel of Italy.

Roger II, King of Sicily, may have expelled the Saracens from Sicily along with the Byzantines from Italy, but he retained an admiration for Arab culture and civilisation. His coronation cloak, **above**, woven in Palermo, incorporated Arabic inscriptions, as well as the Arabic *Hegira* date of 628.

At the start of the 11th century, the Italian peninsula south of Rome was split into a patchwork of small states; either administered by Lombard warlords (nominal suzerains of the German kingdom), by the Byzantine Empire, or by semi-independent city authorities owing alternating allegiances to the greater powers. Nearby Sicily was in Muslim hands, ruled by Arab emirs who owed their allegiance to beys in Egypt or Tunis. Norman knights are first mentioned in the region in 1017, when they acted as mercenaries, supporting Lombard separatists against Byzantine authority.

These freebooters included three brothers, the offspring of a Norman lord named Tancred de Hauteville. When the brothers started carving out petty fiefdoms in their own name, they sent representatives back to Normandy to recruit more adventurers to help them. Many younger sons of the less wealthy Norman noble families enlisted. These adventurers included two other Hauteville relatives, Robert and Roger.

By 1038 – the same year George Maniakes began the ill-fated Byzantine conquest of Sicily – Normans had occupied the area around Aversa near Naples. Maniakes, who had suffered

humiliation for the loss of Sicily, returned to Italy in 1042 to face the Normans who were rapidly mopping up the whole of the south. With the aid of a regiment of Varangians and Harald Hadrada, he unleashed a pitiless war on the towns, leaving a trail of smoking ruins in his wake. But palace intrigue was to stall Byzantine progress, when Constantine IX recalled him. In a terrible rage he had his troops proclaim him emperor and led them back across the Adriatic with every intention of attacking Constantinople. Fortunately for the feckless Constantine, Maniakes was mortally wounded in a battle with forces sent against him and died at Ostrovo in Bulgaria.

By the time Constantine died in 1055 the Normans were well on their way to finally eliminating the Byzantine presence in Italy. In 1059 Pope Nicholas II recognised the Norman knight Richard d'Aversa as the Lord of Capua, and Robert Guiscard de Hauteville as the Duke of Apulia. This was the climax of a decade of expansion by the Normans, who gained control of large segments of southern Italy by conquest, annexation and treaty with the popes.

A successful Norman state

Within a year, other Norman adventurers extended their influence by capturing much of Calabria from Byzantium, and in 1071 the Apulian ports of Bari and Brindisi fell to Robert de Hauteville. These were the last Byzantine strongholds in Italy; by the end of the 11th century southern Italy had become a Norman kingdom, distinct from the semi-independent Lombardic city-states of Naples and Amalfi.

In about 1060 Roger, the younger brother of Robert de Hauteville, succeeded where George Maniakes had failed, by invading Sicily and capturing Messina in 1061. He proclaimed himself Count of Sicily (r.1061–1101), and slowly pushed the Saracens back to the south and west. Palermo fell in 1072 and provided an administrative capital for the new Norman Kingdom of Sicily. The Norman conquest of the island was completed by 1091, and Roger set about reorganising his domains, which technically formed part of the lands of the Duke of Apulia.

Roger de Hauteville was succeeded by his son, who became Roger II, Count of Sicily (r.1103–54). When Robert's grandson died in 1127, Roger II seized control of the Duchy of Apulia, and three years later in 1130 Pope

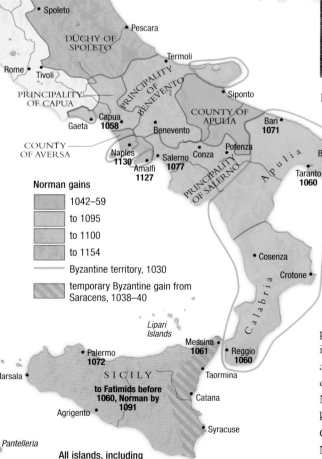

The Norman conquest of southern Italy and Sicily, 1038–1190

Norman gains
- 1042–59
- to 1095
- to 1100
- to 1154
- Byzantine territory, 1030
- temporary Byzantine gain from Saracens, 1038–40

All islands, including Malta, Norman by 1091

Innocent II granted him the title of King of Sicily. The kingdom grew to include the other small Norman states in southern Italy, and by 1154 it extended as far north as the border of the Papal State, providing the papacy with a loyal semi-independent vassal to the south of Rome, and a Christian bulwark against Arab or Byzantine invasion.

The Kingdom of Sicily was to remain a unified state until it became embroiled in the struggle between the German Empire and the papacy. In that time the kingdom's economy improved through trading links with the Muslims and, ironically, with Constantinople, and it became one of the richest of the feudal states. In 1194, Norman rule in Italy came to an end when the kingdom was occupied by the Hohenstaufen German Emperor Henry VI, but by that time Norman expansion into the Balkans and to the very heart of the Byzantine Empire was complete.

With typical Norman brashness, Roger II publicised his coronation as King of Sicily – which included all of southern Italy to the borders of the Papal State – in Byzantine style, as this image of Christ placing the crown on his head shows. It was a deliberately provocative picture that might have been viewed as a warning to the Byzantines to expect more of the Italian Normans… and there was indeed much more to come from this quarter.

The Latin-Greek Split

At the end of the reign of Constantine IX a bitter spat between the heads of the Eastern and Western Churches over the finer points of doctrinal practices led to a confrontation in which a cardinal and two archbishops perpetrated an uncanonical act born of spite. It led to the final and lasting schism between the two great Christian Churches. For Byzantium, the timing could not have been worse.

Guiscard vs Leo; the battle for Italy

The two Churches had been growing apart for centuries. At the root – apart from a struggle for Latin or Greek territorial primacy – was the fundamental differences in their approaches to Christianity. The Byzantines, for whom their emperor was Equal of the Apostles and doctrinal matters could be settled only by the Holy Ghost speaking through the Ecumenical Council, were appalled at the arrogance of the pope in formulating dogma and claiming both spiritual and temporal supremacy. By the same token, the disciplined – at times even austere – minds of Rome were repelled by the Greek love of theological

discussion and speculation, which had unintentionally spawned many heresies.

The disaster that was about to fall on Christianity was largely the fault of Patriarch Michael Cerularius, who had been enthroned in 1043. Formerly a civil servant, he had entered a monastery to further his ambitions, but he was a mediocre theologian and a rigid, narrow-minded bureaucrat lacking in any charm. Had there been a Photius on the patriarchal throne, calamity might have been avoided.

The situation worsened when the German Pope Leo IX was captured by Normans in 1053. Leo had acted to prevent further Norman expansion by taking the sword to them, and advanced from Mantua towards Benevento, requesting Byzantine aid – but it was not forthcoming. The papal forces met those of Robert Guiscard near the small town of San Paolo di Civitate on the Apulian border (the battle is sometimes wrongly called Civitella) on 18 June. It went badly for Leo, who was incarcerated in Benevento for a year. His capture by the Normans provoked anger in Rome that Byzantine forces had not turned up for the fight.

In an attempt to restore good relations the local Byzantine commander, Argyrus, urged the emperor to make an alliance with the papacy against the Normans, and Constantine IX concurred. Cerularius, however – whose narrow ecclesiastical view feared a papal return to supremacy – vehemently disagreed. He had learned that the Normans, with papal approval, were enforcing Latin customs on the Greek churches of south Italy, and tit-for-tat ordered the Latin communities of Constantinople to adopt Greek customs. When they refused, he closed them down. Worse, he accused certain practices of the Catholic Church to be sinful and 'Judaistic'.

The pope's bullies

Leo from his captivity responded with a spirited defence of Latin usages in a letter addressed only to 'Michael of Constantinople'. In a second response – which only went with his legates to Constantinople – he promoted the patriarch to

Map

Italy in 1053

- to Byzantine Empire
- to Normans (Robert Guiscard)
- to Lombards
- mixed Lombard/Greek population
- Papal State
- to Fatimids
- temporary Byzantine gain from Saracens, 1038–40 (Maniakes)
- Leo IX's advance and intended route

Mantua
Po
Modena
Bologna
Ravenna
Rimini
Arno
Pisa
KINGDOM OF ITALY (KINGDOM OF GERMANY)
Spoleto
Tiber
Pescara
DUCHY OF SPOLETO
Rome
PAPAL STATE
Civitate 18 June 1053
Fortore
PRINCIPALITY OF CAPUA
PRINCIPALITY OF BENEVENTO
Siponto
PRINCIPALITY OF BENEVENTO
COUNTY OF APULIA
Bari
COUNTY OF AVERSA
Capua
Gaeta
Benevento
Naples
Amalfi
Salerno
Conza
Potenza
Apulia
Brindisi
Taranto
PRINCIPALITY OF SALERNO
Otranto
Cosenza
Crotone
Calabria
Lipari Islands
Messina
Palermo
Reggio
SICILY
Taormina
Catana

1025–28	1030	1032	1034	1038	1038–40	1042	1042
Poor reign of Basil's brother Constantine VIII; his daughter Zoe becomes the real power	Zoe's husband, Romanus III, loses control of Aleppo, but George Maniakes regains it soon after	George Manikaes returns Edessa to the empire for the first time since the days of Heraclius	Zoe has Romanus III murdered and marries young Michael IV	Norman adventurers occupy territories in south Italy near Naples and Aversa	George Maniakes invades Sicily, but is forced to leave the island to deal with the Normans in Italy	When Michael IV dies, Zoe adopts obscure Calaphates as Michael V; he lasts four months	New Emperor Constantine IX recalls Maniakes, who rebels and leaves Italy to the Normans

112

'archbishop' but continued in a stream of slurs and castigation. Constantine, however, was still eager to see an alliance and indicated his willingness to receive Leo's legates. In this, the usually sensible pope chose unwisely, perhaps because he was still fuming, or because he was already terminally ill. Humbert, Cardinal of Mourmoutiers, was opinionated and anti-Greek; the two others, Cardinal Frederick of Lorraine and Archbishop Peter of Amalfi, had both fought at Civitate and bore a grudge against the Byzantines for having let them down.

Constantine received them politely on their arrival in April 1054; Cerularius was rude, and when he got to receive Leo's second missive of invective, infuriated. But a few weeks later, Leo died. His legates, as his personal appointees, were automatically relieved of their mission, and should have returned to Rome, but instead they stayed on, becoming more arrogant with each passing day. When a monk named Nicetas Stethatus criticised certain of the Latins' usage, Humbert launched into a tirade, calling Stethatus

a 'disciple of the malignant Mohamet'.

And then in an astonishing display of folly, the three ex-legates marched into St Sophia on 14 July in full canonical regalia and, before the clergy assembled for the Eucharist, laid down the Bull of excommunication before taking their leave of the city. This fatal blow, struck by the disempowered legates of a dead pope using an uncanonical and inaccurate instrument, meant the lasting separation of the Eastern and Western Churches. And it came at a moment when there was need greater than ever before of unity between the two Churches.

There was a sad postscript for Argyrus in Italy. When the mob heard of the excommunication of their patriarch and their Church, they blamed Constantine, who made Argyrus the scapegoat for having instigated the moribund alliance and had those of his family in the city arrested and he was recalled in disgrace. For the Normans, the dismay the affair caused among the army of Argyrus was just what they needed to complete the eviction of Byzantine power from Italy.

Byzantine altarpiece with the Virgin Mary and Christ child flanked by angels and warrior-saints. Veneration of the Virgin Mary in the Greek Church represented a distinct difference between Constantinople and Rome at the time. Although a few churches in the West had been consecrated to the Virgin before the 10th century, her cult was not considered particularly important until much later in the medieval period.

The Gathering Seljuk Storm

In Asia Minor the Byzantine Empire had recovered great swathes of territory from the Arabs, but when Constantine IX reduced troop strengths and disarmed the existing military elites of Armenia, the shortsighted move left the whole eastern frontier vulnerable to a terrible new threat. In a short space of time the Seljuks were to radically alter the balance of power in Islam's favour.

I n northeastern provinces of the Islamic world the Seljuk Turks had started to play an important role during the early 11th century. Their name was that of a noble family in a clan forming part of the Turkic Ghuzz tribe, which dominated the steppes north of the Caspian and Aral seas. After the Ghuzz converted to Islam, the Seljuks and their followers served as soldiers for various eastern dynasties.

During the first half of the 11th century, however, the Seljuks reached Khurasan and, campaigning on their own behalf, took control of Nishapur in 1038. Toghril Beg, the Seljuk leader, proclaimed himself champion of Sunni Muslims

and of the Abbasid Caliph. With his highly effective and largely Turkish army, Toghril Beg swept aside resistance by the Shi'a Buwayhids and entered Baghdad in 1055 – the year Constantine IX died – where he was proclaimed sultan by a grateful Abbasid Caliph.

Within a few years the Seljuks controlled Iran, Iraq and much of Syria. Meanwhile other bands of adventurers, not necessarily Seljuk or even Turkish, started raiding the edges of Byzantine lands in eastern Anatolia. As early as 1046 Toghril Beg himself had attacked Byzantine territory, but it was a failure, and although raids into Armenia – some very serious – were to continue, Byzantium was not the Seljuks' real aim. As recent converts to Islam, even more so as Sunnis, they had a proselyting strength, and saw themselves as rightful heirs to the lands conquered during and immediately after the time of the Prophet Mohammed, in particular, the heretical Shi'a lands of the Levant and Fatimid Egypt.

Nevertheless, the continuing weakening of the Armenian position under Constantine

Great Seljuk sultanate

Seljuk tributaries with Islamic population

other Islamic region

nomadic Islamic community

disputed between Seljuks and Fatimids

Byzantine Empire

other Christian state

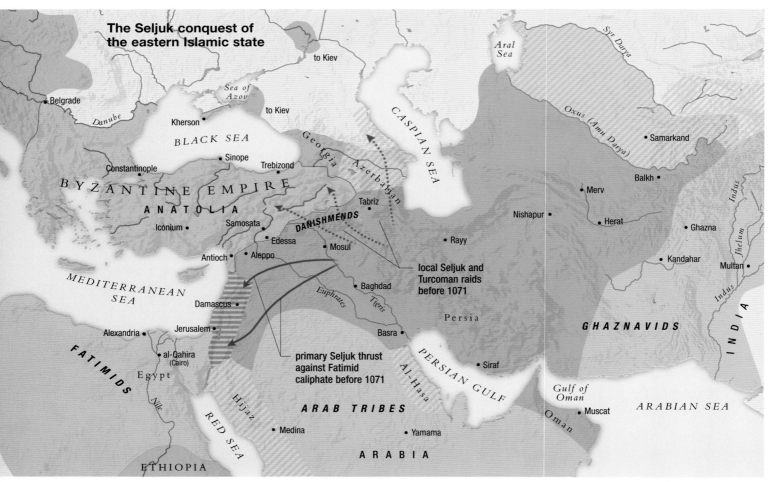

The Seljuk conquest of the eastern Islamic state

local Seljuk and Turcoman raids before 1071

primary Seljuk thrust against Fatimid caliphate before 1071

Monomachus and Constantine Ducas made for a continual temptation to the Seljuks, a prize ripe for the taking… and what was Byzantium doing to prevent this? The answer is nothing. The following 15 years amounted to a period of civil war between the bureaucratic party in Constantinople, the disaffected Anatolian barons and the Armenian princes disgruntled at the loss of their militias by imperial fiat.

Heading for momentous disaster

On 11 January 1055 the septuagenarian Theodora, still refusing to marry, ruled alone. By her firm administration she controlled the unruly nobles but marred her reputation by excessive severity towards private enemies. When she died on 31 August 1056 – probably of a burst appendix – the bureaucrats chose an elderly patrician by the name of Michael Bringas to succeed her; a nonentity in their hands. But Michael VI did not please the military feudal aristocracy and rebellion broke out immediately, championing the Cappadocian Isaac Comnenus.

After barely 13 months on the throne, Michael was deposed following a battle in Phrygia. He spent the rest of his life in a monastery. Isaac I Comnenus (r.1057–59) was an experienced and shrewd strategist at most levels, and he might have restrained the overbearing bureaucracy and reversed the decay of military power had he lived longer. But shortly after completing a successful campaign against the Magyars and Pechenegs, he was struck down by a fever that killed him.

On his deathbed Isaac was persuaded to appoint a member of the bureaucratic party named Constantine Ducas as his successor. Constantine X's eight-year reign was as desultory as any in the empire's history, notable for the loss of Italy, with the exception of Bari, and the succession of Toghril Beg's nephew Alp Arslan as sultan of the Seljuks in 1063. Constantine's wife, Eudocia – the niece of Michael Cerularius, who had been deposed from the patriarchy in 1058 – dominated both her husband and their son,

Michael Ducas, who succeeded his father in 1067… although not quite.

Before he died, Constantine made Eudocia swear not to marry again, but with him out of the way she tricked Patriarch John VIII Xiphilinus into giving her dispensation from her promise on the grounds that she wanted to marry the patriarch's brother. She then promptly selected Romanus Diogenes, a distinguished member of the Anatolian military aristocracy. They were married, and he was crowned Romanus IV (r.1068–71). Still in early middle age he had much to recommend him. As governor of Serdica he had won victories over the Pecheneg invaders. He had been accused of conspiring against Constantine X (but this could be viewed as a positive attempt to remove a monarch whom he believed was leading the empire to destruction). He held vast estates in Cappadocia – a theme that was already in the front line facing the Seljuks. Eudocia is said to have wept tears of joy, but not over the prospect of her handsome new husband: she had raised a soldier to the throne to save the empire.

'That Terrible Day' – Manzikert

The monumental battle of 1071 that changed the course of European history might never have taken place if Emperor Romanus had negotiated. But the human dynamics of the situation were unstoppable and the outcome altered the map of Asia Minor forever.

† Scholars give the 5th, 12th, 19th or 26th for the battle, but a contemporary account says the third night before the battle was moonless, which in 1071 would have been on the 23rd, making the 26th the most likely date.

When Romanus IV Diogenes was crowned on 1 January 1068, he faced serious problems. Turcoman attacks on the eastern frontier were increasing in intensity – despite a truce recently made with Alp Arslan, while in the capital his accession had earned him the undying hatred of both the Ducas family and the bureaucratic party. He had inherited a demoralised and poorly trained army, but spending too much time in the East exposed him to an almost certain coup in Constantinople. Nevertheless, improving the army's morale had to be his primary task.

By 1071 he was ready to face the Seljuks with a force of some 70,000. This was no longer the magnificent army of Basil II – less than half were Byzantine born; its bulk consisted of foreign mercenaries, the Varangian Norsemen, heavily armoured Norman and Frankish knights in search of adventure, Slavs, and Turks from the steppes of southern Russia: Pechenegs, Cuman and Ghuzz. The expedition crossed the Bosphorus in the second week of March 1071, and then headed east. Romanus sent the greater part of his force towards the northern shore of Lake Van under the command of the experienced general Joseph Tarchaniotes, while the emperor and his senior general Nicephorus Byrennius continued with the remainder towards the little fortress town of Manzikert, which had been recently occupied by Alp Arslan's forces. The Seljuk garrison gave him little problem and soon surrendered.

However, the events surrounding Tarchaniotes and his contingent are shrouded in mystery. It may be that, as a secret Ducas supporter, Tarchaniotes simply abandoned his emperor and dispersed his soldiers. On the other hand, he was commanding the mass of Turkish irregulars and, faced with fighting their own kind, perhaps they went over to the enemy. In any event, Romanus now had to face the Seljuks with less than half his army.

And what of Alp Arslan? All the moves he had made during 1070 point to his belief that the truce was still in force. He had repeatedly distanced himself from the Turcoman raiders, and

after taking Manzikert had marched southwest to Amida and Edessa, which he besieged. His ultimate target, therefore, was not Byzantium, it was the Fatimid caliphate. But when news arrived of the massive Byzantine army's approach, Arslan was obliged to alter his plans, turn about and return to Manzikert.

On Wednesday 24 August,† two days before the actual battle, Romanus sent out skirmishers to drive off what he believed to be a small band of Turkish marauders. To the emperor's annoyance they soon requested reinforcements and he sent Byrennius with a larger detachment. To his horror Byrennius found himself engaged with a considerable proportion of the Seljuk army, and by nightfall it was clear that Romanus would have to commit his entire force at daylight.

But the expected battle did not take place on the next day. A delegation from Alp Arslan arrived in the Byzantine camp and offered peace. The sultan could see no point to a war; his eyes were set on Fatimid Egypt, and the only bone of contention was Armenia, could they not agree to an equable division? Romanus never hesitated. This was his chance to rid the empire of the Turkish menace, but his obduracy points out that while he was a brave and capable general, he was not a clever politician, for here was an opportunity to exploit the Sunni-Shi'a schism to his own advantage. His refusal made battle certain.

Treachery loses the day

Romanus drew up his array by the book, in a long line several ranks deep, with cavalry on the wings. He took the centre, with the generals Bryennius on the left and Alyattes on the right. The private armies of the great landowners made up the rearguard, under the command of Andronicus Ducas, the nephew of the late emperor. This seems a grave risk on Romanus's part, the young man having made no secret of his loathing, but perhaps the emperor thought it wiser to have him under watch rather than stirring up trouble in Constantinople. It *was* a grave risk, and it *was* a terrible mistake.

The imperial army advanced across the steppe towards the Seljuks, who steadily withdrew into a crescent, allowing their archers to shower arrows on the flanking cavalry – mostly Franks and Normans. Angered by the impudent archery, the impetuous western knights charged after the Seljuk horsemen into the foothills and straight

into prepared ambushes. Romanus and the centre kept advancing into a void and, frustrated by the lack of enemy, with the sun setting and his camp left unguarded, he ordered the withdrawal.

It was the moment Alp Arslan had been waiting for. His main force now swept down from the hills onto the steppe and fell on the Byzantines. Many of the mercenary troops fled the field in panic, assuming that the withdrawal signal meant the emperor had been killed or captured, and this allowed the Seljuks to split the front ranks from the rearguard. The day might still have been saved, but treacherous Andronicus spread the word that Romanus was dead and the battle lost, and the flower of imperial arms joined the ignominious flight. Only the emperor remained with his Varangians around him. Romanus fought valiantly until the end, and his capture.

A 10th-century Byzantine church stands on a promontory above Lake Van not far from modern-day Malazgirt, scene of the worst military defeat in Byzantine history.

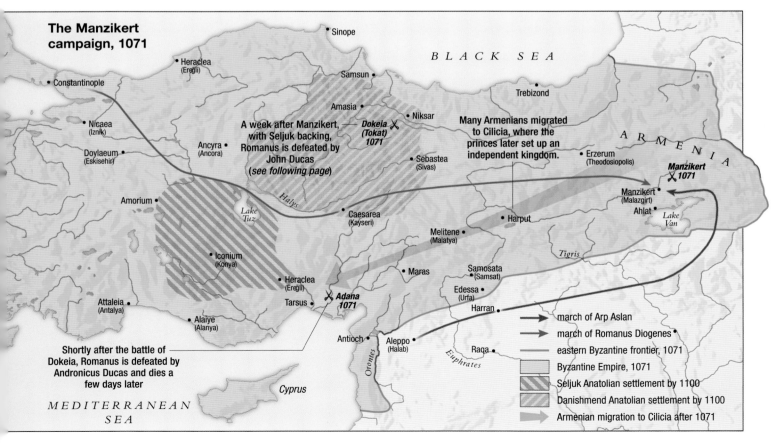

The Manzikert campaign, 1071

Sinope

BLACK SEA

Constantinople

Heraclea (Eregli)

Samsun

Trebizond

Nicaea (Iznik)

Amasia

Niksar

Doylaeum (Eskisehir)

Ancyra (Ancora)

Dokeia (Tokat) ✗ *1071*

A week after Manzikert, with Seljuk backing, Romanus is defeated by John Ducas *(see following page)*

Many Armenians migrated to Cilicia, where the princes later set up an independent kingdom.

A R M E N I A

Erzerum (Theodosiopolis)

Manzikert ✗ *1071*

Amorium

Lake Tuz

Halys

Sebastea (Sivas)

Caesarea (Kayseri)

Harput

Manzikert (Malazgirt)

Ahlat

Lake Van

Melitene (Malatya)

Tigris

Iconium (Konya)

Maras

Samosata (Samsat)

Attaleia (Antalya)

Heraclea (Eregli)

Tarsus

Adana ✗ 1071

Edessa (Urfa)

Harran

march of Arp Aslan

Alaïye (Alanya)

Antioch

Aleppo (Halab)

Raqa

Orontes

Euphrates

march of Romanus Diogenes

eastern Byzantine frontier, 1071

Byzantine Empire, 1071

Seljuk Anatolian settlement by 1100

Shortly after the battle of Dokeia, Romanus is defeated by Andronicus Ducas and dies a few days later

MEDITERRANEAN SEA

Cyprus

Danishmend Anatolian settlement by 1100

Armenian migration to Cilicia after 1071

The Seljuk Sultanate of Rum

The battle of Manzikert was the worst disaster the Byzantine Empire had suffered in its 750 years of existence – so shattering a defeat that the Greeks thereafter only referred to it as 'that terrible day'. In one catastrophic day the empire lost its major recruiting and grain-producing region, and the vital trade route between Constantinople and the riches of the East. Yet even this could have been avoided if the rot at the empire's heart had not ensured the inevitable.

Alp Arslan treated his captive with the respect and hospitality Islam demanded of a host for his guest. The sultan wanted to get on with his primary objective, subjection of the Fatimids, and offered Romanus a generous treaty, considering the circumstances. He asked for a million and a half gold pieces ransom, a modest annual tribute,

a marriage between his son and one of Romanus's daughters, and the surrender of Manzikert, Edessa and Antioch. Of Armenia, he made no demands. He also recognised the importance of returning Romanus to Constantinople as soon as possible before some other and unknown quantity should take the throne.

Manzikert came as a second terrible blow for Constantinople. A month after Romanus had left for the East the Normans led by Robert Guiscard finally took Bari after a siege lasting 32 months. It was the end, after five centuries, of Justinian's Byzantine Italy. That at least was clear; what was not was what had happened to the emperor. No one knew if he lived or not, but even if he did, it was decided Romanus could no longer be

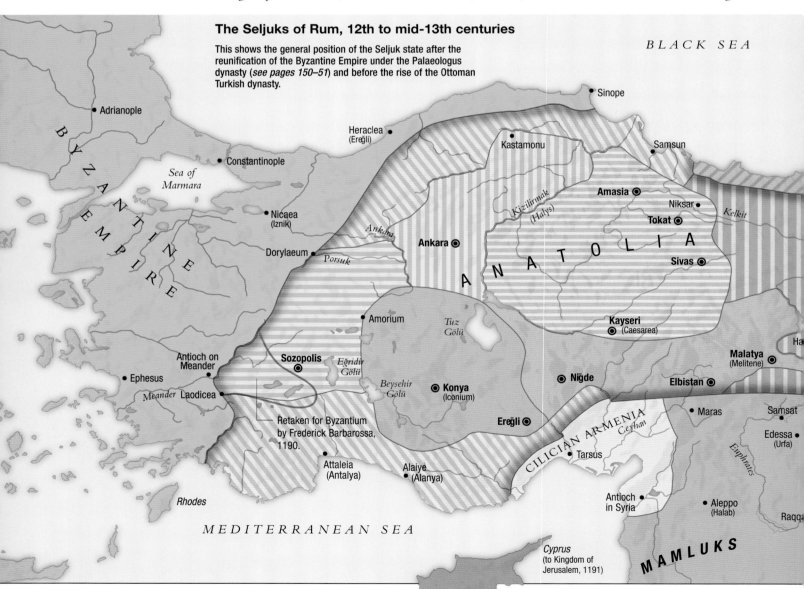

The Seljuks of Rum, 12th to mid-13th centuries

This shows the general position of the Seljuk state after the reunification of the Byzantine Empire under the Palaeologus dynasty (*see pages 150–51*) and before the rise of the Ottoman Turkish dynasty.

Retaken for Byzantium by Frederick Barbarossa, 1190.

emperor. The obstacle was Empress Eudocia. She had already showed willing to favour the military over the bureaucratic party, so the Ducas family opted for her arrest and the elevation of her son Michael VII Ducas (r.1071–78). Since the feeble-minded youth's chief interest lay in trifling academic pursuits, he would safely be under the control of the Caesar John Ducas.

Only a week after the battle of Manzikert, Romanus set out for Constantinople, gathering the remnants of his scattered army as he went. John Ducas was, however, ready for him. There were two battles, one near Tokat (Dokeia) and one near Adana in Cilicia, where he confronted Andronicus Ducas. Romanus lost both and surrendered, renouncing his claim to the throne. Both his eyes were put out, and he died a few days later of the terrible wounds.

Predictably, Michael VII – or rather his counsellors – repudiated the treaty with the Seljuks negotiated between Romanus and Alp Arslan, although with what military confidence to support their arrogance is hard to imagine. Arslan died of an assassin's attack in November 1072, so it was his son Malik-Shah who gave the order for the Seljuks to cross the frontier in the summer of 1073 and take what they could. The chaos that reigned within the empire and the collapse of the defensive structure based on themes and landed militia ensured that the tens of thousands of Turcoman tribesmen advanced into Anatolia without hindrance.

Prelude to the Crusades

By 1080 Sultan Malik-Shah controlled a vast area of Anatolian territory from the Hellespont to Cilicia, which the Seljuks called the Sultanate of Rum in recognition of its former ownership by Rome. The empire held on precariously to the Mediterranean and Black Sea coastal strips, as well as part of western Asia Minor, but it had lost a considerable portion of its grain producing area. As a result the emperor was forced to raise the price of wheat by 25%, which earned Michael popular odium and his nickname *Parapinakes* ('Minus a quarter').

In 1072 troubled erupted among the Slavs, which was quickly put down by Nicephorus Bryennius who, having fought with distinction at Manzikert, had been made Dux of Dyrrachium. But by 1078, fed up with Michael VII's inept government, he raised the standard of revolt and marched on Constantinople. Simultaneously, from the East came the *strategos* of Anatolikon Theme, Nicephorus Botaneiates, for the same reason.

Neither made a direct assault, knowing that the inflated price of food would soon bring the emperor down, and it did. Riots broke out and Michael resigned the throne with hardly a struggle to retire into a monastery. Botaneiates, first into the city, grabbed the throne, captured his rival and had him blinded. It was a poor start to an even poorer reign and Nicephorus III (r.1078–81), already in his mid-70s, presided over the further disintegration of Byzantium, unable to quell any of the numerous revolts he had inherited and for which he was largely to be blamed as the inspiration.

Administration collapsed and anarchy ruled, and the Seljuks conquered and established their sultanate. The empire desperately needed a man of vision and ability, and at the last second found him – the brightest young general of his time, Alexius Comnenus, nephew of Isaac I.

Reverse of a gold coin depicting Michael VII Ducas and his two sons.

Byzantine 'Empire of Trebizond' becomes vassal of Seljuks in 1243

GEORGIA

Trebizond

Köse Dag 1243

Coruh

ARMENIA

Erzerum

Aras

Manzikert 1071

Ahlat

Lake Van

Murat

Tigris

MESOPOTAMIA

Mosul

frontier of Seljuk state, c.1243

Seljuk provincial capital

Seljuk territory, 1100

Byzantine territory, 1240

Byzantine territory lost to Seljuks by 1182

disputed by Seljuks, Danishmend Turks, Byzantines; annexed by Seljuks by 1180

Danishmend territory, annexed by Seljuks by 1174

Danishmend territory, annexed by Seljuks by 1180

Seljuk conquests of Byzantine and Cilician territory, 1182–1240

Seljuk conquests of neighbouring Islamic and Crusader States, 1182–1240

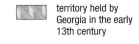
Byzantine 'Empire of Trebizond'

Christian Georgia, c.1240

territory held by Georgia in the early 13th century

other Islamic territory

The Byzantine Economic Crisis

At a time when the Byzantine Empire confronted the worst military crisis of its existence it also faced one no less serious in the area of economy. The once mighty Mediterranean manufacturing and trading machine was in decline, and revenues fell at a moment when liquidity was at a premium.

Constantinople was faced with competition for a stable currency from all fronts, not least the Arabs who quickly established the gold *dinar* right across the Mediterranean trading area. This example is a *dinar* of al-Mutamid, the ruler of Seville in Spain between 1069 and 1090.

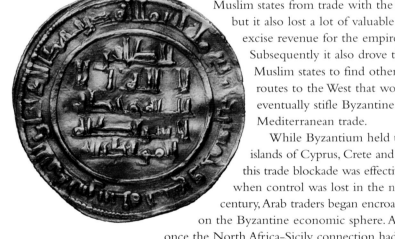

The trade monopoly in the West for high quality products, which continued to be held during the eighth and ninth centuries by Byzantine goods (*see pages 30-1*), had been lost by the tenth. In the 11th century, Byzantine economic supremacy no longer went uncontested. As early as 700, the Umayyad caliph, Abd al-Malik, began minting gold coins (*dinar*) in an attempt to unseat the Byzantine gold *nomisma* as the world's currency. In response, the empire placed a ban on Arab manufactured goods, and only raw materials were allowed entry through Attaleia. This had the effect of cutting off the Muslim states from trade with the West, but it also lost a lot of valuable excise revenue for the empire. Subsequently it also drove the Muslim states to find other routes to the West that would eventually stifle Byzantine Mediterranean trade.

While Byzantium held the islands of Cyprus, Crete and Sicily, this trade blockade was effective, but when control was lost in the ninth century, Arab traders began encroaching on the Byzantine economic sphere. And once the North Africa-Sicily connection had been established, Byzantine commerce with southern Italy was threatened. The Italian mercantile ports, particularly Venice, were also threatened, but they made pacts with the North African Muslims, supplying timber for ship-building and iron for arms manufacture in return for lucrative concessions on luxury goods that had once come only from Constantinople. In effect, the blockade on Arab commerce had become an Arabian one on Byzantine commerce with the West.

In turn, a new textile industry grew up in Italy, supplying the rest of Europe, leading to a further decline in Byzantine revenues, while the Normans – after evicting the Arabs – began their own silk manufacturing in Sicily. To the east, the situation was no better. Early conflict with the Rus closed entrepôts to Byzantine trade with the

Baltic states, while the Russian traders used the river systems to link up directly with their Khazar neighbours to the southeast, who acted as middlemen with the Arab states, thus cutting Byzantium out of the equation entirely.

Recession and inflation

The economic recession came at the same time that military expenditure rose, particularly in relation to the upkeep of mercenaries, putting further strain on the empire's citizens. The feudal magnates also destroyed the planned economy of former years, and wages rose alarmingly due to the lack of slaves through conquest. The government was forced into depreciating the *nomisma* by lowering its gold content, which had the effect of driving up prices further. As we have seen in 1080, with the loss of Anatolia to the Seljuks, Michael VII was forced to raise the price of wheat by 25%, making greater devaluation necessary.

The confidence of European states in Byzantine currency was greatly shaken by this continual devaluation. The net result was a gradual replacement of the *nomisma* as an international currency by newer, more confident coinage: the Florentine *fiorino*, the Milanese *ambrogio* and the Venetian *zecchino* in particular. With Byzantine credit destroyed, there was a further reduction in overseas trade.

The economic decline had other consequences. In order to meet the need for increased military strength, which could no longer be met from the economy or the now feudalised agriculture, the empire resorted to bartering its sovereign rights in return for military aid from other powers. No longer was any attempt made to protect the home market by tariffs, and thus Venice benefited the most, and by special treaties obtained free trading rights in Byzantine lands, which in time would bring the empire to its knees.

This, then, was the economic situation Alexius I Comnenus faced. As a consequence he had also inherited only a poorly equipped and heterogenous army and a small, neglected fleet – so ineffectual that in 1081 when Robert Guiscard attacked across the Adriatic (*see the next chapter*) he was obliged to appeal to Venice for naval aid. If the empire were to survive, both military arms had to be strengthened and reorganised, and neither could be achieved without cost. His first years were to be spent fighting, but finding the money was to dominate and sour the last years of his reign.

Facing: Medieval European portraits of Constantinople, mostly constructed from hearsay, never got the mighty city's scale right, but perhaps it was an unconscious reflection on how far the Byzantine capital's fortunes had fallen in the minds of men by the start of the 12th century.

Byzantium's isolation from
international trade, last half 11th century

Legend:
- Byzantine Empire
- Islamic states
- Normans (England, Normandy, Sicily)
- France
- Germany
- Hungary
- Spanish Christian states
- Pisan territory
- Venetian trade routes
- Genoan trade routes
- overland trade routes
- Holy Roman Empire
- major trade centre

Map labels:

ENGLAND · London

NORMANDY

KINGDOM OF GERMANY · Frankfurt · Prague · Nuremberg

POLAND

RUSSIAN PRINCIPALITIES · Kiev

Baltic-Russian-Oriental trade route

Tana

Catalan Counties · ARAGON · NAVARRE

FRANCE · Paris

LEÓN-CASTILE

Geneva · Innsbruck · HUNGARY

Lyons

KINGDOM OF ITALY · Genoa · Venice

Marseilles · Pisa

Kherson

Byzantine Black Sea trade is increasingly handled by Venice and Genoa

BYZANTINE EMPIRE · Varna · Sinope · Trebizond

Barcelona

Corsica (Pisa)

Rome · PAPAL STATE

ALMORAVIDS · Valencia · Palma

Sardinia (Pisa)

Málaga

Constantinople

Durazzo · Thessalonica

KINGDOM OF SICILY

SELJUK SULTANATE OF RUM

Lesser Armenia

HAMMADIDS · ZIRIDS · Tunis

Palermo

Syracuse

Attaleia · Antioch

Famagusta

Candia

Alexandria

FATIMIDS

God Wills It – The Crusades

Alexius Comnenus I (r.1081–1118) was to rule for 37 years during a time when the Byzantine Empire needed his strong hands on the wheels of government. And yet he was unable to make the empire safe, and when he appealed to the West for aid against the threat of Islam, he unwittingly invited in the very men who would one day prove to be Constantinople's undoing – the crusaders.

Alexius, the nephew of Isaac I Comnenus, had been fighting the enemies of Byzantium since he was 14, and since then, whether Seljuks or Byzantine usurpers, he had never lost a battle. And he did not lose ten years later, when his and his brother Isaac's troops hailed him emperor instead of the aged and weary Nicephorus Botaneiates, who abdicated in the young general's favour. But ironically – as a warrior – in a reign full of military struggle he was to acquit himself better as a diplomat than as a soldier.

The indefatigable Norman, Robert Guiscard, had been greedily eyeing up Byzantium for several years since conquering Bari, even attempting marriage alliances with Michael VII. By 1080 he had given up on diplomacy and planned to invade the Balkans, and in May 1081 his fleet crossed the Adriatic with some 1,300 Norman knights, supported by Saracens from Sicily and several thousand soldiers of mixed descent from Italy.

The destination was Durazzo, the ancient Roman port of Dyrrachium and Illyria's chief port, and from where the ancient Via Egnatia crossed the Balkan peninsula direct to Constantinople. The Normans' entry was prevented, however, by the appearance of a fleet under the command of Doge Domenico Selvo, and superior Venetian seamanship scattered the Norman ships. Selvo then led his men into Durazzo to bolster the Byzantine garrison, and Duke Robert was forced to besiege the city for all of the summer.

This delay enabled Alexius to raise an army and march to the rescue. The battle was joined a little to the north of the city on 18 October. Despite an initially successful onslaught of the emperor's Varangian Guard – now mostly composed of Anglo-Saxon English soldiers who had fled their country after Hastings in 1066 and desired vengeance on the Normans – the poorly trained Byzantine army broke, and the day was lost.

The Normans expanded their power throughout the western provinces under Bohemund of Taranto, Duke Robert's eldest son, while his father returned in haste to Italy to deal with a rebellion engineered by Alexius. To counter him, Alexius needed a proper army, but there was no money. And then, in a repeat of the situation in 618 when Patriarch Sergius had come to the rescue of Heraclius, the wealth of the orthodox Church (this time less willingly) was placed at the emperor's disposal.

Refreshed, rearmed and encouraged, a new army marched out and drove Bohemund out of the Balkans. Duke Robert did not give up. He was back in 1084, but this time his enemy was an epidemic of typhoid, which devastated the Norman ranks and eventually killed Robert on 17 July 1085. For the time being the Norman threat had evaporated, but Bohemund of Taranto was far from finished with Byzantium.

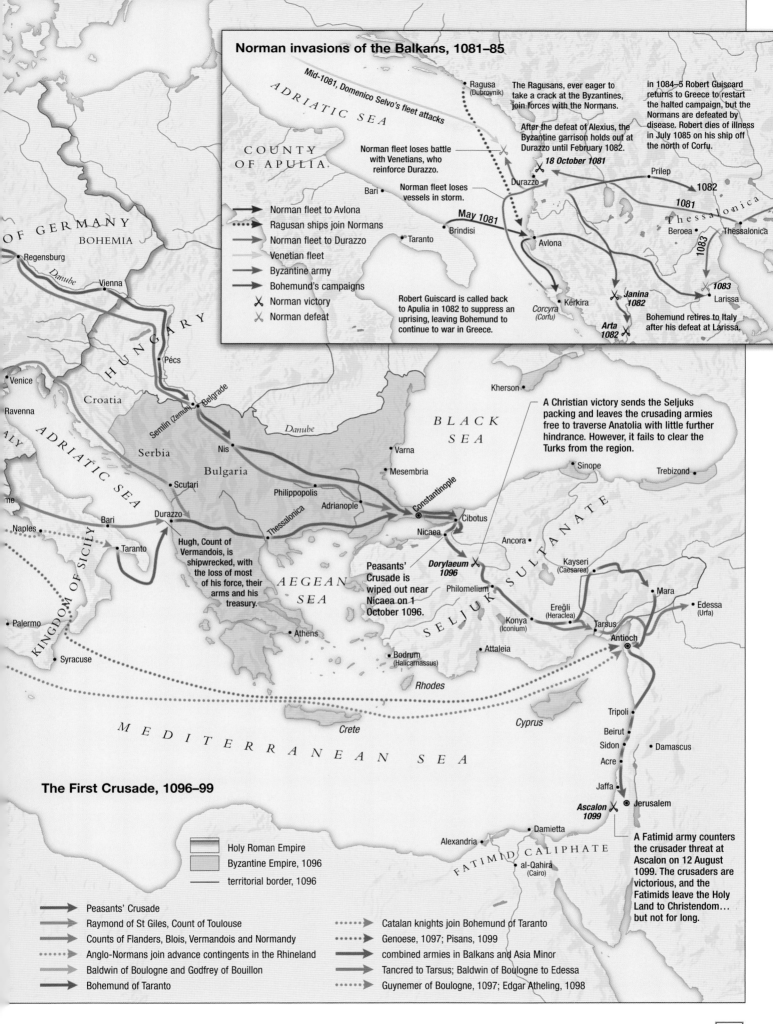

Norman invasions of the Balkans, 1081–85

Mid-1081, Domenico Selvo's fleet attacks

The Ragusans, ever eager to take a crack at the Byzantines, join forces with the Normans.

After the defeat of Alexius, the Byzantine garrison holds out at Durazzo until February 1082.

in 1084–5 Robert Guiscard returns to Greece to restart the halted campaign, but the Normans are defeated by disease. Robert dies of illness in July 1085 on his ship off the north of Corfu.

Norman fleet loses battle with Venetians, who reinforce Durazzo.

Norman fleet loses vessels in storm.

18 October 1081

ADRIATIC SEA

COUNTY OF APULIA

Ragusa (Dubrovnik)

Durazzo

Prilep

1082

1081

Thessalonica

Beroea

Thessalonica

Bari

May 1081

Brindisi

Taranto

Avlona

Robert Guiscard is called back to Apulia in 1082 to suppress an uprising, leaving Bohemund to continue to war in Greece.

Corcyra (Corfu)

Kérkira

Janina 1082

Arta 1082

Larissa

1083

Bohemund retires to Italy after his defeat at Larissa.

Legend:
→ Norman fleet to Avlona
⋯ Ragusan ships join Normans
→ Norman fleet to Durazzo
→ Venetian fleet
→ Byzantine army
→ Bohemund's campaigns
✕ Norman victory
✕ Norman defeat

OF GERMANY

BOHEMIA

Regensburg

Danube

Vienna

HUNGARY

Pécs

Venice

Croatia

Ravenna

ADRIATIC SEA

Semlin (Zemun)

Belgrade

Serbia

Nis

Danube

Bulgaria

Scutari

ITALY

Bari

Durazzo

Naples

Taranto

KINGDOM OF SICILY

Palermo

Syracuse

Hugh, Count of Vermandois, is shipwrecked, with the loss of most of his force, their arms and his treasury.

Philippopolis

Thessalonica

Adrianople

AEGEAN SEA

Athens

Bodrum (Halicarnassus)

Rhodes

Crete

KHERSON

BLACK SEA

Varna

Mesembria

Constantinople

Cibotus

Nicaea

Sinope

Trebizond

Ancora

A Christian victory sends the Seljuks packing and leaves the crusading armies free to traverse Anatolia with little further hindrance. However, it fails to clear the Turks from the region.

Dorylaeum 1096

Peasants' Crusade is wiped out near Nicaea on 1 October 1096.

Philomelium

SELJUK SULTANATE

Kayseri (Caesarea)

Ereğli (Heraclea)

Konya (Iconium)

Tarsus

Mara

Edessa (Urfa)

Antioch

Attaleia

Cyprus

Tripoli

Beirut

Sidon

Damascus

Acre

Jaffa

Ascalon 1099

Jerusalem

MEDITERRANEAN SEA

Damietta

Alexandria

FATIMID CALIPHATE

al-Qahira (Cairo)

A Fatimid army counters the crusader threat at Ascalon on 12 August 1099. The crusaders are victorious, and the Fatimids leave the Holy Land to Christendom… but not for long.

The First Crusade, 1096–99

Legend:
Holy Roman Empire
Byzantine Empire, 1096
territorial border, 1096

→ Peasants' Crusade
→ Raymond of St Giles, Count of Toulouse
→ Counts of Flanders, Blois, Vermandois and Normandy
⋯ Anglo-Normans join advance contingents in the Rhineland
→ Baldwin of Boulogne and Godfrey of Bouillon
→ Bohemund of Taranto
⋯ Catalan knights join Bohemund of Taranto
⋯ Genoese, 1097; Pisans, 1099
→ combined armies in Balkans and Asia Minor
→ Tancred to Tarsus; Baldwin of Boulogne to Edessa
⋯ Guynemer of Boulogne, 1097; Edgar Atheling, 1098

A Plea to the Pope

Defeating the Normans had assured Alexius stability in his rule by appeasing the temper of the military elite and stamping his authority on the bureaucracy, and with a crushing defeat of the Pechenegs he could at last contemplate the recovery of Asia Minor. But there was a major obstacle, he did not possess enough soldiers for the task. There had to be a way, and he found it.

No sooner had Alexius ejected the Normans from his dominions than the Pechenegs invaded. For more than two centuries these most ferocious of the barbarian tribes had been a nuisance, largely appeased by presents, pacts, treaties and tributes. In recent years the empire's

finances had not matched the Pechenegs' greed and in 1087 an army of about 80,000 invaded. After several battles in which both sides won victories, the Pechenegs stood to the northwest of Constantinople. Chaka, the Turkish Emir of Smyrna, seized the opportunity to launch a naval attack in an attempt to claim the throne. He quickly captured the key islands of Rhodes, Chios, Lesbos and Samos, and began sailing along the Hellespont. Fortunately, Alexius had been building up the navy in the Marmara to a sufficient extent that for the moment it kept Chaka at bay.

As for the Pechenegs, Alexius, whose manpower was almost non-existent, bribed the Cumans to the empire's aid, and together they fought a great battle at Levunium on 28 April 1091, at which the Pechenegs were virtually wiped out. The Byzantine navy drove the emir's fleet back, and he would no doubt have tried again had he not been murdered by his sultan, Kilij Arslan, in 1092.

This event underpinned a development in Anatolia that was to Byzantine benefit. In less than 20 years the Seljuk Sultanate of Rum had begun to disintegrate, with semi-autonomous emirs squabbling between themselves – often set at each other's throats through Byzantine diplomacy. A reconquest began to look distinctly possible, apart from one thing – manpower. Alexius retained a healthy respect for the martial abilities of the Frankish and Norman knights he had encountered. He needed this kind of military assistance from the West, and on a large scale.

Impressing Piacenza

In late 1094, Alexius received an embassy from Pope Urban II, who was hoping to improve relations between the Latin and Greek Churches. This had a practical aspect, Urban needed friends in his battle over the Investiture Crisis with the German emperor, Henry IV (r.1056–1106). This was basically an argument over whether the pope or the emperor had the right to appoint high ecclesiastics in western European states. Henry had seized Rome and installed an anti-pope, and it was to be another five years before Urban

Chaka's seizure of the Aegean islands, 1089–91

BLACK SEA

Adrianople

Thrace

BYZANTINE EMPIRE

Strymon
Macedonia

Heraclea • Constantinople • Chalcedon

Sea of Marmara

Thassos

Samothrace Gallipoli • Cyzicus

Imroz

Hellespont • Brusa

Lemnos

SELJUK
SULTANATE
OF RUM

Lesbos • Mytilene

A Scyros

Gediz

By the end of the 11th century, the Seljuk state was already disintegrating into many petty fiefdoms ruled by local emirs.

E
G
E Chios • Chios • Smyrna
(Izmir)

Hellas

Andros • Ephesus

Meander

Kea Tenos N Samos

Ikaria

Mikonos

Paros

Naxos S Kos • Bodrum
(Halicarnassus)

Siphnos E

A

Rhodes • Rhodes

—— Islands seized from the empire by Chaka

—— thwarted Seljuk fleet

—— Byzantine fleet

Carpathos

MEDITERRANEAN SEA

Crete

The feudal system in western Europe had created an entire hierarchy of petty lords, nobles and their knights, who squabbled endlessly over land issues. It was this state of almost military anarchy – fuelled by the similarly self-centred kings – that the papacy wanted to end by bringing all the armed secular powers under papal control. The call for help from Alexius Comnenus was, literally, a Godsend for Pope Urban II, seen here in an early 15th-century manuscript illumination.

could return himself to the Lateran Palace.

Urban had begun the reconciliation process as early as 1089 when he lifted the perpetual ban of excommunication on Alexius and the whole empire, and the emperor's response of reopening the Latin churches in Constantinople that Patriarch Michael Cerularius had closed in 1053 brought both sides closer together. The visiting papal legates invited Alexius to send representatives to address the Council of the Roman Church, due to be held at Piacenza in the following March. Alexius accepted at once, because he realised this was the golden opportunity, with papal blessing, to press the Byzantine need for western mercenaries to help him regain Anatolia – and perhaps even more.

During the winter of 1094–5, Alexius, together with his ministers and clerics, drafted an appeal for help. It spoke of the suffering of Christians in the East, the threat to Christendom and, no doubt, the opportunities offered by

conquest. It also hinted at a possible union of the two Churches. In Piacenza the Byzantine ambassadors did their work well – perhaps, as will be seen, too well – impressing the Latin delegates and most especially the pope.

Urban was concerned to find a way to harness the latent martial energy of the feudal nobility and channel it in a way that could benefit the Church. Alexius's plea offered a means to do just that. It also might be used to consolidate his spiritual authority over Christendom, by uniting all Christian secular nobles under the banner of a common cause.

Urban decided to grasp the opportunity. By calling for a campaign against the infidel Muslims, he felt he could benefit both Europe and the Church. He also naïvely believed that he would be able to control the crusaders once the expedition got underway. And for his part, little did Alexius know that he had just opened Pandora's Box.

A Rag-Tag Beginning

On 27 November 1095 Pope Urban II addressed a Council of bishops and senior clergy in Clermont, central France. Since a major announcement was expected, thousands flocked to listen and the dais had to be moved into an adjacent meadow, so that everyone could hear Urban's words. It was a speech that would alter the course of history.

For years, Urban had preached that killing was a grave sin, even if it took place as an act of war. It placed the soul of the slayer at risk unless he performed penance to the Church. Now, through a neat theological twist, the pope conceived of the 'just war'; the killing of the

Pope Urban II pulls his masterstroke and at Clermont proposes to the massed clergy and princes of Europe a crusade against the infidels; from a 14th-century miniature.

'enemies of Christ' was a penance in itself, an act of piety and devotion.

His address was well prepared and there were even written copies for distribution. He began by reminding the kings and nobles that he was invested by the permission of God and they must now 'keep the Church in all its orders entirely free from the secular power of princes'. And then he went on to the real meat of the address to the packed nobles, that 'there still remains for you a very necessary work. For you must hurry to aid your brethren in the East'.

Graphic detail of the iniquities and depravity of the Muslim enemy helped work up a healthy enthusiasm for the task Urban was outlining, no less than the total extermination of Islam and the 'vile race' that practised the faith. He urged his listeners, 'Enter upon the road to the Holy Sepulchre, wrest that land from the wicked race

and make it subject to yourselves. Jerusalem is the navel of the world.'

All this was going much too far for Alexius. He had hoped for a substantial contingent of Western troops under his command, not the full-scale crusade Urban was promoting. Besides, Jerusalem was still considered a part of the empire, and regaining it was a job for the imperial army, not a host of undisciplined brigands, who would demand food and shelter, ignore his authority and probably still expect to get paid. In an attempt to limit the inevitable ravaging of the countryside by the rabble armies, Alexius began laying in supply depots along the Via Egnatia; it was to prove an invaluable precaution.

But in Clermont Urban had achieved his goal of re-establishing ecclesiastical supremacy over the temporal powers; the violent nobles and their retinues who threatened the stability of Europe had been converted into Soldiers of Christ, under the spiritual guidance of the papacy. Pope Urban had set the Crusades in motion.

The People's Crusade

Peter the Hermit, an itinerant monk whose charismatic personality inspired thousands with crusading zeal, was first to rally to the pope's cry. In March 1096, he left Amiens in northern France, bound for Jerusalem via Cologne in Germany, accompanied by a growing host of the faithful; mostly French peasants and their families, but also Germans and Italians.

The People's Crusade of several columns somehow made its way across Europe and along the Danube through Hungary without serious mishap until it reached Semlin (Zemun). Here, over some argument, a full-scale battle broke out with Hungarian troops. Astonishingly, the peasants won, and were left unmolested to cross the Sava to Belgrade; however, the later stragglers and isolated groups were massacred.

At Belgrade the crusaders were denied food, and the rag-tag army ran amok, setting fires and doing great damage before order was restored. Worse came when a straggling band of German crusaders burned houses near the city of Nis, and were promptly set on by the Byzantine garrison. Almost 10,000 crusaders were brutally killed or led into captivity in a three-day killing spree before Peter could defuse the situation.

Alexius forgave the 'pilgrims' their excesses and had the various groups escorted to a camp outside Constantinople. As soon as they were amalgamated on 6 August, the peasants were ferried across the Bosphorus into Asia Minor, before they could cause any further trouble to the capital.

Around 30,000 men, women, and children were now loose on the Asian continent. Peter the Hermit pleaded for them to wait until the main crusading army arrived, but he was ignored. A base camp was established at the small village of Cibotus, and there the crusaders divided into two groups, one French, the other mixed German and Italian. They ravaged the countryside looting and indiscriminately killing the locals, all of whom were Christian Greeks. Both groups then marched on Nicaea, the local Seljuk capital, where the Turkish garrison, led by Sultan Kilij Arslan, decimated the French column.

The Germans avoided Nicaea and occupied the fortress of Xerigordon, which was immediately besieged by the Turkish army.

Xerigordon fell in late September, and all who were unwilling to convert to Islam were massacred. The Turks then ambushed those who had remained at Cibotus. A number of young girls and boys who had survived were taken by the Turks to use for their own purposes, but the remaining adults were slaughtered. In all, only a handful escaped the disaster, including Peter the Hermit, who was still in Constantinople when the massacre took place.

The People's Crusade was over.

Peter the Hermit jumps the gun in this 14th-century manuscript illumination as he gathers the rabble of Europe behind him. It was the very last thing that Alexius Comnenus was wishing for.

This 13th-century illustration depicts the Peasants' Crusade marching along the banks of the Nisava outside the walls of Nis in the Bulgarian Theme. Having heard of how raucous German elements of the crusade had fired Belgrade, the governor of Nis ordered his garrison to fall on the peasants. It was said that as many as 10,000 of the amateur crusaders were slain before Emperor Alexius intervened to save the remainder.

All the Princes of Europe

Over the next nine months from the late summer of 1096, Alexius's worst fears were to be realised, as he became unwilling host to another 70,000 men, led by some of the richest and most powerful feudal princes of the West. Byzantium was fortunate in having an emperor possessed of the intelligence and tact to meet them.

Hailing from Europe's wealthiest province, Raymond of Toulouse's crusader army was the largest and best equipped. It was not, however, very well behaved towards the Christians of the Balkans as it passed down the Dalmatian coast on its way to Constantinople.

In the early stages of the crusades – as indeed it would remain throughout the period – it was essential that Alexius establish his suzerainty over the princes, in the western feudal manner. He was not fooled for a moment by the crusaders' high-minded aims, whom he knew were bent on setting up their own independent fiefdoms in the East. So it was also vital to establish that they could not do so on territory that properly belong to the empire.

In the first arrival, Hugh, Count of Vermandois, brother of King Philip I of France, he was fortunate. Anna Comnena, Alexius's daughter, records that he described himself to her father as 'king of kings, and the greatest of those under heaven'. The chronicler William of Tyre called him 'Hugh the Great', but most contemporaries agreed with Anna's verdict that he was 'a pompous upstart'. His arrival at the Byzantine court failed to match his lofty pretensions, however.

He was shipwrecked on the eastern coast of the Adriatic, cast ashore on Byzantine soil half-naked and barely alive, and almost all of his followers were lost in the wreck. Hugh was conveyed to Constantinople where Alexius showered him with gifts… and guarded him closely. Hugh swore an oath of loyalty to Alexius, promising to return to the emperor any former Byzantine lands he recaptured. The next crusaders to arrive were a lot less tractable.

Godfrey of Bouillon, the Duke of Lower Lorraine and his brother Baldwin of Boulogne had come overland through Hungary without trouble to their large army. They entered the Byzantine Empire and, under armed escort, arrived outside Constantinople two days before Christmas. Here, the army remained for another four months, waiting for the other contingents. Unlike Hugh, Godfrey – who claimed to be the direct descendant of Charlemagne – refused to swear allegiance to the emperor, and Alexius cut off the food supplies. The brothers' response was to ravage the countryside until the supplies were resumed. In March 1097, after an uneasy truce, Alexius cut off the provisions again in an effort to force Godfrey to swear fealty. This time Godfrey attacked the city, which proved to be a tougher proposition than the unresisting countryside. The assault was repulsed and Godfrey obliged to take the oath in order to get his army fed. On Easter Sunday Godfrey, Baldwin and their senior knights made their oaths and banqueted with Alexius. The next day he shipped the lot of them over the Bosphorus.

A former enemy, a new friend

On 9 April 1097, three days after Godfrey's contingent stepped onto Asia Minor, Bohemund of Taranto arrived, after crossing the Adriatic Sea then marching through Byzantine Greece. This poacher turned game-keeper was the leader Alexius most feared. And yet everything went well. A Greek speaker from his time spent within the empire's borders and well versed in Byzantine court protocol, he promised to swear the oath without demurral. Unlike Hugh, Anna Comnena

praised his behaviour and striking appearance, but it concealed a simple policy. Bohemund desired the crusade's leadership, and knew that Alexius's friendship and support would help. In freely giving an oath he had no intention of keeping, the wily Prince of Taranto avoided any trouble that might delay him getting his hands on a piece of the Holy Land that the emperor would never see.

A fortnight later Bohemund and his Italian Normans were across the Bosphorus and Constantinople waited in trepidation for the next crusaders. Raymond IV of Saint-Gilles, Count of Toulouse and Marquis of Provence, had lost an eye fighting the Moors in Spain. To him, the crusade was merely a continuation of this struggle. His domain in south France was the richest province in the kingdom, and consequently he commanded the largest retinue in the expedition. They had marched via Lyons and reached Constantinople by way of Italy and Serbia. Unfortunately, the taste of his men for indiscriminate rape and pillage brought them into repeated conflict with their imperial escorts, so Alexius had little hope of a friendly meeting. In

the event this too went better than anticipated.

True, neither Raymond nor his companion Adhemar of Monteil, Bishop of Le Puy, to whom Pope Urban had entrusted the spiritual well-being of the crusade, would swear an oath of fealty to Alexius. But confronted by two skilled diplomats, the emperor agreed to compromise. Raymond swore only to respect the emperor's life and honour, safeguard Byzantine property and restore her lost provinces. The relationship between Raymond and Alexius became founded on mutual respect, and both were to profit from their friendship.

The last contingent to arrive was led by Robert, Duke of Normandy, eldest son of William the Conqueror, who had travelled through Italy, then followed the route taken by Bohemund. He was accompanied by his brother-in-law Count Stephen of Blois and his cousin Count Robert II of Flanders. Robert had no hesitation in swearing the full oath, and together with Raymond and his contingent, the Normans were duly ferried across the Bosphorus.

Crusader knights pack two ships under the care of a priest at the helm. While the majority of crusaders travelled overland to reach Constantinople, Guynemer of Boulogne sailed around Spain and across the Mediterranean to join the army already encamped about Antioch.

The First Crusade

Alexius was under no delusion about the crusaders. They were now engaged against his enemies the Seljuk Turks, but their long-term ambitions were not so certain. They had made clear their dislike of the Byzantines and the feeling was mutual. It was one matter to allow a foreign – if ostensibly friendly – army into the empire, it would be a great deal harder to get it out again.

Facing right: The crusaders lay siege to Antioch, a bitter business that dragged on for seven months. When they finally broke through, the unholy rape and pillage began, sparing neither Muslims nor Jews.

To Sultan Kilij Arslan, the crusaders were no more a threat than the rabble of the People's Crusade. This fatal error was based on assumptions that the *Ifranj* (derived from 'Varangian', the word came to cover all 'foreigners' as well as the Franks) were still the primitives who had made up isolated bands of mercenaries in the region for some time. The crusaders quickly laid siege to the Turkish regional capital Nicaea, and Arslan brought up his army, intent on defeating the besiegers. But the Seljuks had no troops capable of defeating heavily armoured knights in close combat.

Crusaders advance on Nicaea flourishing the heads of decapitated Turks on their pikes; from the 13th-century *Les Histoires d'Outremer.*

Since one face of Nicaea was protected by Lake Iznik, Alexius assisted the siege by supplying several boats, which were transported overland and then floated on the lake, completely cutting off the city. He also sneaked a diplomatic embassy into Nicaea by water to persuade the defenders of their hopeless position, and on 19 June 1097 the garrison surrendered. Alexius lavished gifts on

the crusaders for returning western Asia Minor to Byzantine control.

On 1 July the combined forces of Bohemund and Raymond of Toulouse smashed Arslan's army at Dorylaeum. The cost of the victory was high – almost 4,000 crusaders killed or wounded; Turkish losses were significantly higher. However, the battle of Dorylaeum broke Seljuk resolve and the crusaders faced no further serious opposition as they marched through the rest of Anatolia.

On 3 June 1098 Antioch fell after a bitter siege that lasted seven months, and finally on 15 July 1099, amid scenes of unbelievable carnage, the crusaders fought their way into Jerusalem. Muslims were cut down, irrespective of gender or age. The Jewish population took refuge in the city's principal synagogues, but the victorious Christians had little time for religious niceties. The synagogues were burned to the ground and those inside were immolated in the fires. The slaughter continued until only Christians remained alive in Jerusalem. Bishop Daimbert of Pisa wrote to the pope, saying: 'If you desire to know what was done with the enemy who were found there, know that in Solomon's Porch and in his Temple our men rode in the blood of Saracens up to the knees of their horses.'

The foundation of Outremer

Raymond of Toulouse, as the oldest and richest of the leaders, was expected to become Jerusalem's ruler, but refused the honour, which fell to Godfrey of Bouillon. Godfrey would not call himself king, preferring instead the title Defender of the Holy Sepulchre. Two of the great leaders were not present at the thanksgiving service of 1099. Godfrey's brother Baldwin of Boulogne had diverted at Antioch and made himself Count of Edessa, while Bohemund – after a quarrel with Raymond – had remained at Antioch and established his independent principality. In Constantinople the news of Jerusalem's recovery was greeted with delight, although Alexius did not expect to receive the ancient patriarchy into his hands. Still, it had been in Muslim hands for almost four centuries and was distant enough not be concerned about. Antioch, however, was another matter.

The city, having been retaken from the Arabs in 969, had been an integral part of the empire, and its inhabitants were overwhelmingly Greek-speaking Orthodox Christians. Now it was in

succeed. Greatly strengthened, the mighty fortress of Durazzo held out against him, and while a Byzantine fleet blockaded the Normans from the Adriatic, Alexius brought his army up and surrounded them. His forces reduced by famine and disease, Bohemund surrendered in September on the banks of the River Devol. By treaty, he acknowledged the emperor's suzerainty over the Principality of Antioch and retired to obscurity in Apulia. There, he died three years later and his three-year-old son Bohemund II succeeded him.

the hands of a Norman adventurer who, despite his oath, clearly had no intention of surrendering it to Byzantine authority. Bohemund's immediate enemies, however, were the Turks, and on one of his several raids into the surrounding regions, he was captured in the summer of 1100 and his nephew Tancred became regent.

In July of the same year, Godfrey died to be succeeded by his brother Baldwin, who handed the County of Edessa to his cousin, Baldwin of Le Bourg. Unlike Godfrey, Baldwin had no qualms about taking the title King of Jerusalem. He then negotiated the ransom of Bohemund from the Turks. In the intervening period between his capture and ransom in 1103, Byzantine forces managed to retake several coastal cities including Adana and Tarsus, and from Latakia down to Tripoli. This, plus a crushing defeat by the Turks at Harran in 1104, decided Bohemund to leave Tancred in charge of the principality while he returned to Italy to raise reinforcements.

This he did, but after having succeeded in persuading Pope Paschal II that the real enemy of the Crusader States was not the infidel Turk but Alexius Comnenus, Bohemund turned his new army towards the Adriatic and another invasion of the empire. This started in 1107, but Bohemund was not to

Above right: At Antioch the massacred infidel citizens' naked bodies were hung up in a grisly display.

Below: The siege of Jerusalem – crusaders scale the city's walls as Christ looks on from above.

Enemies On All Fronts

Alexius's fiscal policy was harsh and needed to be, given the huge expenditure necessary for imperial defence. The First Crusade had not delivered the desired effect of increasing security for the empire and in fact had left the frontiers more vulnerable than ever. The emperor's policies made him deeply unpopular among his subjects.

Right: Alexius I Comnenus halted further debasement of the Byzantine *solidus* by introducing the gold *hyperpyron*, or 'highly refined' coin.

Below: Having lost in the Balkans, Bohemund of Taranto retired to Apulia, where he died in 1110. He was buried in his oddly oriental-looking mausoleum at Canosa, with its Arabic designs and inscribed on the tomb the single word: BOAMVNDVS.

Having shepherded probably more than 100,000 men at arms from one frontier to the other, Alexius could take stock of what had been gained from the crusade so far; in truth, not much. Western Asia Minor had been regained, but as the crusading armies swept on down to Syria, the Lebanon and Palestine, they had little further effect against the Turks in Anatolia, and left Byzantine frontiers as vulnerable as before their arrival. And they were soon followed in 1101 by yet another four expeditions, all making a similar drain on imperial finances.

These were: 20,000 Lombards led by Archbishop Anselm of Milan; another French army under Count William of Nevers; an independent contingent of French knights with Stephen of Blois, who had fled the siege of

Antioch and was now shamefacedly returning; and a large Franco-German force under the joint-command of Welf, Duke of Bavaria and William, Duke of Aquitaine. All met with disaster in the middle of Anatolia, and served only to stir up the Turks to further raids on Byzantine territory. The need to raise money became acute.

But the empire's economy was in a mess. In 1092 Alexius made an attempt to halt the continued debasement of the *nomisma*, which had reached such a state that there were six different *nomismata*, of six different base metals in circulation. The financial chaos was worsened by the fact that the imperial exchequer insisted that all payments made to it were in the original gold standard, thus placing unreasonable strain on every level of commerce. His gold *hyperpyron* ('highly refined') was to become the standard Byzantine coin for another two centuries, but it was not until 1109 that he managed to restore some sort of order by establishing a proper rate for the whole coinage.

A tricky succession

Nevertheless, recovery was slow, so measures were taken to heavily tax the aristocracy (excepting his own family, to whom he gave too generously), the senatorial families and the rich monasteries. Conscription was introduced and this fell heavily on the peasantry. They began to live in dread of the imperial recruiting agents stealing their young men when they desperately needed them working in the fields. These and many other measures made him unpopular, but they were needed.

As has been related, as a result of Alexius's efforts the renewed Norman threat of Bohemund was ended by force of Byzantine arms, and

Antioch regained in consequence. However, the Treaty of Devol held for three years before Prince Tancred, acting as regent for Bohemund II, repudiated it, and it was to be the emperor's son John who would once more restore the city to Byzantium.

Struggles were to be unceasing along the ill-defined Asian border between 1111 and 1117 and, as Turkish attacks resumed, a fleet of Genoese and Pisan ships began ravaging the Ionian coast. The two Italian trading cities – bitter rivals to Venice – were making fortunes supplying the Crusader States in Outremer, and Alexius bought them off by offering not to impede their trade and by giving them trading rights in Constantinople along the lines Basil II had given the Venetians in 992. Against the Turks Alexius himself led his armies deep into disputed territory on several occasions, but the inconclusive battles wore him down and his health was failing fast.

He also suffered anxieties the succession of his son John Comnenus. His wife Irene Ducas had conceived a hatred of John – even though he was also her son – and she wished the succession altered in favour of Caesar Nicephorus Bryennius, the husband of her daughter (and the older sibling) Anna Comnena. Alexius had grown to distrust Irene, and often made her accompany him on campaign in order to keep an eye on her, but she never left his side in the last days as he sank. However, on 15 August 1118, by some trickery, Alexius managed to send her from his room and promptly called John to his bedside. He gave his son the imperial ring, after which John hastened to Patriarch John IX Agapetus, who crowned him John II Comnenus, a scant hour before his father's death.

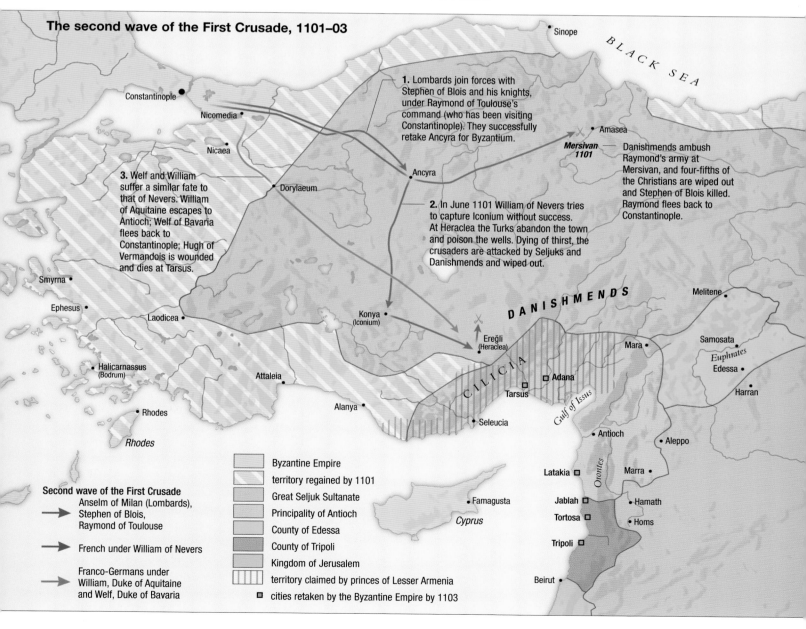

The second wave of the First Crusade, 1101–03

1. Lombards join forces with Stephen of Blois and his knights, under Raymond of Toulouse's command (who has been visiting Constantinople). They successfully retake Ancyra for Byzantium.

2. In June 1101 William of Nevers tries to capture Iconium without success. At Heraclea the Turks abandon the town and poison the wells. Dying of thirst, the crusaders are attacked by Seljuks and Danishmends and wiped out.

3. Welf and William suffer a similar fate to that of Nevers. William of Aquitaine escapes to Antioch; Welf of Bavaria flees back to Constantinople; Hugh of Vermandois is wounded and dies at Tarsus.

Danishmends ambush Raymond's army at Mersivan, and four-fifths of the Christians are wiped out and Stephen of Blois killed. Raymond flees back to Constantinople.

Mersivan 1101

BLACK SEA

Sinope
Constantinople
Nicomedia
Nicaea
Dorylaeum
Ancyra
Amasea
Smyrna
Ephesus
Laodicea
Konya (Iconium)
Ereğli (Heraclea)
Melitene
Mara
Samosata
Euphrates
Edessa
Harran
Halicarnassus (Bodrum)
Attaleia
Tarsus
Adana
CILICIA
DANISHMENDS
Gulf of Issus
Alanya
Seleucia
Antioch
Aleppo
Rhodes
Rhodes
Latakia
Marra
Jablah
Famagusta
Hamath
Tortosa
Homs
Cyprus
Tripoli
Beirut
Orontes

Second wave of the First Crusade
Anselm of Milan (Lombards), Stephen of Blois, Raymond of Toulouse

French under William of Nevers

Franco-Germans under William, Duke of Aquitaine and Welf, Duke of Bavaria

Byzantine Empire
territory regained by 1101
Great Seljuk Sultanate
Principality of Antioch
County of Edessa
County of Tripoli
Kingdom of Jerusalem
territory claimed by princes of Lesser Armenia
cities retaken by the Byzantine Empire by 1103

Byzantium and Outremer

On account of his mild and just reign, John Comnenus II is sometimes called the Byzantine Marcus Aurelius, but like that great warrior-philosopher of the second century he also devoted his reign to fighting the empire's enemies, eventually restoring Byzantium to its former extent before the disaster at Manzikert. Sadly, the Comnenian dynasty gave Byzantium but a brief respite against disintegration.

Mosaic of Emperor John II Comnenus and his mother, the dowager Empress Irene Ducas. Irene loathed her son and never missed an opportunity to blacken his name, but his success as a ruler defeated her schemes to have her daughter Anna Comnena's husband, the Caesar Nicephorus Bryennius, made emperor in John's place.

John II Comnenus (r.1118–43) is also known as *Kaloioannes* ('John the Beautiful'), not for his appearance – which was said to be ugly – but for the piety of his character. He quickly banished luxury from the court, and rigorously practised what he preached. Unlike his father, whose nepotism had several times almost been his undoing, John kept his family at arms length. As a military commander, he proved second to none. He scored victories over the Seljuks in 1119 by recapturing the Phrygian city of Laodicea taken by the Turks in 1071. He subjected the resurrected Pechenegs so thoroughly in 1121 that they were never again a problem, and repulsed Serbs and Hungarian invasions in 1128. But in Asia Minor, it was not just Turks who received the dynamic emperor's attention. He had a score to settle over Antioch.

The principality's short existence had been a confused one. When Tancred died in 1112, the regency passed to his cousin, Roger of Salerno, who took power at a dangerous moment. Ilghazi,

emir of Mardin, had recently also made himself emir of Aleppo. A skilled military commander, Ilghazi invaded Antioch and on 28 June 1119, 24km (15 miles) from Aleppo, the Seljuks surrounded Roger's crusaders and massacred them to a man. Baldwin II (r.1118–31) of Jerusalem – who had raced belatedly to the rescue – assumed direct control of the principality, but only division within the Seljuk alliance prevented the Muslims from pouring in. Ilghazi died three years after the battle, allegedly from the effects of alcohol.

In October 1126 Baldwin welcomed young Bohemund II to Antioch, 15 years after his father's death, and married him to his daughter Alice. She soon bore him a daughter, Constance, but four years later Bohemund lay dead at the hands of the Turks. This coincided with the accession of Fulk I (r.1131–43) to the Kingdom of Jerusalem, who proclaimed himself regent of Antioch in the name of Constance. However, Alice looked to the empire for security, and in 1135 offered Constance's hand to Manuel Comnenus, the youngest of John's four sons.

The match was politically ideal for the emperor, so it is easy to imagine his fury when King Fulk – appalled at the idea of a Frank marrying a Greek – insisted she marry one of his feudal lords, Raymond of Poitiers, the ceremony taking place in 1136.

Crusader treachery

John Comnenus gathered his battle-hardened troops and marched for Antioch, sweeping up the loose federation of squabbling principalities that made up Lesser Armenia in the process. When the Byzantine host besieged Antioch in August 1137, Raymond – who was only newly arrived from his comfortable home in France and with little sympathy for his principality, and with no hope of a crusader army reaching him – offered terms. Fulk, whose hands were now occupied with holding at bay Imad el-Din Zengi, Atabeg of Mosul and effective master of all northern Syria, gave his consent, and Antioch capitulated.

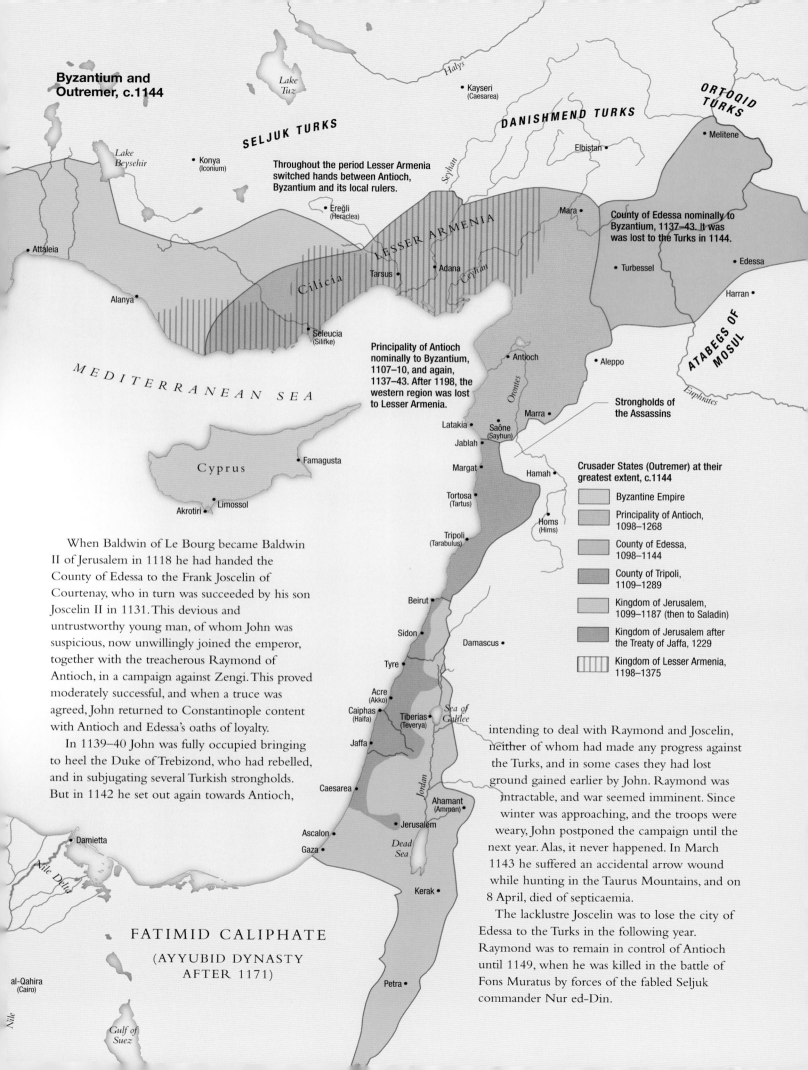

Byzantium and Outremer, c.1144

SELJUK TURKS

DANISHMEND TURKS

ORTOQID TURKS

• Melitene

Halys

• Kayseri
(Caesarea)

• Elbistan

Lake
Tüz

Lake
Beyşehir

• Konya
(Iconium)

Throughout the period Lesser Armenia
switched hands between Antioch,
Byzantium and its local rulers.

• Ereğli
(Heraclea)

• Mara

Seyhan

LESSER ARMENIA

County of Edessa nominally to
Byzantium, 1137–43. It was
lost to the Turks in 1144.

• Attáleia

Cilicia

Tarsus •

• Adana

Ceyhan

• Turbessel

• Edessa

• Alanya

Harran •

• Seleucia
(Silifke)

Principality of Antioch
nominally to Byzantium,
1107–10, and again,
1137–43. After 1198, the
western region was lost
to Lesser Armenia.

• Antioch

• Aleppo

ATABEGS OF
MOSUL

Euphrates

M E D I T E R R A N E A N   S E A

Orontes

Strongholds of
the Assassins

• Marra

Latakia •

Saône
(Sayhun) •

Jablah •

Margat •

Hamah •

Cyprus

• Famagusta

Tortosa
(Tartus) •

Homs
(Hims) •

**Crusader States (Outremer) at their
greatest extent, c.1144**

Akrotiri •

• Limossol

Tripoli
(Tarabulus) •

Byzantine Empire

Principality of Antioch,
1098–1268

County of Edessa,
1098–1144

County of Tripoli,
1109–1289

Kingdom of Jerusalem,
1099–1187 (then to Saladin)

Kingdom of Jerusalem after
the Treaty of Jaffa, 1229

Kingdom of Lesser Armenia,
1198–1375

When Baldwin of Le Bourg became Baldwin
II of Jerusalem in 1118 he had handed the
County of Edessa to the Frank Joscelin of
Courtenay, who in turn was succeeded by his son
Joscelin II in 1131. This devious and
untrustworthy young man, of whom John was
suspicious, now unwillingly joined the emperor,
together with the treacherous Raymond of
Antioch, in a campaign against Zengi. This proved
moderately successful, and when a truce was
agreed, John returned to Constantinople content
with Antioch and Edessa's oaths of loyalty.

In 1139–40 John was fully occupied bringing
to heel the Duke of Trebizond, who had rebelled,
and in subjugating several Turkish strongholds.
But in 1142 he set out again towards Antioch,

• Beirut

Sidon •

Damascus •

Tyre •

Acre
(Akko) •

Tiberias
(Teverya) •

*Sea of
Galilee*

Caiphas
(Haifa) •

Jaffa •

Jordan

Caesarea •

Ahamant
(Amman) •

Ascalon •

• Jerusalem

Gaza •

*Dead
Sea*

FATIMID CALIPHATE

(AYYUBID DYNASTY
AFTER 1171)

• Damietta

Kerak •

Nile Delta

al-Qahira
(Cairo) •

Nile

*Gulf of
Suez*

Petra •

intending to deal with Raymond and Joscelin,
neither of whom had made any progress against
the Turks, and in some cases they had lost
ground gained earlier by John. Raymond was
intractable, and war seemed imminent. Since
winter was approaching, and the troops were
weary, John postponed the campaign until the
next year. Alas, it never happened. In March
1143 he suffered an accidental arrow wound
while hunting in the Taurus Mountains, and on
8 April, died of septicaemia.

The lacklustre Joscelin was to lose the city of
Edessa to the Turks in the following year.
Raymond was to remain in control of Antioch
until 1149, when he was killed in the battle of
Fons Muratus by forces of the fabled Seljuk
commander Nur ed-Din.

A Brilliant Comnenus

Like his father, Manuel Comnenus was a fine general, with a quicksilver mind and enormous energy. Unlike his father, he enjoyed a luxurious court; but most disastrously, his obsession with affairs of the West left the empire with even more enemies than it had 37 years before at his accession.

A gold *hyperpyron* of Manuel I Comnenus. He holds an orb and sceptre, and the hand of God crowns him. His name and title (*despotes* – the word for emperor at this time) are on the right; on the left *porphyrogenitus* indicates his being born to a reigning emperor.

In 1142, as he was preparing to bring Raymond to heel, tragedy struck John II Comnenus at Attaleia. His eldest son, Alexius, fell ill with a virus and died. John ordered his second and third sons, Andronicus and Isaac, to escort the body back to Constantinople, keeping Manuel with him. On the return sea voyage Andronicus fell victim to the illness, and also died; and so it was that John chose his youngest to succeed him on the grounds that he possessed a better temperament than Isaac.

Endowed with a fine physique and great personal courage, Manuel devoted himself whole-heartedly to a military career. His first business was Prince Raymond of Antioch, who had insultingly claimed back his principality the moment John had died. When, in 1144, the inept Joscelin of Courtenay lost Edessa to Zengi and

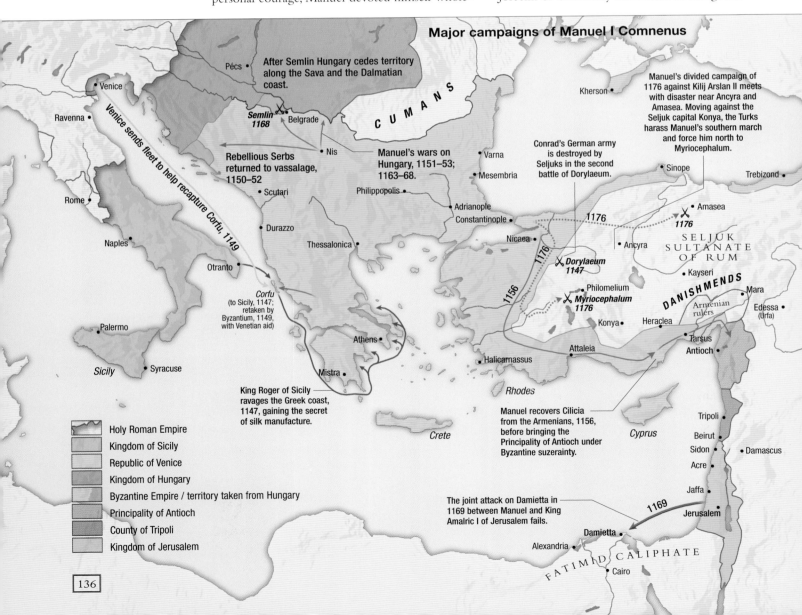

Major campaigns of Manuel I Comnenus

After Semlin Hungary cedes territory along the Sava and the Dalmatian coast.

Manuel's divided campaign of 1176 against Kilij Arslan II meets with disaster near Ancyra and Amasea. Moving against the Seljuk capital Konya, the Turks harass Manuel's southern march and force him north to Myriocephalum.

Venice sends fleet to help recapture Corfu, 1149

Rebellious Serbs returned to vassalage, 1150–52

Manuel's wars on Hungary, 1151–53; 1163–68.

Conrad's German army is destroyed by Seljuks in the second battle of Dorylaeum.

Semlin 1168

King Roger of Sicily ravages the Greek coast, 1147, gaining the secret of silk manufacture.

Corfu (to Sicily, 1147; retaken by Byzantium, 1149, with Venetian aid)

Manuel recovers Cilicia from the Armenians, 1156, before bringing the Principality of Antioch under Byzantine suzerainty.

The joint attack on Damietta in 1169 between Manuel and King Amalric I of Jerusalem fails.

Dorylaeum 1147

Myriocephalum 1176

1176

1156

1169

SELJUK SULTANATE OF RUM

DANISHMENDS

Armenian rulers

CUMANS

FATIMID CALIPHATE

Holy Roman Empire
Kingdom of Sicily
Republic of Venice
Kingdom of Hungary
Byzantine Empire / territory taken from Hungary
Principality of Antioch
County of Tripoli
Kingdom of Jerusalem

Places: Venice, Ravenna, Rome, Naples, Palermo, Syracuse, *Sicily*, Otranto, Pécs, Belgrade, Nis, Scutari, Durazzo, Thessalonica, Philippopolis, Adrianople, Constantinople, Nicaea, Varna, Mesembria, Kherson, Sinope, Trebizond, Amasea, Ancyra, Kayseri, Mara, Heraclea, Konya, Philomelium, Tarsus, Antioch, Edessa (Urfa), Attaleia, Halicarnassus, Athens, Mistra, *Rhodes*, *Crete*, *Cyprus*, Tripoli, Beirut, Sidon, Acre, Jaffa, Damascus, Jerusalem, Damietta, Alexandria, Cairo

turned towards Antioch, Raymond fled to the emperor to beg support, and was forced to swear allegiance to Manuel. News of the alliance dissuaded Zengi from attacking the principality, and in the following year a drunken eunuch murdered the great Atabeg, relieving the Crusader States of their most fearsome enemy. Also in 1145 Manuel drove the Seljuks out of Isauria.

The fall of Edessa prompted the Second Crusade, and despite his fondness for Westerners, Manuel was disquieted at the thought of more foreigners marching through his territories. The German emperor-elect, Conrad III of Germany, and King Louis VII of France led the crusaders. There was the drearily familiar bad feeling between Franks and Greeks on their line of march, which nearly precipitated a conflict between Manuel and his unwelcome guests. Within weeks of their crossing to Asia Minor in 1147, news arrived that a Seljuk army had wiped out the Germans at Dorylaeum. Conrad escaped and managed to get back to Constantinople, where he remained for months as an honoured guest. Louis eventually made his way to Antioch, harassed by Turkish ambushes and attacks across an Anatolia still under Seljuk control, and thus to the debacle of Damascus (*see the following page*).

Plans for Italy, humbling of Venice

In the same year the Norman King Roger of Sicily sent a war fleet against the empire. Sailing from Otranto, it captured Corfu, rounded the Peloponnese and ravaged the eastern coast of Greece as far as Euboea. It also brought back to Sicily the secrets of silk manufacture, which was to become an important Norman industry thereafter. Manuel made a treaty with Venice, and together they recovered Corfu in 1149. Then Manuel and Conrad – Byzantium and Germany – made a pact to jointly attack the Kingdom of Sicily, but it was postponed by a war with Serbia and Hungary, and Conrad's death in 1152 ended the alliance between the two empires. Conrad's nephew and successor, Frederick of Swabia, entertained none of his uncle's friendliness towards Byzantium, and the conquest of southern Italy became problematical (*see the following page*)

On his northern frontier Manuel forced the rebellious Serbs to vassalage (1150–52) and made repeated attacks on the Hungarians with a view to annexing their territory along the Sava. In the wars of 1151–53 and 1163–68 he led his troops into Hungary but failed to consolidate the gains; in 1168, however, a decisive victory near Semlin (Zemun) resulted in a peace by which Dalmatia and other frontier strips were ceded to Byzantium.

The Saracen enemy, left to right: Syrian emir 12th–13th centuries, mamluk warrior, Turcoman auxiliary, and mamluk askar. Syrian emirs favoured knee-length mail hauberks covered by rich fabrics. Initially, the Franks failed to recognise the garments as armour and referred to the Muslims as being unarmoured. The Turcoman carries an axe – often preferred instead of a sword in close combat. Askars carried a javelin for use as a shock weapon and also carried a bow and a sword, or small axe or mace.

Much of Manuel's time was absorbed by affairs of the West, but in 1158–59 he sought revenge on Reynald of Châtillon, who had succeeded Raymond as Prince of Antioch. Reynald – a mercenary Frank of the worst sort – had attacked and plundered Cyprus in 1156. Manuel marched across Cilicia, returning it to Byzantine hands, and defeated Reynald to reclaim Antioch. He was less successful against the Fatimids when, in 1169, he sent a joint expedition with King Amalric (Amaury) I of Jerusalem to Egypt, which retired after an ineffectual attempt to capture Damietta. As part of this alliance, Manuel married his niece, Maria Comnena, to Amalric.

The growth of Venetian power in the Mediterranean had become a cause for concern in Constantinople, and Venetian irritation at trade treaties concluded with their Pisan and Genoese rivals, not to mention the loss of Dalmatia which Venice considered her own preserve, led to a war in 1172. But between Byzantine wiliness and a plague epidemic, the expedition was a disaster. It cost Doge Vitale Michiel his office and his life, and rent Byzantine-Venetian relations for 14 years.

Despite successes against Sultan Kilij Arslan II in 1159, the Turks were not defeated. After almost 20 years biding his time, Arslan struck again in 1176 and overwhelmed the Byzantine army at the battle of Myriocephalum. This disaster, though partly retrieved in the campaign of the following year, had a serious effect on Manuel; from then he took no part in military matters as his health declined. Manuel I Comnenus died on 24 September 1180.

The Abortive Conquest of Italy

Emperor Manuel I dreamed of recovering Italy, and his friendship with German Emperor Conrad III made this vision a reality. Unfortunately, his obsession with the West lost many advantages he might have gained in the East, and before it was over the empire was embroiled in the Hungarian Wars.

After the fiasco at Dorylaeum in 1137, Conrad fell ill and it was Manuel – noted for his medical skills – who personally nursed him back to health. The resulting friendship was enduring – for the first time in over six centuries there was a possibility of true peace between the two Roman empires, and Manuel's niece Theodora married Conrad's brother, Duke Henry of Austria.

In 1149 the Second Crusade ended in ignominy after squabbling between the princes of

Having suppressed his rebellious nobles in Germany, Holy Roman Emperor Frederick Barbarossa marched his army into Italy to ensure the allegiance of troublesome northern cities like Milan, and to force Pope Hadrian IV to crown him emperor; illustration from a 12th-century manuscript.

Outremer and Louis VII led to a pointless attack on Damascus and a rout of the Christians by Nur ed-Din. Two outcomes are worth noting: Louis divorced his wife Eleanor of Aquitaine for having an affair with Raymond (who was to die in battle this same year); and Louis conceived a hatred for the emperor, unfairly blaming Manuel for all the ills that had beset his army. Eleanor was famously to marry King Henry II of England and become the mother of Richard the Lionheart.

Meanwhile, Manuel and Conrad conceived of a plan to conquer the Kingdom of Sicily from Roger. Manuel's reasons were clear enough,

Conrad accurately suspecting the wily Norman of financing German rebels against his sovereignty. Roger had also been busy further poisoning King Louis VII of France by suggesting a European league against Byzantium. War loomed, but Conrad's death on 15 February 1152 deprived Manuel of a valuable ally and brought him a potential enemy in the new emperor-elect, Frederick Barbarossa. Frederick wanted the Kingdom of Sicily for himself and had no intention of sharing it. However, events turned out differently.

In his own feudal lands he faced open rebellion, and in Rome papal suspicion of his autocratic manner. For three years Frederick battled to consolidate his rule at home, and in northern Italy to finally enforce his coronation by the unwilling and tough-minded Englishman, Pope Hadrian IV. In 1154 Roger died, to be succeeded by his son William. The Norman nobles of Apulia – envious of the 'jumped-up' Hautevilles – were in almost open rebellion. The opportunity this promised was open to both Frederick and Manuel. To thwart a possible southward expansion by Frederick, Manuel sent envoys in 1155 to Frederick at Ancona to suggest a joint attack on the Kingdom of Sicily. But by this time the German troops were too weary to follow their emperor and Frederick passed on the campaign.

King William, a far less able ruler than his father, offered a peace to Manuel, but the emperor wanted nothing less than conquest, and without German aid, determined to go it alone. He was helped by Italian unrest at the Sicilian domination, and by Pope Hadrian's equal determination to see William overthrown. Byzantine gold poured into south Italy through the hands of the generals Michael Palaeologus and John Ducas to finance local rebellion, and there were initial successes. First Bari fell in 1155, followed by Trani and Giovinazzo.

Finally, King William brought his army to Apulia, but was defeated at Andria. Encouraged, Hadrian raised a troop of mercenaries and marched south. By the end of the year all of Campania and most of Apulia was in Byzantine

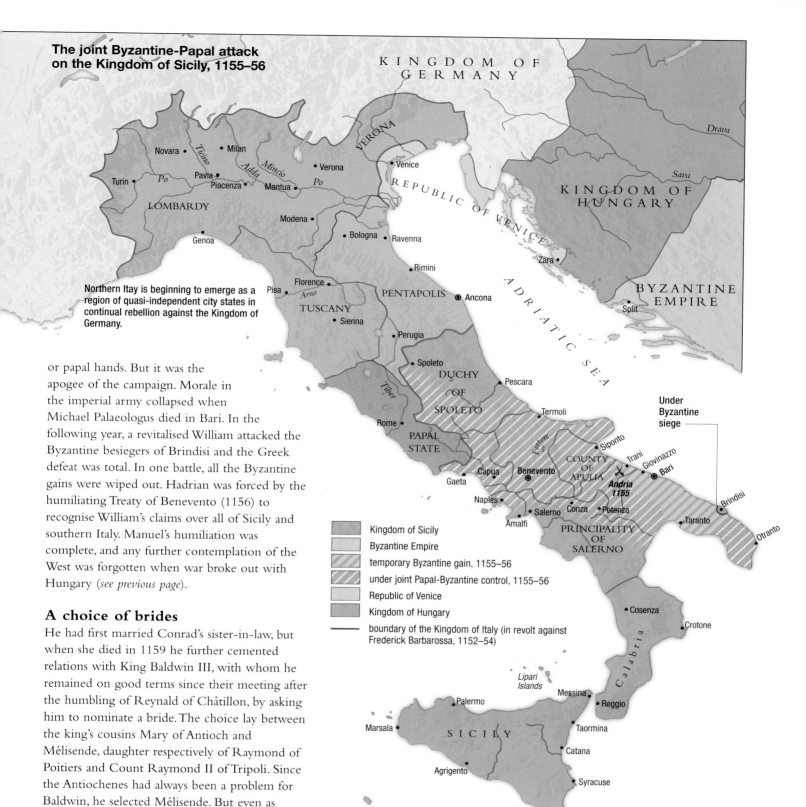

The joint Byzantine-Papal attack on the Kingdom of Sicily, 1155–56

Northern Italy is beginning to emerge as a region of quasi-independent city states in continual rebellion against the Kingdom of Germany.

Under Byzantine siege

■	Kingdom of Sicily
■	Byzantine Empire
▨	temporary Byzantine gain, 1155–56
▨	under joint Papal-Byzantine control, 1155–56
■	Republic of Venice
■	Kingdom of Hungary
—	boundary of the Kingdom of Italy (in revolt against Frederick Barbarossa, 1152–54)

or papal hands. But it was the apogee of the campaign. Morale in the imperial army collapsed when Michael Palaeologus died in Bari. In the following year, a revitalised William attacked the Byzantine besiegers of Brindisi and the Greek defeat was total. In one battle, all the Byzantine gains were wiped out. Hadrian was forced by the humiliating Treaty of Benevento (1156) to recognise William's claims over all of Sicily and southern Italy. Manuel's humiliation was complete, and any further contemplation of the West was forgotten when war broke out with Hungary (*see previous page*).

A choice of brides

He had first married Conrad's sister-in-law, but when she died in 1159 he further cemented relations with King Baldwin III, with whom he remained on good terms since their meeting after the humbling of Reynald of Châtillon, by asking him to nominate a bride. The choice lay between the king's cousins Mary of Antioch and Mélisende, daughter respectively of Raymond of Poitiers and Count Raymond II of Tripoli. Since the Antiochenes had always been a problem for Baldwin, he selected Mélisende. But even as preparations were made, there was a change of plans. In 1160 Nur ed-Din captured Reynald and his hated wife Constance assumed control of Antioch. The Antiochene nobles appealed to Baldwin to replace her with her son Bohemund. The matter should have been referred to Constantinople, but Baldwin made the decision, and an angered Manuel rejected Mélisende in favour of Mary. Thus it was her son, Alexius II Comnenus, who succeeded Manuel in 1180.

Of the five Comnenus emperors, Manuel was the most brilliant, and yet through bungled diplomacy he succeeded in uniting most of his neighbours against him, rather than playing one off against the other. His victories were devalued by the defeats his subordinates sustained. The expense of keeping up his mercenary establishment and the sumptuous magnificence of his court put a severe strain on the state's finances. And the subsequent rapid collapse of the Byzantine Empire was largely due to his brilliant but unproductive reign – as well as the terrible string of emperors who followed him.

The Muslim Recovery of Jerusalem

When Manuel died the realm was at peace, but it was – as usual – divided by political intrigue. The teenage Alexius II Comnenus (r.1180–83), whose mother Empress Mary of Antioch had married him to a 12-year-old French princess, was an unimpressive child. He was first of a string of emperors of little or no ability who would bring the empire to its knees before Western enemies.

The chronicler Nicetas Choniates described Alexius II as 'so puffed up with vanity and pride, so destitute of…ability as to be incapable of the simplest task.' In any case, he was under the regency of Mary. As the first Latin regent to run the empire, she was neither popular nor did her conduct help her. Conservative elements within the Byzantine court feared an increase in Latin influence so many supported the coup by the late emperor's cousin, Andronicus I Comnenus (r.1183–5).

Not only did the 64-year-old Andronicus seize the imperial mantle and kill Alexius and his mother, he also claimed the pubescent bride. The new emperor promptly launched a state-organised persecution and massacre of western foreigners, including many of the Venetian merchants stationed in Constantinople, which caused a flood of refugees to Italy and Hungary, begging for help. It also caught up a certain Enrico Dandolo, a Venetian merchant whose ill treatment before he fled the city was to leave him with a hatred of Byzantium that would have dire

consequences for the empire.

King William II of Sicily, who had succeeded his father in 1166, landed at Durazzo on the Adriatic in 1185, hoping to attract opponents of the tyrant Andronicus. The resulting invasion of the empire failed, but not until after the capture and sack of Thessalonica. Unfortunately for William, the ensuing uprising in Constantinople was all too successful and Andronicus was murdered by a Byzantine mob. His nephew became Isaac II Angelus (r.1185–95), and a rejuvenated Byzantine army repulsed the Norman Sicilians.

It was the only good outcome. During his time, Cyprus was lost to the rebellious Byzantine warlord Isaac Comnenus, and the court and government became rife with corruption as 'offices were sold like vegetables'. Oppressive taxation drove the Bulgarians and Vlachs to revolt in 1186, which resulted in the second Bulgarian Empire and an end to Byzantine authority in the Balkans. In the following year the Muslims under the charismatic command of Saladin recaptured Jerusalem from the crusaders.

A minor Kurdish warrior, Saladin had risen to power in Zengi's army and in 1170 made himself master of Egypt under the Ayubbid banner. In May 1187, having eradicated his Zengid overlord of Damascus, Nur ed-Din, Saladin also controlled Syria and turned his attention to the Holy Land. His pretext for invading was the breaking of a four-year truce

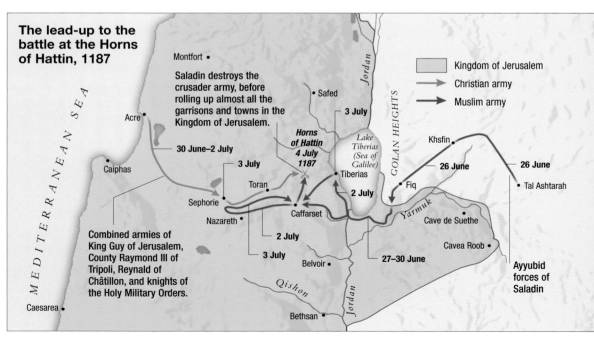

The lead-up to the battle at the Horns of Hattin, 1187

Saladin destroys the crusader army, before rolling up almost all the garrisons and towns in the Kingdom of Jerusalem.

Combined armies of King Guy of Jerusalem, County Raymond III of Tripoli, Reynald of Châtillon, and knights of the Holy Military Orders.

Montfort

Safed

3 July

Acre

30 June–2 July

Horns of Hattin 4 July 1187

Lake Tiberias (Sea of Galilee)

Khsfin

26 June

26 June

3 July

Tiberias

Tal Ashtarah

Caiphas

Toran

2 July

Fiq

Sephorie

Nazareth

Caffarset

Cave de Suethe

2 July

Cavea Roob

3 July

Belvoir

27–30 June

Ayyubid forces of Saladin

Qishon

Caesarea

Bethsan

MEDITERRANEAN SEA

Jordan

GOLAN HEIGHTS

Yarmuk

Jordan

Kingdom of Jerusalem
Christian army
Muslim army

Jaffa, Beirut, Caiphas (Haifa), Sidon and the cities of Galilee. Tyre managed to hold on, as did the northern cities of Tripoli and Antioch. Wheeling south, Saladin took Ascalon by storm and Gaza surrendered, and on 2 October 1187 Jerusalem capitulated after a 12-day siege. In pointed contrast to the crusader's sack of 88 years previously, Saladin's entry to Jerusalem went unmarked by bloodshed, and there was no looting. Although the inhabitants were held to tribute, Saladin freed many and paid the ransoms himself for many others. He was the hero of the Islamic world and the Kingdom of Jerusalem had virtually ceased to exist.

Pope Urban III died of shock on hearing the news, and his successor Gregory VIII immediately called on the mightiest kings of Europe to lead a Third Crusade. As the forces gathered, it became clear to Isaac that the coming crusade would prove a more dangerous threat to his empire than either of its predecessors.

negotiated by Count Raymond III of Tripoli, acting as regent for the sickly child-king Baldwin VI. On the boy's death in 1186, Guy of Lusignan emerged the successor from a power struggle, and his chief advisor, the intemperate Reynald of Châtillon, began attacks on Muslim caravans. The truce was over.

On the Horns of Hattin

In late June 1187 Saladin invaded Galilee and besieged Tiberias (Teverya), trapping Count Raymond's wife inside. By this time Guy had gathered his army near Acre. Raymond counselled caution, but Guy listened to Reynald, a man who would suggest a course of action, however absurd, without counting the consequences. He was all for rescuing the damsel, pointing out that Raymond was obviously not man enough to care for his own wife. The king ordered the army to march on Tiberias – and straight into Saladin's arms.

On 3–4 July, Muslim skirmishers herded the crusaders to a point just below the mountainous outcrop known as the Horns of Hattin, and there Saladin sprang his trap. Although Count Raymond escaped, most of his knights were cut down. The Bishop of Acre was killed in the battle and the True Cross was lost. While King Guy and his leading nobles were taken prisoner and sent to Damascus, Saladin had Reynald executed, followed by the leaders of the Christian Military Orders.

The defenceless realm was now swiftly mopped up. Acre fell on 7 July (incidentally freeing Isaac II's brother Alexius III, who was a hostage there), followed by the coastal cities of

Byzantine Force of Arms

Contingents of the First Crusade arrived at Constantinople in 1097, but Byzantium had been fighting against Islam since the eighth century. Although the defeat of the Byzantines by Seljuks at Manzikert left the empire weakened, the army still had an extensive role to play.

The Byzantine army had declined by 1097. What had once been a powerful standing army organised along recognisably ancient Roman legionary lines, was now largely composed of mercenaries. At the height of its power in the sixth century at the conclusion of Justinian I's expansionist reign, the Byzantine army was the most powerful military force in the Mediterranean. Byzantine warships ensured the stability of the sprawling empire. That all ended in 1071 at Manzikert, and what little military force survived the Seljuk invasion was destroyed in the dynastic and feudal power struggle that lasted a decade. When Alexius I Comnenus seized the throne in 1081, he tried to rebuild his country's defences.

The Byzantines had relied on Anatolia for much of their revenue and military manpower. With this resource largely lost to the Turks, Alexius was forced to rely on foreign troops to augment his army. Because the men were regulars, under strict discipline and training, it was still a formidable force of some 20,000. This was divided into heavy cavalry, light cavalry, light infantry and the Imperial Guard, better known as the Varangians. The standing army no longer operated throughout the empire as had once been the case. Each theme was expected to look after itself, and conscript its own *thema* (militia).

Even at the provincial level, the vestiges of ancient Roman military organisation were visible in the numerical division of a *thema* in order to provide a chain of command and the discipline

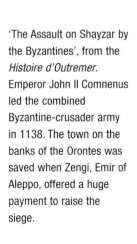

'The Assault on Shayzar by the Byzantines', from the *Histoire d'Outremer*. Emperor John II Comnenus led the combined Byzantine-crusader army in 1138. The town on the banks of the Orontes was saved when Zengi, Emir of Aleppo, offered a huge payment to raise the siege.

required in a well-run army. At the base level, a *numerus* (equivalent to a modern company) numbered 300–400 men, itself split into several platoons. Between five and eight *numeri* made up a *turma*, and each *thema* consisted of between two and three *turmae*. It was Byzantine policy to vary the numbers of the component parts to make it harder for an enemy to calculate the exact strength of a *thema*. Although the *thema's* task was to provide defence for its own theme, the province was also expected to reinforce the standing army.

In 1097, the total strength of the Byzantine army has been calculated at about 70,000 men. This figure does not take into account the large number of support units, which consisted of supply and siege train personnel, drovers, pack animal handlers, medical corps and a highly skilled engineer corps. The latter found itself often thrown together with the crusaders, especially in the early years, when the Franks had neither the materials nor the skills of the Byzantines in siege warfare.

A heterogenous force

The mercenary composition of the Byzantine army included Turks, Russians, Norsemen, Anglo-Saxons, Danes, Franks and Normans. The Turks operated as skirmishers and light cavalry, the Franks and Normans as heavy cavalry. For obvious reasons, neither of the latter was used in any Holy Land campaigns, although Turks were used to escort crusaders across some stretches of Anatolia. The elite force was the Varangian Guard, composed at various times of Vikings and Anglo-Saxons.

Vikings had served in the Byzantine army and navy since the mid-ninth century, and by 1097, Varangians were the best paid of all Byzantium's soldiers. Norsemen from all over Russia and Scandinavia came to Constantinople to join the guard, which was so popular, they had to pay a membership fee to get in. Because of their renowned loyalty, Byzantine emperors felt secure under Varangian protection – a comfort in a court of volatile intrigue. The Varangians accompanied John II Comnenus to Antioch in 1137 when the emperor decided it was time to force the prince of Antioch to pay homage and desist in his depredations of Lesser Armenia, a territory that should have been returned to Byzantium. The Varangians also fought against crusaders in the 1204 sack of Constantinople.

Scholars of language have pointed out that the word Varangian may have come to have a wider meaning by the time of the Crusades. Since it is derived from the word Viking, which essentially means 'to go travelling', it was probably applied to any foreigner in the service of the emperor, or even more widely to any foreign merchant or pilgrim passing through.

The Byzantine army combined forces with the Franks in an assault on the Emir of Shayzar in 1138, and were successful. In 1142 and again in 1157, the Byzantine army advanced on Antioch, though on the last occasion the prince – Reynald of Châtillon – was disposed to paying homage to Manuel I Comnenus in order to get rid of the annoying emperor. Franks and Byzantines again combined for the 1158–9 campaign against Reynald, which resulted in his humbling. This army, much despised by the crusaders, was to keep the Byzantine Empire alive for another 400 years, long after the crusaders had gone home.

Left to right:
Byzantine peltast, Varangian guardsman, and Byzantine cavalryman. The peltast first appeared in the 12th century as a mid-weight armoured infantryman. Earlier Rus Varangians favoured the heavy double axe, wielded with the shield slung over the shoulder, but by the 13th century the Varangian Guard was mostly comprised of other nationals and swords were more commonly used. Cavalrymen wore distinct colours for each *turma* (squadron).

The Third Crusade

The leaders of the Third Crusade were no less than German Emperor Frederick Barbarossa, and the great European rivals Richard II Lionheart of England and Philip II Augustus of France. Of these, it was Frederick, no friend of Byzantium, who posed the greatest threat to Isaac II, for the English and French contingents elected to sail to Outremer.

Frederick Barbarossa's accidental death by drowning in a river in the west Taurus Mountains is depicted in the *Gotha Manuscript* of the *Saxon Chronicle*; second half of the 13th century.

Now they were reconciled after a 17-year struggle for supremacy, the pope may have thought Frederick's crusading zeal stemmed from guilt, but in fact he saw the crusade as a means of bringing to heel the German nobility who – unlike their Frankish counterparts – had a healthy disregard for the principles of the feudal system. The German army, numbering about 100,000, set out from Regensburg in May 1189. The king of Hungary obliged the Germans with free passage, but Isaac II Angelus proved more difficult. Despite reluctant assurances to Frederick, he blocked the mountain passes into Byzantine territory. To be fair to Isaac, he was already aware that Frederick was intriguing with the rebellious Serbian princes, not to mention the Seljuk Sultan of Konya.

The Germans were therefore obliged to fight their way towards Constantinople, taking the surrender of towns and cities as they descended to the Thracian plain. When the Germans arrived outside the capital they found the gates barred against them. Frederick immediately declared war on Isaac, defeating a Byzantine army in Thrace and campaigning in Macedonia before entering winter quarters in Adrianople. By this time the Byzantines had taken enough and Isaac made peace, agreeing to ferry the crusaders over to Asia Minor.

In March 1190, Frederick led his army east and defeated the Turks near Philomelium before capturing Konya. The sultan (who had earlier rebutted Frederick's overtures) provided supplies to the near-starving crusaders, then hurried them on their way towards Cilicia. But then tragedy struck. While crossing the fast-flowing Calycadmus (Göksü) in the Taurus on 10 June 1190, Frederick drowned in the river current. Over half of his army had already perished on the long march. Now the survivors struggled on to Antioch, where many elected to return home by sea, while the few who remained finally reached Acre in October, providing meagre reinforcements for the depleted army of Outremer.

Since their sea journeys bypassed the empire altogether, Richard and Philip play little part in this story, beyond Richard's stop in Cyprus. His fleet was blown ashore by a storm, and the English king took the opportunity to seize the island from the despot Isaac Comnenus, a grandson of John II Comnenus, handing it over first to the Templars and then later to Guy of Jerusalem.

The bitter political row between Richard and Philip continued in Outremer and robbed the crusade of much-needed unity. Philip soon returned to Europe, but Richard the Lionheart's often merciless progress and his rivalry with Saladin made for many legends. His main impact

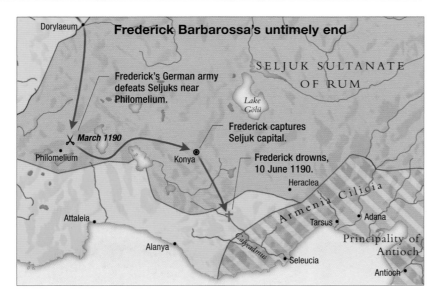

Frederick Barbarossa's untimely end

Dorylaeum

Frederick's German army defeats Seljuks near Philomelium.

SELJUK SULTANATE OF RUM

Lake Gölü

March 1190

Philomelium

Frederick captures Seljuk capital.

Konya

Frederick drowns, 10 June 1190.

Heraclea

Armenia Cilicia

Attaleia

Adana

Tarsus

Alanya

Calycadmus

Principality of Antioch

Seleucia

Antioch

on the future of the Byzantine Empire lay in an observation made towards the end of the moderately successful Third Crusade. Richard II identified Egypt as the best place for any further landings, and when Pope Innocent III called for the Fourth Crusade, Egypt was to be its target… at least, that is what he thought.

That meant ships, lots of them, and so the pope turned to Venice. In 1201, when papal envoys approached the doge – who by this time was Enrico Dandolo, the hater of Byzantium – for assistance in transportation, Venice's Council of Ten considered the proposal and agreed, but at an exorbitant cost. They also demanded half of everything captured on sea or land. Dandolo, however, had a different target in mind. The crusaders' objective of Egypt was unacceptable; it would disrupt Venetian trade with the Orient. Dandolo had a target closer to home in mind – Constantinople.

The Fourth Crusade starts

Innocent had insisted that Europe's kings devolve their authority to six papal legates. But this was a weakness: the legates were unable to command wily Dandolo and it was soon clear that it was the doge not the pope who was in control of the Fourth Crusade. Unable to pay the Venetians the full contracted sum, Dandolo offered to postpone the crusaders' bill in return for their military help to recover the Venetian city of Zara on the Adriatic coast, which had just been seized by the king of Hungary. There were violent objections

to attacking a Christian state, but as thousands of Venetians offered to join the crusade, the legates were forced to acquiesce.

Some 200 crusader ships arrived off Zara on 10 November 1202 and for the next two weeks siege machines bombarded the walls, from land and sea. Eventually the city surrendered, the Venetian flag was raised over its walls and the plunder was divided. Horrified at the news, Innocent excommunicated Dandolo and the Venetians.

Meanwhile, in Constantinople, Isaac Angelus had been blinded and imprisoned by his brother, who took the imperial mantle as Alexius III (r.1195–1203). Isaac's son, another Alexius, escaped to Zara and offered inducements if the crusaders would help him regain his patrimony. These included placing the Orthodox Church under Rome's authority, huge financial incentives, and 10,000 soldiers to accompany the crusaders to Egypt, the expedition's declared destination. One legate, the Abbot of Veaux, raised objections to another attack on a Christian state, but the majority of the Venetians and crusaders recognised the offer's possibilities. The target was switched, and the crusaders set sail for the Byzantine capital.

Lotario d'Anagni, Pope Innocent III, was a power-broker who came closest to bringing the monarchs of Europe into line since Urban II. He crowned a German emperor and then tried to depose him. He opposed King Philip II of France's marriage and King John of England's refusal to submit to papal authority. Both countries were excommunicated until the kings submitted to the authority of the Holy See. But he was no match for the wily Venetian politician, Doge Enrico Dandolo, who subverted papal authority over the Fourth Crusade for his own brutal ends.

Opening stage of the Fourth Crusade, 1202

Fleet sets sail, 8 November 1202

KINGDOM OF HUNGARY

Hungary seizes Venetian Zara, 1201; crusaders and Venetians recapture the city after a short siege in 1202.

The fleet continues towards Constantinople, 1203

VERONA
Venice
• Verona
VENETIAN REPUBLIC
• Modena
• Bologna • Ravenna
ADRIATIC SEA
• Rimini
Florence
PENTAPOLIS • Ancona
Zara
Split
BYZANTINE EMPIRE
• Sienna
• Perugia
• Spoleto
Duchy of Spoleto • Pescara
PAPAL STATE
Rome •
KINGDOM OF SICILY
Termoli

Christian Sack of Constantinople

When the crusaders arrived off Constantinople on 24 June 1203, many of them 'gazed very intently at the city, having never imagined there could be so fine a place in all the world.' The citizens were as stunned by their arrival as the crusaders were by the city's opulence, a sight that excited even greater greed and drove them to the most shameful act of the entire crusading era.

Above: Constantinople under attack; from a church wall painting. The city had suffered many sieges from barbarians and Seljuk Turks, but the mighty walls of Theodosius had always kept the enemy at bay. Not so in 1204, as the Christian crusader army assaulted them.

The usurper Alexius III watched the Venetian galleys row past the walls, displaying Prince Alexius on board, and heard the crew cry out 'Here is your natural lord.' The crusaders captured the suburb of Galata, breaking the boom that defended the inner harbour, the Golden Horn. On 17 July a simultaneous land and sea assault was launched against the city with the doge – in spite of his almost 90 years in the lead – but the attack was repulsed by the Varangian Guard. Despite this success, Alexius III was alarmed beyond reason and fled the city that night.

Leading Byzantine elements immediately freed the blinded Isaac II and set him on the throne. He deputed his son to co-rule with him in the hope of calming down crusader alarm at this unexpected development. It was an unenviable task. The crusaders were adamant. A papal legate met with Isaac and Alexius IV and informed Isaac that they were expected to abide by the terms of the agreement negotiated with his son. While the crusaders waited for their money and troops, the Byzantine court tried to raise the funds. With the exchequer empty, Alexius IV toured the empire soliciting contributions, under the watchful eye of a squadron of crusader knights.

By January 1204, anti-crusade feelings had risen to fever pitch within Constantinople and the citizens rebelled. Isaac and Alexius were swept from their thrones, murdered, and replaced by the anti-Western figurehead Alexius V Ducas Murzuphlus. Alexius V (r.1204) made it clear that he had no intention of paying the crusaders and began organising the city's defences.

The Venetians had seen enough. Screaming treachery, they persuaded their fellow crusaders that the only recourse remaining was to attack Constantinople. For the crusaders, clerics justified the action by claiming they were unifying the Christian Church. Warriors who fell fighting would benefit from forgiveness of sins as though their opponents were Muslim infidels.

The first attack, on 19 April, was a failure because of an unfavourable wind that kept the attackers from the sea wall, while Byzantine artillery bombarded the Venetian ships with boulders. The simultaneous land attack was also repulsed. A second attack came on 12 April, again a simultaneous assault by land and sea. The Venetians lashed their ships together, protecting them from artillery fire by wooden screens. This time the wind was in the crusaders' benefit, and the giant ships slammed against the city's sea wall.

A new Latin state

A Venetian soldier was the first to enter a wall tower, and while he fought the mercenary defenders, two French knights joined him to defend the foothold. A small gate was discovered and opened, and a flood of attackers poured through. By nightfall the emperor had fled and Constantinople was in crusader hands.

The murder, rape and looting continued for three days. When it was over, the crusaders held a Thanksgiving service. The haul of booty was immense. Holy relics were taken to adorn the churches of western Europe, and the crusaders filled their purses. Many returned home with their booty but thousands more remained to rule their new-found Latin Empire.

Planning for its administration had already been done. The crusaders and the Venetians would each appoint six delegates, and this electoral committee would choose a new emperor. It was expected that this would be a Frank, so the patriarch would be Venetian. The emperor would receive a quarter of the city and of the empire, the balance would be divided equally, one half going to Venice and half in fief to the crusading knights. In this way, the doge knew, Byzantium would never again be capable

of challenging Venetian maritime supremacy.

Dandolo's huge achievement made Venice a leading European power, but its consequences were to be ultimately devastating. In one fell swoop he had destroyed the great bulwark of European security, and when in only a few years a new Islamic foe arose from Asia Minor there would be no defence against them: the Ottomans would conquer to the very gates of Vienna.

On 16 May 1204 the easy-going Count Baldwin of Flanders and Hainault was crowned in St Sophia, ruler of the Latin Empire of Byzantium, also referred to as Romania. The Latins were to rule in Constantinople for nearly 60 years, while the real Byzantine rulers eked an existence at the furthest ends of their former realm.

A medieval drawing depicts the final moments as the Venetian and French soldiery break into Constantinople.

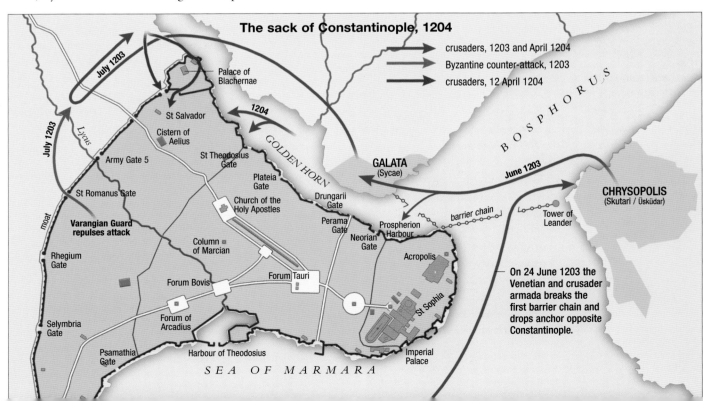

The sack of Constantinople, 1204

→ crusaders, 1203 and April 1204
→ Byzantine counter-attack, 1203
→ crusaders, 12 April 1204

On 24 June 1203 the Venetian and crusader armada breaks the first barrier chain and drops anchor opposite Constantinople.

Emperors of Romania

The offspring of greed and treachery, the Latin Empire of Constantinople was a monstrosity. In the 57 years of its existence it achieved nothing apart from contributing to the collapse of the crusading ideal, and enjoyed no distinction or glory. Of its seven rulers, only one rose above the mediocre; the wonder is that it lasted as long as it did.

Baldwin of Flanders was elected as leader of the new government in Constantinople, effectively becoming the region's first Latin emperor. His actual title was Emperor of Romania, the Latin name for the former Byzantine Empire, a term that emphasised the supremacy of the Roman Church over Greek Orthodoxy. For the Venetians, who formed the

A fresco in Ayasofya, the Church of the Holy Wisdom, built in the 13th century, at Trebizond (Trabzon, Turkey), depicts the Last Supper. The smallest of the split up Byzantine states, Trebizond continued to be a wealthy Christian trading centre until it was finally overwhelmed by the Ottomans in 1461, eight years after Constantinople's fall to the Turks.

majority of the elective council, Baldwin seemed the ideal candidate, lacking the power or influence to oppose their piecemeal appropriation of the best provinces in the Aegean basin. The Venetians coveted a lot more than Byzantine territory.

Of the official plunder from Constantinople most was claimed by Doge Dandolo. Venice also claimed the hinterland of Constantinople, the Adriatic coast of Greece and almost all of the most productive islands in the Aegean Sea, with a few crusaders who were willing to become puppet regional administrators. The twinned islands of Andros and Naxos became the Duchy of the Archipelago, province of a Venetian nobleman. Crete also became a Venetian colony

— over five percent of Venice's population settled there during the next two decades.

While all these new provinces owed their allegiance to the doge of Venice, in reality most were virtually independent. The new Empire of Romania simply provided an overall forum for this collection of states and a legal and constitutional framework for the region. The Aegean coast of Greece was taken over by crusaders from northwest Europe; the new Duke Otto of Athens was a Burgundian and William de Champlitte became Prince of Achaea.

These Latin overlords were, not surprisingly, detested by the Byzantines. The proletariat could do little but sullenly accept the authority of the Roman Church and its rites, and pay their taxes to a Frank rather than a Greek. The aristocracy, on the other hand, was less submissive and many left their ancestral lands in disgust to settle in one of the Byzantine successor states, which became focal points for Greek resistance to Latin domination.

Disintegration and chaos

The Fourth Crusade had not only failed to aid the Christians of Outremer, it also helped drain the Crusader States of their most precious resource – fighting men. Romania became an attractive prospect for the knights and minor nobility of the Crusader States, as well as western Europe, who had hitherto been unable to climb the ladder of feudal society. The ultimate weakness of the Romanian administrative structure was its basis in the European feudal model. Even republican Venice adopted feudalism in Romania, a poor substitute for the old imperial system of regional government. The Latin Empire was gradually eroded by two of the Byzantine successor states, the Empire of Nicaea and the Despotate of Epirus (*see following pages*), and by failing to wipe them out, the Latins sowed the seeds of their own destruction.

The Latin emperors were a poor lot. Baldwin's successful campaign against Theodore of Nicaea that established a Latin foothold in Asia Minor, was interrupted when the Bulgarian Czar Kalojan invaded Thrace in response to a plea from the Byzantine proletariat. In April 1205, Kalojan defeated Baldwin's army at Adrianople and took the emperor prisoner, who died soon afterwards. His brother Henry of Hainault (r.1206–16) spent much of his reign warring with the Bulgarians, and an expedition against the Empire of Nicaea only resulted in a treaty.

When childless Henry died, the crown went his sister Yolanda's husband, Peter of Courtenay, who was in France. He set out immediately but was taken prisoner at Durazzo after a foolish attempt to wrest the port from Theodore Ducas, despot of Epirus. Yolanda arrived in Constantinople in 1217 and ruled as empress regent until her death in 1219 left her feckless elder son Robert on the throne. He failed to hold the hinterland of Thessalonica from the expanding Epirots and otherwise spent his cowardly life in dissipation, leaving his 11-year-old brother Baldwin II (r.1228–61) as his successor. The elderly John of Brienne acted as regent until 1237. On obtaining his majority, Baldwin's realm was little more than the city of Constantinople. His reign was chiefly occupied by begging at European courts for funds to combat his enemies on all sides. Although he returned to Constantinople in 1240 with a substantial army, it melted away for lack of pay.

In 1261 Michael VIII Palaeologus captured Constantinople and Baldwin's rule came to an end. He escaped in a Venetian galley to Apulia and eventually to the Italian court of Charles of Anjou, where he spent the remaining 12 years of his life as a prisoner of Charles.

The Byzantine church of Kata Panaghia, built in the mid-13th century at Arta, one of the major centres of the Despotate of Epirus.

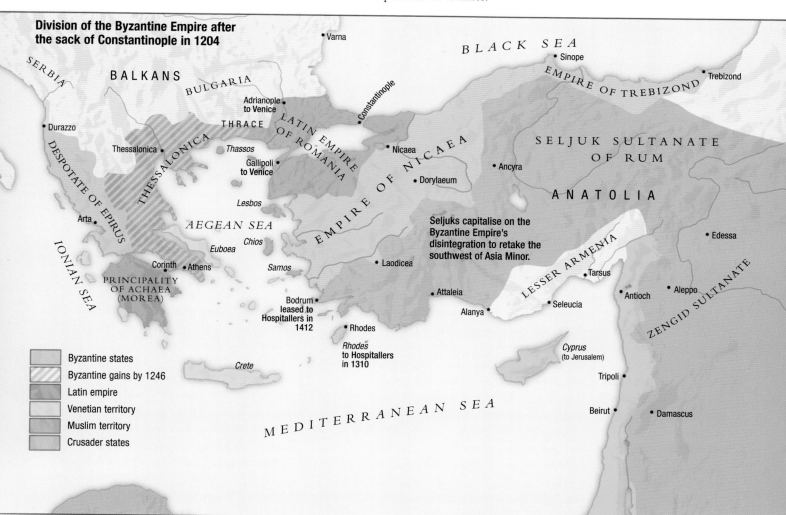

Division of the Byzantine Empire after the sack of Constantinople in 1204

Seljuks capitalise on the Byzantine Empire's disintegration to retake the southwest of Asia Minor.

- Byzantine states
- Byzantine gains by 1246
- Latin empire
- Venetian territory
- Muslim territory
- Crusader states

BLACK SEA

SERBIA
BALKANS
BULGARIA
THRACE
Varna
Sinope
Trebizond
EMPIRE OF TREBIZOND

Durazzo
Adrianople to Venice
Constantinople
SELJUK SULTANATE OF RUM

Thessalonica
LATIN EMPIRE OF ROMANIA
Nicaea
EMPIRE OF NICAEA
Ancyra
ANATOLIA

Thassos
Gallipoli to Venice
Dorylaeum

Lesbos
THESSALONICA

Arta
AEGEAN SEA
Chios
Laodicea
Edessa

DESPOTATE OF EPIRUS
Euboea
LESSER ARMENIA
Tarsus

IONIAN SEA
Corinth
Athens
Samos
Attaleia
Seleucia
Antioch
Aleppo

PRINCIPALITY OF ACHAEA (MOREA)
Bodrum leased to Hospitallers in 1412
Alanya
ZENGID SULTANATE

Rhodes
Rhodes to Hospitallers in 1310
Cyprus (to Jerusalem)
Tripoli

Crete
Beirut
Damascus

MEDITERRANEAN SEA

Phoenix Byzantium

The Frankish rulers of Greece and the Aegean Islands were detested by a local population who longed for the prosperity and stability they had enjoyed as part of the Byzantine Empire. Isolated centres joined forces into a revitalised Byzantium, whose enemies were the Christians who occupied their former capital.

The three surviving Byzantine provinces of Nicaea and Trebizond in Anatolia and Epirus in Greece served as rallying points for Greeks who resented living under Latin rule. The Empire of Trebizond was founded by the grandsons of Andronicus, Alexius and David Comnenus, days before the fall of Constantinople in April 1204 as a breakaway state. It was too remote to have any serious influence on events and did little more than exist on the shores of the Black Sea.

Michael Comnenus Ducas founded the Despotate of Epirus (as it was later known) in 1204, and in 1224 his half-brother Theodore

Later Byzantine rulers showed themselves being crowned by the patroness of Constantinople, the Virgin Mary, rather than by Christ as had earlier emperors. This symbol of the ownership of the city, even while in foreign hands, extended to all the far-flung Byzantine states. **Above:** A poor billon coin of Manuel (1230–40), Emperor of Thessalonica and Despot of Epirus. Next to it is a far better minting of a gold *hyperpyron* of John III Ducas Vatatzes.

conquered Thessaly from the Franks, founding the Empire of Thessalonica. This effectively severed land communications between Constantinople and the rest of the Latin Empire. In 1230 Theodore was defeated by Czar John I Asen of Bulgaria, and Thessalonica became a Bulgarian puppet-state. This left the future of Byzantium in the hands of the Empire of Nicaea. In 1208, the imperial title was given to Theodore Lascaris, son-in-law of Emperor Alexius III. Previously Theodore had been attacked by the Latin emperor Baldwin I, but the Franks became distracted by Bulgar attacks and any further Latin expansion was averted.

In 1214, the Latin and Byzantine emperors signed a peace treaty, leaving the Franks to fight the Bulgars and giving the Byzantines a chance to recover. The first ruler of Nicaea to be dubbed

Byzantine Emperor was John III Ducas Vatatzes (r.1222–54), who began a campaign to win back the old imperial seat.

In 1235, the Bulgars signed a peace treaty with John, which left Thessalonica in an uncertain state, a bone of contention between Nicaea and Epirus. The Bulgars were facing a serious invasion by the Mongols, who had swept out of the Asian steppes to the north and south of the Caspian Sea into central Europe and Asia Minor. In the Middle East they gave a hard time to Christians and Muslims alike, but after defeating the Turks they retired further east. With the Mongols gone, the Turks in disarray and the Bulgar nation crippled, the Byzantines were free to concentrate on fighting the Latin occupiers of the Peleponnese and Constantinople.

The Byzantines return

By this stage, with the crusading impetus failing, the Latin Empire was crumbling into a mess of local jealousies, although it managed to cling on in isolated pockets around the Aegean. The year 1241 proved to be a watershed as the Nicaean emperor John III Vatatzes was recognised as the Byzantine *basileus*. In 1249 he negotiated a peace treaty with the elderly Theodore of Thessalonica, which handed his generally only nominal control of the province to Nicaea. The Byzantines were ready for their comeback.

The highly successful John Vatatzes, who more than any had prepared the way for the return of Constantinople, died in 1254, and his competent but unhealthy son Theodore II Lascaris survived him by only four years. His son, John IV Lascaris, was only a child. It was time for a strong man to take over, and by popular consent that man was the best general of his day, Michael Palaeologus. The detested regent, George Muzalon, was murdered and in November 1258 at Nicaea Michael was raised on a shield in the ancient Roman manner and crowned Michael VIII Palaeologus – founder of Byzantium's last dynasty.

His first act was to declare war. Apart from Constantinople there were now only pockets of Latin resistance in the Peleponnese, and there was Epirus, which had separated from Thessalonica some years before; the despot Michael II was campaigning successfully to take Macedonia. Early in 1258 Manfred of Sicily, the bastard son of German Emperor Frederick II, invaded Epirus, and the despot, rather than give up his

Macedonian campaign when Thessalonica looked to be on the point of falling, offered to form an alliance with him against Nicaea. Michael's offer included the hand of his daughter Helena and – as her dowry – the conquered territory. Manfred agreed, and supplied Michael with a contingent of German knights.

Almost immediately William of Villehardouin, the Latin prince of Achaea, joined the alliance. The emperor waited no longer, and in 1259 a large Byzantine army commanded by his brother John Palaeologus soundly defeated the alliance at Pelagonia. The Latin defeat sealed Thessalonica's fate. To discomfit detested Venice, Michael signed a treaty with Genoa: in return for free trade in the Black Sea the Genoese fleet were to keep the Venetians at bay. With Constantinople cut off from relief, Michael's army captured the city in July 1261. Constantinople was in Byzantine hands once more.

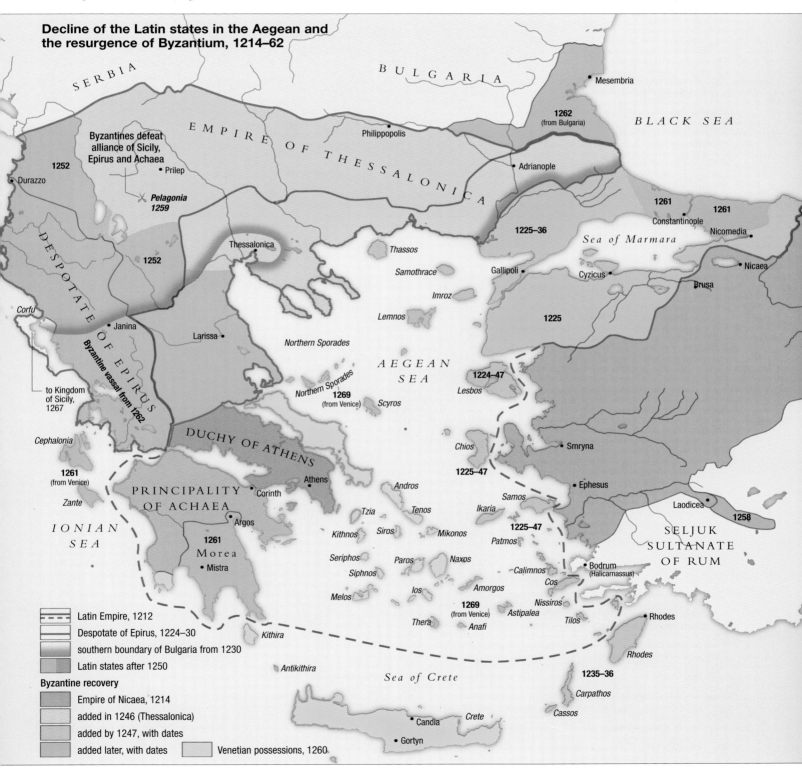

Decline of the Latin states in the Aegean and the resurgence of Byzantium, 1214–62

SERBIA

BULGARIA

- Mesembria

EMPIRE OF THESSALONICA

BLACK SEA

1262
(from Bulgaria)

- Philippopolis

Byzantines defeat alliance of Sicily, Epirus and Achaea

- Prilep

1252

- Durazzo

- Adrianople

✕ Pelagonia **1259**

1261

1261

Constantinople

Nicomedia •

1225–36

Sea of Marmara

DESPOTATE

Thessalonica

1252

- Thassos

Gallipoli •

• Nicaea

Cyzicus •

Brusa •

- Samothrace

Corfu •

OF

- Imroz

1225

- Janina

Lemnos

Byzantine vassal from 1262

- Larissa •

Northern Sporades

EPIRUS

AEGEAN SEA

1224–47

to Kingdom of Sicily, 1267

Northern Sporades

Lesbos

1269
(from Venice)

Scyros

Cephalonia

Chios •

• Smryna

DUCHY OF ATHENS

1225–47

1261
(from Venice)

- Athens

- Andros

Ephesus •

Zante

• Corinth

PRINCIPALITY

Samos •

Laodicea •

IONIAN SEA

OF ACHAEA

- Argos

- Tzia

- Tenos

Ikaria •

1225–47

1258

1261

Kithnos •

Siros •

Mikonos •

SELJUK SULTANATE OF RUM

Morea

Siphnos •

Patmos •

• Mistra

Seriphos •

Paros •

Naxos •

Calimnos •

Bodrum (Halicarnassus) •

Cos •

Melos •

Ios •

Amorgos •

Nissiros •

1269
(from Venice)

Astipalea •

Tilos •

• Rhodes

Thera •

Anafi •

Kithira •

Rhodes

Antikithira •

Sea of Crete

1235–36

Carpathos •

Cassos

Candia •

Crete •

• Gortyn

Latin Empire, 1212

Despotate of Epirus, 1224–30

southern boundary of Bulgaria from 1230

Latin states after 1250

Byzantine recovery

Empire of Nicaea, 1214

added in 1246 (Thessalonica)

added by 1247, with dates

added later, with dates   Venetian possessions, 1260

The Last Dynasty of Byzantium

The final incarnation of the Byzantine Empire was to last for almost two centuries and endure a string of ten dynastic emperors. If all were as able and committed as the first, Michael VIII Palaeologus, Byzantium may well have survived for much longer, and the Ottomans been kept from Europe. But they were not, even though none faced difficulties as complex or extreme as those that confronted Michael.

T he most immediate of many problems facing the first Byzantine emperor in Constantinople for almost 60 years was its defence. Greece was still under Frankish domination, Serbia and Bulgaria were hostile, as was Epirus even though it was Greek. The seas were controlled by the fleets of Venice and Genoa, and the new pope, Urban IV, was unlikely to be a friend of the man who had overthrown the Latin Empire. Meanwhile there was still Manfred of Sicily; Michael VIII was well aware that Manfred had not forgotten his dowry and would come to collect it as soon as he was able. Any combination of these Western powers would easily strangle the resurrected empire if the land and sea walls were not repaired.

The weakest section of the wall was that running along the Golden Horn where the crusaders had breached it in 1203 and 1204. This was first fortified with a wooden wall, but later Michael rebuilt it as two defensive stone walls. Next he arranged for the great chain that in former years had prevented hostile shipping from even entering the Golden Horn to be replaced. And then to ensure that enemy ships never even penetrated as far as this, he began an intensive ship building programme, distrusting Byzantium's current reliance on the Genoese, his only Western allies.

Next there was the reconstruction of the government and the city itself. Both were awesome tasks. So many Greeks had left when the crusaders came that entire sections of the city were empty, and capable administrators had to be found and trained, or persuaded to leave the dubious security of Nicaea. The imperial army was set to rebuilding the devastated buildings, many still the burned out ruins from the sack. By 1262, while there was still a long way to go, much had been accomplished, although it was clear that Constantinople would never again be the splendid jewel it had been before 1204.

Having started or dealt with the immediate

tasks, Michael the warrior became the emperor diplomat. His first mission was one of conciliation to Urban, but Michael's assessment of the pope had been correct. The envoys were given a hostile reception. Urban was under pressure from the exiled Latin Emperor Baldwin I to mount a crusade to restore Byzantium, with

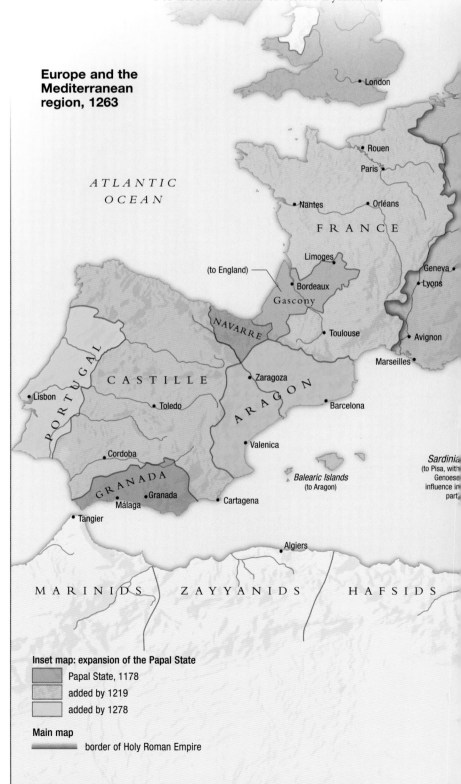

Europe and the Mediterranean region, 1263

ATLANTIC OCEAN

London
Rouen
Paris
Nantes
Orléans
FRANCE
Limoges
(to England)
Bordeaux
Gascony
Geneva
Lyons
NAVARRE
Toulouse
Avignon
Marseilles
PORTUGAL
CASTILLE
Zaragoza
ARAGON
Lisbon
Toledo
Barcelona
Valenica
Cordoba
Sardinia
(to Pisa, with
Genoese
influence in
part)
Balearic Islands
(to Aragon)
GRANADA
Granada
Cartagena
Málaga
Tangier
Algiers

MARINIDS   ZAYYANIDS   HAFSIDS

Inset map: expansion of the Papal State

- Papal State, 1178
- added by 1219
- added by 1278

Main map

border of Holy Roman Empire

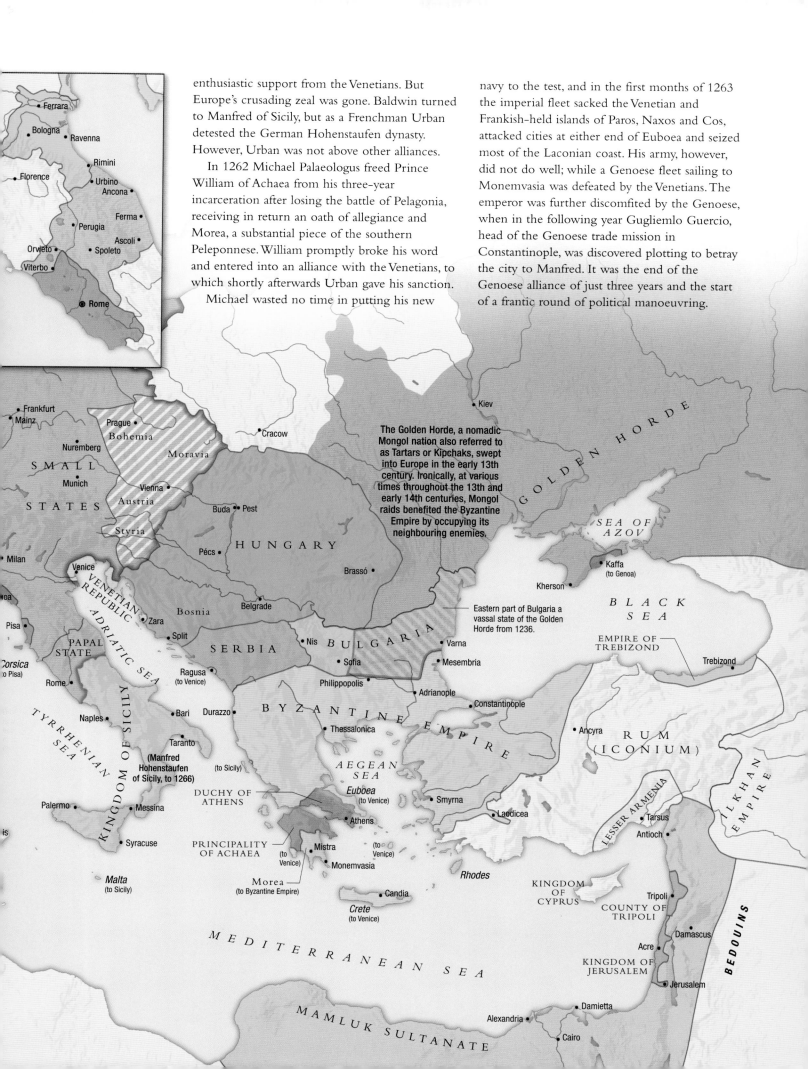

enthusiastic support from the Venetians. But Europe's crusading zeal was gone. Baldwin turned to Manfred of Sicily, but as a Frenchman Urban detested the German Hohenstaufen dynasty. However, Urban was not above other alliances.

In 1262 Michael Palaeologus freed Prince William of Achaea from his three-year incarceration after losing the battle of Pelagonia, receiving in return an oath of allegiance and Morea, a substantial piece of the southern Peloponnese. William promptly broke his word and entered into an alliance with the Venetians, to which shortly afterwards Urban gave his sanction.

Michael wasted no time in putting his new navy to the test, and in the first months of 1263 the imperial fleet sacked the Venetian and Frankish-held islands of Paros, Naxos and Cos, attacked cities at either end of Euboea and seized most of the Laconian coast. His army, however, did not do well; while a Genoese fleet sailing to Monemvasia was defeated by the Venetians. The emperor was further discomfited by the Genoese, when in the following year Gugliemlo Guercio, head of the Genoese trade mission in Constantinople, was discovered plotting to betray the city to Manfred. It was the end of the Genoese alliance of just three years and the start of a frantic round of political manoeuvring.

The Golden Horde, a nomadic Mongol nation also referred to as Tartars or Kipchaks, swept into Europe in the early 13th century. Ironically, at various times throughout the 13th and early 14th centuries, Mongol raids benefited the Byzantine Empire by occupying its neighbouring enemies.

Eastern part of Bulgaria a vassal state of the Golden Horde from 1236.

Michael VIII Palaeologus

Michael Palaeologus is best remembered for the recovery of Constantinople, but his monument should be the fact that he managed to keep Byzantium's grasp on the reduced empire. An outstanding general in his youth, he became a master of diplomacy in his maturity – perhaps the most brilliant that Byzantium ever produced; he failed only in his religious policy.

In 1261 – with Prince William still in control of much of Greece and the Epirots holding out along the Adriatic – the emperor needed friends more than ever. So he pulled the master stroke that was to earn him the hatred of his subjects. He made Pope Urban an offer he could not refuse: to unify the Greek Church with Rome, with the pope as the spiritual head of both. Urban accepted, but died in October 1264 before

its consummation, and through a series of obdurate popes it was to be a decade before the plan came to fruition.

In 1265 another unwelcome development occurred in Italy. Before his death Urban had chosen Charles, count of Anjou, the brother of King Louis IX of France, to bring an army and oust the despised Manfred from Sicily. With its capital now at Naples, the kingdom reached to the border of the now expanded Papal State. The new pope, Clement IV – another Frenchman with a hatred for the anti-papal Hohenstaufens – completed the arrangements. Against Charles' 30,000 troops, Manfred stood little chance, and went down fighting in February 1266 at Benevento.

Charles was the opposite of his saintly brother Louis, cold, arrogant and ambitious, and Michael

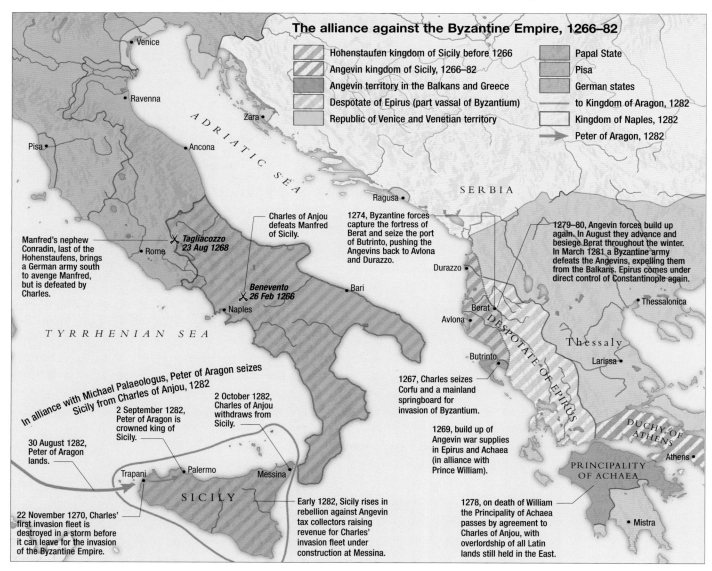

The alliance against the Byzantine Empire, 1266–82

- Hohenstaufen kingdom of Sicily before 1266
- Angevin kingdom of Sicily, 1266–82
- Angevin territory in the Balkans and Greece
- Despotate of Epirus (part vassal of Byzantium)
- Republic of Venice and Venetian territory
- Papal State
- Pisa
- German states
- to Kingdom of Aragon, 1282
- Kingdom of Naples, 1282
- Peter of Aragon, 1282

Manfred's nephew Conradin, last of the Hohenstaufens, brings a German army south to avenge Manfred, but is defeated by Charles.

Tagliacozzo 23 Aug 1268

Charles of Anjou defeats Manfred of Sicily.

Benevento 26 Feb 1266

1274, Byzantine forces capture the fortress of Berat and seize the port of Butrinto, pushing the Angevins back to Avlona and Durazzo.

1279–80, Angevin forces build up again. In August they advance and besiege Berat throughout the winter. In March 1281 a Byzantine army defeats the Angevins, expelling them from the Balkans. Epirus comes under direct control of Constantinople again.

1267, Charles seizes Corfu and a mainland springboard for invasion of Byzantium.

In alliance with Michael Palaeologus, Peter of Aragon seizes Sicily from Charles of Anjou, 1282

2 September 1282, Peter of Aragon is crowned king of Sicily.

2 October 1282, Charles of Anjou withdraws from Sicily.

30 August 1282, Peter of Aragon lands.

1269, build up of Angevin war supplies in Epirus and Achaea (in alliance with Prince William).

22 November 1270, Charles' first invasion fleet is destroyed in a storm before it can leave for the invasion of the Byzantine Empire.

Early 1282, Sicily rises in rebellion against Angevin tax collectors raising revenue for Charles' invasion fleet under construction at Messina.

1278, on death of William the Principality of Achaea passes by agreement to Charles of Anjou, with overlordship of all Latin lands still held in the East.

Palaeologus rightly suspected that they would not be friends. In 1267 Charles took Corfu and part of the coast of Epirus, and signed a treaty with William of Achaea. Michael now pulled off another coup: a renewed treaty with Genoa and – astonishingly – another with Venice, equally alarmed that King Charles might blockade the Adriatic. Genoa, however, was persuaded into Charles' camp two years later as he prepared a vast invasion fleet in Sicily. But on 22 November 1270, one of the worst storms in living memory sank it, together with most of the Angevin army on board. The empire was saved.

On 6 July 1274 the long postponed union of the two Churches took place in a formal ceremony held at the Council of Lyons. Once the news had sunk in, the Byzantine population rebelled in fury; what had seemed to Michael the only logical action he could take to provide security, his subjects saw as the worst of betrayals. The prisons soon filled with rioting Orthodox Greeks, while others fled to Epirus, where the despot claimed to be the champion of Orthodoxy.

Contemporary fresco painting of Pope Clement IV investing Charles of Anjou with the Kingdom of Sicily in 1266. The destruction of Manfred of Sicily brought Hohenstaufen domination of southern Italy to an end, but it did nothing to improve the Byzantine Empire's relations with the West.

If at first you don't succeed...

Ten years after the loss of his fleet, Charles made another bid to conquer the empire. William of Achaea had died in May 1278, leaving the overlordship of all Latin lands in the Balkans to Charles, while Epirus concluded a treaty under pressure to cede him many strongholds. In 1280 the Angevin force moved eastwards across Albania and besieged the Byzantine fortress of Berat. The garrison held out through the winter until Michael Palaeologus led a relief army and conclusively defeated the Angevins, including the heavily armoured Latin knights.

In the same year a partisan Frenchman, Simon de Brie, became Pope Martin IV. He had no care for the unified Church and, having excommunicated Michael, spurred Charles onto a full-scale amphibious assault on the Byzantine Empire. Furious ship-building began at Naples and Messina to carry a vast army of knights, men-at-arms and siege engines. But Michael had a secret weapon – a concord with King Peter III of Aragon (r.1276–85). Peter's wife was the daughter of Manfred, and he hated the Angevin for seizing his Hohenstaufen patrimony of Sicily. The emperor supplied Peter's agents with plenty of gold to fan the flames of discontent among the hard-pressed Sicilians, who were having everything taken from them for the coming invasion by Charles' greedy quartermasters.

In March 1282, with Charles' armada lying at anchor in Messina harbour, a revolt broke out in Palermo, leading to a massacre of the Angevin garrison. Rebellion soon engulfed the island and the warships at Messina were fired. In August King Peter arrived at Palermo and was crowned king of Sicily. With his fleet destroyed and many soldiers killed, Charles was no match for the massive Aragonese army, and he was driven from Sicily forever.

So, by diplomacy, Michael Palaeologus had once again saved the empire. After a moderately successful campaign against the Turks, he died in his 59th year while leading an expedition against rebels in Thessalonica, proclaiming Andronicus, his son and co-emperor, as his successor.

The Palaeologi Nightmare

For a further 170 years, Palaeologi continued to rule in Byzantium, but it was a period during which the emperors spent more time in dynastic strife than dealing with the foes on all sides. No longer able to dominate their neighbours, nations and freebooters capitalised on the internal strife to reduce Byzantine territory ever more as each year passed.

A gold *hyperpyron* of Andronicus II Palaeologus, with the Virgin Mary crowning the emperor.

Andronicus II (r.1282–1328) – the longest-reigning of the Palaelogians (excluding the split reign of John V) – devout in his orthodoxy, overturned Michael's union with the Church of Rome. While this pleased many, it was not enough for a group of extremists known as Arsentites, after the deposed Patriarch Arsenius Autoreianus, who called for the execution of all those who had betrayed their Church. They were to cause Andronicus a deal of trouble, but nowhere near as much as the Venetians, Genoese and Catalan adventurers. Andronicus allowed the navy, so painstakingly rebuilt by his father, to decay, which gave the rival states of Venice and Genoa free reign of the seas, and their internecine fighting even took place in the

Bosphorus without care for the Byzantines.

During his reign, the Ottoman Turks became an unstoppable power in Anatolia, and the hired Catalan mercenaries under Roger de Flor (*see pages 158–59*), who did at least halt the Ottomans, turned on their hirer with devastating results. From 1320 onwards the emperor was engaged in war with his grandson and heir Andronicus III. His violent behaviour resulted in the emperor disinheriting him, and the young Andronicus rebelled. The civil war ended when Andronicus II accepted his grandson as his colleague in 1325.

Three years later the unsatisfactory joint-rule ended with the abdication of Andronicus II. Andronicus III (r.1328–41) was chiefly engaged in war with the Ottomans, but only to the effect that the Turks conquered almost all of Asia Minor. He annexed large regions in Thessaly and Epirus, but they were lost before his death to the rising power of Serbia under Stephen Dushan, and his reorganisation of the defunct navy resulted in the recovery of Lesbos and Chios from the Genoese.

He was succeeded by his son, John V (r.1341–76), whose first reign became entangled with that of John VI Cantacuzenus. From 1328

Crushed between Serbs and Ottomans, the Byzantine Empire, 1346

Under Stephen Dushan (Stefan Dušan, r.1331–55) Serbia expanded rapidly, gaining the rest of Macedonia, Albania, Epirus and Thessaly. Dushan styled himself Emperor of the Serbs, Greeks, Bulgarians and Albanians.

Philippopolis • BULGARIA

BYZANTINE EMPIRE

BLACK SEA

• Adrianople

SERBIA

Durazzo (to Venice)

Constantinople

Thessalonica (to Byzantium)

Sea of Marmara

Izmit (Nicomedia)

Gallipoli • OTTOMAN EMPIRE • Cyzicus

Iznik (Nicáea)

(to Byzantium)

(to Byzantium)

• Brusa

Butrinto •

• Janina

(to Kingdom of Naples)

Larissa

AEGEAN SEA

Tenedos (variously to Byzantium and Venice)

Lesbos (to Byzantium, 1339; to Genoa, 1346)

(to Byzantium)

ANATOLIA

FRAGMENTS OF SELJUK EMIRATES

DUCHY OF ATHENS

Euboea (to Venice)

Chios (to Byzantium, 1339; to Genoa, 1346)

• Smyrna (to Knights of St John, 1344)

(to Kingdom of Naples)

PRINCIPALITY OF ACHAEA   Corinth

(to Catalans)   • Athens

• Ephesus

(to Genoa)

• Argos

IONIAN SEA

Morea

• Mistra

(to Venice)

(to Byzantium)

Duchy of Naxos (to Venice)

Knights of St John

• Philadelphia (to Byzantium)

• Bodrum (Halicarnassus)

Rhodes

Cantacuzenus had been entrusted with the supreme administration of affairs, but while campaigning in Thrace, declared himself emperor on John's accession. Since John V was only nine, his mother led the six-year civil war against Cantacuzenus, during which the rivals called in the aid of the Serbians and Ottoman Turks, and engaged mercenaries of every description. It was only by the aid of the Ottomans, with whom he made a disgraceful bargain, that Cantacuzenus brought the war to a termination favourable to himself, and acceptance of a joint rule in 1347.

The empire shrinks, bit by bit

This was the year that Constantinople was stricken by the Black Death, brought by ships escaping from the plague-ridden Genoese colony of Kaffa in the Crimea. The epidemic carried off well over half of the population, evidence surely that the city's protectoress, the Holy Virgin, had deserted them after more than a thousand years. And as further evidence, the survivors could point to the way the empire was shrinking: a little bit of former Thrace, some islands in the northern Aegean (but not Chios, which the Genoese took back in 1346) and a strip of coast around Thessalonica, otherwise surrounded by the dominions of Stephen Dushan. However, John VI was too ready to seek the aid of foreigners who, when he was unable to pay them, nibbled more of the empire away. Cantacuzenus lost any popularity and retired to a monastery in 1354.

John V's sole reign was marked by the gradual dissolution of imperial power through the rebellion of his son Andronicus IV and by the advance into Thrace of the Ottomans. In 1366, while undertaking a personal embassy to the king

of Hungary, John was captured by the Bulgars, and was only rescued by the effort of his cousin Amadeus (*see page 165*). In 1369 he travelled to Rome seeking Pope Urban V's assistance against the Turks and submitted himself to the Roman Church, which did nothing to endear himself to the Byzantines and resulted in no advantage. Returning via Venice, again seeking funds, he ceded the island of Tenedos (Bozcaada) at the mouth of the Hellespont to the Venetians, but even this deal collapsed (*see page 163*).

In 1373, having failed to secure papal or Venetian support, John was finally forced to accept the empire's status as a subject-state of the Ottomans. This ignominy so enraged John's son Andronicus that he rebelled against his father, but failed in his attempt to remove the emperor, and was thrown into prison. Three years later the Genoese helped him to escape, deposed John V and crowned Andronicus, who in turn crowned his infant son John VII. The Venetians then intervened and overthrew Andronicus IV in 1379, restoring John V to the throne. Andronicus rebelled again in 1385, but was equally unsuccessful and died soon afterwards.

When John V died on 16 February 1391, aged 58, he was a broken wreck, effectively the vassal of every enemy. He had been on the throne too long, an emperor who was neither intelligent nor far-sighted, and one too willing to submit to his Turkish suzerains. His longevity, however, ensured that it was his son Manuel who succeeded him and not his nephew John VII. The Byzantine Empire was now reduced virtually to the city of Constantinople, and that it was to hold out for yet a further 60 years was due to the determination of the last three emperors who ensured it went down fighting.

Typical of most Aegean islands in the 13th and 14th centuries, mountainous Chios changed hands several times between the Byzantine Empire, Turks and the ever rapacious Genoese.

Catalan Freebooters in Byzantium

The Spanish had become involved in Byzantine affairs before, when Michael VIII Palaeologus invoked the help of Aragon to invade Sicily and neutralise Charles of Anjou. But that had been at a distance; in the reign of Andronicus II Palaeologus a Spanish corps known as the Grand Company of Catalans made a distinctive mark within the empire's frontiers.

The Grand Company of Catalans owed its existence to Peter III of Aragon, who recruited a band of Spanish mercenaries – most but not all from Catalonia. Later, they fought for

IOANNES·ACVTVS·EQVES·BRITANNICVS·DVX·AETATIS·
VAE·CAVTISSIMVS·ET·REI·MILITARIS·PERITISSIMVS·HABITVS·EST

·PAVLI·VCIELLI·OPVS·

his son Frederick against the claim of Charles II of Anjou, but when a treaty was signed in 1302 and their services were no longer required, they looked for a new employer. By this time their leader was a swashbuckling adventurer and former pirate named Roger de Flor, and he sent envoys to Andronicus offering their services to the emperor, knowing he sorely needed military aid.

The Catalans reached Constantinople in September 1303 – at a high price. The men were to receive four months' wages in advance, at double the usual rate of pay; Roger demanded the rank of *megas dux* (grand duke) and the hand in marriage of the emperor's niece Maria. Andronicus II agreed to these exorbitant demands, and the wedding took place. But the Catalans celebrated by fighting with the local Genoese community, and Andronicus quickly shipped them over the Bosphorus to get them out of the city. In Anatolia they soon proved their worth, and by the spring of 1303 the Turkish army was on the retreat everywhere.

On the other hand, Andronicus began to realise that he had unleashed forces he could not control; the Catalans showed little respect for their employers, took their own decisions, and kept all the plunder they took. They also fell out with the several hundred Alan cavalry, supposedly fighting at their side. When the Alans discovered that the Catalans received more pay than themselves, they mutinied. In a sharp skirmish the Alans suffered 300 casualties, including the son of their chieftain, after which the remainder left. Undaunted, Roger de Flor attacked the Turkish besiegers of the important frontier town of Philadelphia, slaughtering 18,000 Turks and driving off the remnant.

By this time, his considerable fleet had not been idle – the islands of Chios, Lemnos and Lesbos were now in Catalan hands. The unprincipled adventurer could look back on two years in which he had allied himself to the imperial family and secured much of southwestern Asia Minor. He continued raiding deep into Turkish territory as far as the Taurus Mountains before returning to Bithynia, where the Catalans turned to strike south, passing

1204	1204–61	1259–82	1266	1274	1282	1303–08	1352
The Fourth Crusade is hijacked by the Doge of Venice and turns on Constantinople	Period of the Latin Empire, or Empire of Romania, finally defeated by Byzantine Nicaea	Reign of Michael VIII Palaeologus; recovery of most Byzantine territory from the Latins	Charles of Anjou defeats Manfred of Sicily, establishing an Angevin kingdom in southern Italy	The Greek and Latin Churches are united at the Council of Lyons; it does not last for long	In alliance with Michael VIII, King Peter of Aragon seizes Sicily from the Angevins	Roger de Flor's Catalan freebooters come to Byzantium's aid – and end up ravaging the empire	The mercantile war between Genoa and Venice culminates in a naval battle at Constantinople

through Sardis, Magnesia and Ephesus before crossing the Hellespont to land at Neapolis in Gallipoli. By this point it was obvious to Andronicus that the Catalans were little better than freebooting brigands.

Worse still, the imperial coffers were empty, and the Catalans were owed a years' back pay. In compensation Roger demanded the whole of Byzantine Anatolia in fief, and Andronicus was forced to concede it. The grand duke's ambition now knew no bounds and his eyes were clearly set on little less than the crown; but the Alans had not forgotten his treatment of them. In April 1305, as Roger was visiting Adrianople, a band of Alans fell on the Catalans, and Roger was killed. But there was no relief in this for Andronicus.

The desperation of Thrace

The depleted Grand Company boosted their numbers with disaffected Turkish and Bulgar soldiers, and then set out from Gallipoli to drive across Thrace, taking a terrible vengeance. The province had suffered from many ravagers over the centuries, but none so bad as the Catalans. Every town, village and hamlet in their path was burned; so savage were their massacres and vile their atrocities that it seemed they would depopulate Thrace. Thousands of panic-stricken refugees streamed into Constantinople, fleeing from their blazing cornfields.

And then – as had happened to barbarian pillagers many times before – the wasteland the Catalans created could no longer support them. In the summer of 1308 they turned west towards Thessalonica. Having failed to capture the city, the Grand Company destroyed several smaller towns and plundered the monasteries of Mount Athos before descending into Thessaly and then, in 1310, into Boeotia. Here, they found a new employer, Walter of Brienne, the French Duke of Athens, one of the prominent leaders of the Romanian Latin Empire. Walter hired them to satisfy his cherished dream of taking Thessalonica from John Ducas II, but he soon discovered that the Catalans were dangerous employees. When peace came in 1311 he attempted to dismiss them, and on 15 March the Catalans annihilated his army on the muddy banks of the Cephissus river. Walter and most of his knights were killed, and the victors advanced to Athens, where they set up their own Duchy. It was to last another 77 years.

In less than a decade, the Catalans had inflicted as much damage to the empire as the Turks had done in a century – and they had been paid to do it. Andronicus II had been forced to debase the coinage and impose still heavier taxes on his already desperate subjects to pay the Catalans. And the flood of refugees to Constantinople meant the city faced famine with the thousands of extra mouths to feed. The blow the Catalans had inflicted on the empire they had come to save was one from which it would never recover.

Facing: There is no reliable portrait of the captain of the Grand Company, Roger de Flor, but the leader of a band of mercenaries rose to the heights of being recorded in the visual history, in the equestrian portrait of Sir John Hawkwood, by Paolo Uccello. Hawkwood, an English veteran of the first half of the Hundred Years War, commanded the White Company. In a long career mostly spent in northern Italy he hired his services to the Pisans, the Viscontis of Milan, the papacy and the Florentines, turning coat as suited the depths of the exchequers he plundered. Roger de Flor's career was a splendid inspiration for the likes of Hawkwood, and an indication of just how much wealth could be accumulated as a mercenary warrior in the late medieval period.

Left: The companies of mercenaries cared little for neither the subject people of their enemies nor their employers. In Germany, southern France, northern Italy and the Byzantine Empire the order of the day for the roving bands of professional soldiers was rape, pillage and destruction on a grand scale, as this 15th-century woodcut shows.

Friend and Foe – Genoa

The last decades of the Byzantine Empire belong as much to its occasional friends and more often its enemies – the distinction was often difficult to distinguish – as to Byzantium, adrift on a sea of others' jealousy and mutual greed. Notable among them was the Italian city-state of Genoa, whose rivalry with Venice continually rocked Constantinople.

A woodcut from Hartmann Schedel's *Chronicle* of 1493 shows the city of Genoa. The harbour is in the foreground, with the jetties and dockside warehouses. A Genoese Mediterranean galley with its oars can be seen, as well as a sailing cog from a western nation.

Genoa, a port on the Ligurian Gulf of the Tyrrhenian Sea, grew as a mercantile centre from ancient Roman times. After AD 1052 the city was organised as a commune, governed by consuls and a *podestà* (mayor). By the mid-14th century, except when its rule was in the hands of foreigners, dukes chosen from among the principal merchant families governed Genoa. During the First Crusade the Genoese fleet transported the crusading armies and their supplies to the Holy Land in return for lucrative commercial privileges among the Crusader States.

In the period of the Latin Empire of Constantinople (1204–61) the Romanian emperors favoured the rival Republic of Venice, and Venetian fleets defeated the Genoese in 1257 and 1258. In the same year, however, Genoa took its revenge through an alliance with the Empire of Nicaea, and helped Michael VIII Palaeologus recover Constantinople. In return Genoa received the Ionian city of Smyrna and a monopoly of trade in the Black Sea, with the principal market being Kaffa in the Crimea. In 1262–67 a bitter war with its Italian neighbour and rival Pisa kept Genoa busy in the Mediterranean. A second war of 1282–84 ended with the utter defeat of the Pisans, and then the scene of conflict shifted to the East as the old rivalry with Venice flared up again.

At Laiazzo on the Armenian coast, the Genoese were victorious in 1294. Two years later

Venice retaliated by sacking the Genoese quarter of Galata on the Golden Horn opposite Constantinople. But in 1298 the Venetian fleet was annihilated at Curzola by the Genoese under the command of Lamba Doria. By this point, both mercantile states were exhausted, and an uneasy truce resulted in the so-called Peace of Milan (1299). It was to last for some 40 years, during which the Genoese enclave of Galata in Constantinople expanded greatly at the expense of the Byzantines.

Unwelcome guests

By the start of John VI Cantacuzenus's reign the empire relied completely on Genoese ships of the Black Sea fleet for food supplies, and the balance of trading revenues was overwhelmingly in Genoese favour. In 1348 Genoese customs in Galata were collecting 200,000 *hyperpyra* a year; across the Golden Horn in Constantinople the corresponding amount was only 30,000. John acted by reducing import tariffs to make Constantinople more attractive to foreign merchants; the Genoese resorted to force and

desultory skirmishes continued that wore Byzantine patience.

War between Genoa and Venice was never far away. A cause of irritation was the Genoese recapture of the island of Chios – recently taken from them by Andronicus III – in 1346, which the allied Catalans, Venetians and Greeks wanted to occupy as an outpost against the increasing piracy of the Turks. Forestalled, Venetian anger mounted when the Genoese interfered with Venetian shipping in the Black Sea. War broke out 1350 when Genoa captured Euboea, one of Venice's most valuable colonies.

In May 1351 a Venetian fleet sailed into the Golden Horn to attack Galata, and the Genoese – furious that the Byzantines did not immediately come to their aid – began catapulting boulders over the walls of Constantinople. John reluctantly sided with the Venetians, only to face Genoese wrath when the Venetians suddenly retired. On 28 July there was another naval battle with Genoa, which the Byzantines lost. Three months later a Genoese fleet on its way to Galata sacked the port of Heraclea on the Marmara, sailed through the

A carved relief on a headstone at the old French crusader port of Aigues Mortes depicts a Mediterranean galley, typical of those sailed by the Genoese. Those of Pisa and Venice were virtually identical in design – fast and sleek in war as well as commerce.

burned the few Byzantine ships they could find. In turn, the Byzantines fired the Genoese warehouses and the fighting continued for weeks. The Genoese then brought in reinforcements and attacked Constantinople. Peace was eventually settled when Genoa agreed to pay an indemnity and evacuate land behind Galata that it had illegally occupied over the years. However,

Bosphorus and attacked the Black Sea city of Sozopolis (Roman Apollonia).

By this time Venice was seriously alarmed at the increase in Genoese power, and an accord between themselves, the Aragonese and John Cantacuzenus set the scene for the greatest sea battle the citizens of Constantinople had ever witnessed.

Friend and Foe – Venice

When Attila the Hun devastated northern Italy in 452 the survivors fled to the marshy islands at the northwestern edge of the Adriatic and built Venice, named after the Roman region in which it was situated. In time it grew to become the most powerful trading nation in the Mediterranean.

Detail of a painting by Gentile Bellini (c.1429–1507) showing a procession in St Mark's Square, Venice. The cathedral's architecture clearly shows the oriental-Byzantine style derived from centuries of association with the once-parent empire.

Venice owed its growth to super power status to the conflicts between its western rivals Pisa and Genoa, which had been almost continual since the 11th century, which gave Venetian merchants free reign in the Mediterranean markets. As well as trading in costly silks and spices, the Venetians also produced ships, glass and ironwork, making them one of the most productive industrial cities in the Mediterranean. As a republic, Venice was a rarity in Europe – an independent non-feudal state, free of political bonds with the pope or the German and Byzantine emperors. The republic was ruled by the Great Council, or the Council of Ten,

presided over by the doge.

The Great Council supervised the city's administration, mercantile transactions and systems of justice, and also negotiated trading agreements with other cities and states. Venetian merchants were slow to take advantage of the First Crusade, and it was only when Doge Vitale Michiel saw the booty the Genoese and Pisans were bringing back from Palestine that this changed. Venice more than made up for its tardiness when it came to the Fourth Crusade. By this point Venice had become the greatest power in the Mediterranean – a situation Genoa could never tolerate, and so the many minor wars, escalating in violence until the 1350s.

After the Genoese capture of Euboea, Venice looked to the West for an ally and found him in King Peter IV of Aragon (r.1336–87), who was just as eager to see Genoa's influence in the western Mediterranean lessened. He offered 26 fully armed men-of-war, while John VI

Cantacuzenus, understandably fed up at Genoese duplicity, provided another 12 vessels on the understanding that Galata be razed and the islands seized by Genoa returned to Byzantium.

The Golden Horn aflame

On 13 February 1352 the rival fleets met in the Bosphorus beneath the walls of Galata, the Genoese under the command of Paganino Doria, the allies led by the Venetian Nicolò Pisani – both outstanding admirals. Pisani spotted the way that Doria had drawn up his ships in such a way as to dangerously constrict the allies' approach as a trap. But the impatient Aragonese commander would not listen and attacked, obliging the Venetians and Byzantines to follow. The resulting fight became a contest between Genoa and Venice. The Byzantines disengaged almost at once; the Aragonese did not last much longer.

The battle was fought with great ferocity, with vessels of both sides catching fire, until long into the night. In the end, with the wind against them, it was the Venetians who had to yield, but for Doria the victory was Pyrrhic, for his losses were almost as great. For Byzantium the defeat was total, and John VI could only plead for another peace with Genoa. But for the mercantile rivals the war was not over. Off the coast of Sardinia Genoa suffered a defeat in 1353; in the following year the roles were reversed as Doria twice routed the Venetians in the Adriatic and removed Venetian influence from the Black Sea altogether. The Venetians captured Genoese Beirut and in retaliation Genoa seized Cyprus in 1373.

Two years previously Genoa interfered with the plans of John V Palaeologus, who had offered Tenedos to the Venetians in return for financial support. The significance of Tenedos was two-fold: not only did it command the entrance to the Hellespont, but it was a useful stronghold from which to attack the Turkish 'pirates' of Karasi *beylik* who were causing havoc to Venetian shipping. The Genoese in Constantinople, appalled at the prospect of so valuable a prize falling into their enemy's hands, pressured Andronicus, John's son and regent during his absence in Rome and Venice, and Andronicus refused outright to give up the island.

After John's return to the capital and his imprisonment of Andronicus for rebellion, in 1376 the Venetians asked for Tenedos. Since he was offered substantial financial gain in return, John willingly agreed – to the repeated horror of the Genoese. Their thoughts turned to their ally Andronicus and they arranged his escape from prison. Sultan Murad also offered aid for the restitution of Gallipoli, captured by Amadeus of Savoy ten years before. Andronicus stormed the Palace and overthrew his father John V.

After this point, although neither Venice nor Genoa were finished with the empire, their involvement was to have less impact, and the two rival powers fought each other to a standstill by 1379. On 23 August 1381, both sides gratefully signed the Treaty of Turin: Tenedos was to be neutral ground, and both parties pledged to do everything in their power to bring the Byzantine Empire into the Catholic faith.

The doge presides over a meeting of the Council of Ten (of which he was the most distinguished member), while four scribes seated in front take the minutes; from a 14th-century manuscript illumination.

Rise of the Ottomans

For the last few decades of its existence the crumbling Seljuk Sultanate of Rum was a vassal of the Mongol Il Khans or had a Mongol governor imposed on it. After 1307 Turkish Anatolia fragmented into several beyliks, one of which was to emerge as a power greater even than the Seljuks themselves. The Ottomans were to threaten the survival of the last remnants of the Palaeologian Byzantine Empire.

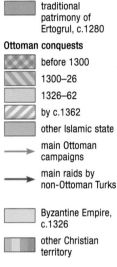

traditional patrimony of Ertogrul, c.1280

Ottoman conquests

before 1300

1300–26

1326–62

by c.1362

other Islamic state

main Ottoman campaigns

main raids by non-Ottoman Turks

Byzantine Empire, c.1326

other Christian territory

The first Ottomans were probably one of the many nomadic Turcoman bands that moved westwards to the Byzantine frontier and caused so much trouble before and after Manzikert. The Ottomans had several myths surrounding their emergence. The legendary Othman – from whom the tribe's name was derived – probably never existed, but coins naming Ertogrul, the earliest historical leader of the Ottomans, date from the 1270s. His tiny territory was in the mountains around Sögüt and included Dorylaeum where the First Crusade had defeated the Seljuks in 1097 and where in 1147 they in turn had wiped out the Germans of Conrad III.

Under Ertogrul's son, Othman Ghazi (r.1281–1324), the Ottoman *beylik* (small Turkish

state) was one of several that emerged from the fragmentation of the Sultanate of Rum. Located close to the Byzantine border, it attracted *ghazis*, religiously motivated warriors fighting in defence of Islam. The first clashes were the result of little more than traditional Turcoman raiding, but gradually the Ottomans took over more and more Byzantine territory. Sometimes they left towns isolated under Byzantine garrisons and governors who only later submitted to Turkish rule.

In many cases these Christian troops and leaders entered Islamic-Turkish service, sometimes converting to Islam at once but often remaining Christian for at least a generation. Such absorption of previous military and aristocratic elites would become a distinctive feature of Ottoman expansion, both in Anatolia and later in Europe. At the same time, other Seljuk *beyliks* were happy to hire themselves out as mercenaries to the Byzantine emperors

The primary focus of Ottoman expansion was northwards; in the reign of Andronicus III they captured Brusa (now Bursa) after a seven-month siege on 6 April 1326, and made it their capital; three years later they blockaded Nicaea after

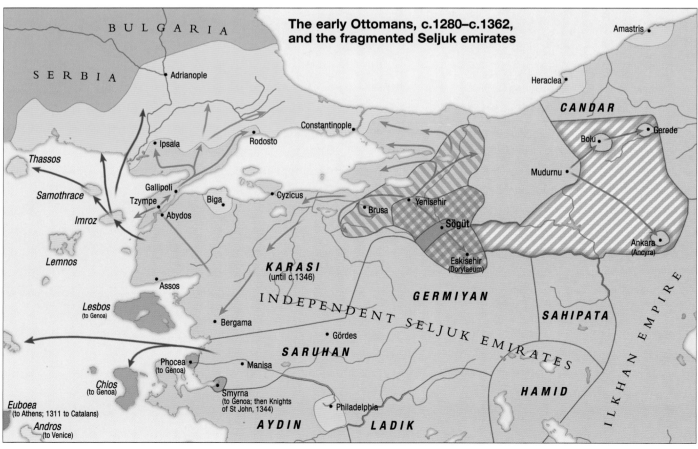

The early Ottomans, c.1280–c.1362, and the fragmented Seljuk emirates

inflicting an indecisive defeat on John VI Cantacuzenus. But the Ottomans were also in competition with neighbouring Turkish *beyliks*. Several of the latter were pursuing similar expansion against other Byzantine territory. In most case these *beyliks* found nowhere else to go once they reached the Aegean coast, so some took their raiding to sea, becoming what European chroniclers inaccurately called 'pirate states'. One of these was the Karasi *beylik* in northwestern Anatolia, whose ships ravaged Byzantine, Venetian and Genoese shipping approaching the Hellespont.

The Ottomans' conquest of Karasi in the mid-14th century opened up two new strategic possibilities. The first was offered by the small Karasi fleet, which enabled Ottoman *ghazis* to raid Byzantine islands and coasts in the same way that other *beyliks* were doing. The second was to place Ottoman troops on the Asiatic shore of the Dardanelles. The enfeebled Byzantine rulers were already inviting Ottoman and other Turkish troops to help them in their self-defeating civil wars. But in 1353 John Cantacuzenus allowed the Ottoman ruler Orkhan (r.1324–60) to garrison the little fort of Tzympe (Çimpe) on the Gallipoli peninsula, on the European side of the Dardanelles; it was the first European settlement. From here

Ottoman troops raided further afield in Thrace: in 1361 Didymotichm fell; in 1362, Adrianople. A large part of the native population was taken into slavery in Asia Minor, its place being taken by Turkish colonists. In the same year Orkhan died to be succeeded by his energetic son Murad I.

Byzantium was not entirely without friends. Amadeus of Savoy, a cousin on John V (he was a half-brother of John's mother Empress Anne), led an amphibious crusade in concert with the Genoese governor of Lesbos against the Turkish bridgehead at Gallipoli in May 1366. The Christians recaptured Gallipoli after two days' furious fighting and the victory had a salutory effect on Byzantine morale, and denied Murad an easy passage for reinforcements from Asia Minor. Amadeus then sailed his small but powerful fleet through the Bosphorus into the Black Sea and laid siege to Varna, demanding the czar release John. Since by this time the Bulgarian military position was weak, the czar bowed to the pressure and the emperor returned to Constantinople.

But Gallipoli was a small success which did not prevent Turkish expansion, and ten years later the Gallipoli bridgehead was re-established. The Ottoman Empire eventually spread over the entire Balkans and much of central and eastern Europe.

Orta Hamam Ottoman public bath, late 14th century, at Bolu in Turkey. Of all the enemies the empire had faced over the centuries, the Ottomans were the most civilised – indeed, they outstripped the sophistication of the late Byzantine period in terms of public welfare. In addition to public hospitals and schools, the Turks built public baths, or *hamams*, like this one wherever they settled.

The Ottoman Menace

The Ottoman conquest of the southern Balkans during the 14th century was one of the most dramatic events in the later medieval period. By 1400 the Ottomans had bypassed Constantinople to sweep through Greece and the southern Balkans, and northwards through Serbia and Bulgaria to the borders of Hungary. Constantinople was only spared from conquest by the timely arrival of a Mongol army.

In the decades leading up to 1400 the Byzantine Empire consisted only of Constantinople and adjoining coastal areas, southern Greece, and some northern Aegean islands. Similarly little was left of the Latin States in Greece, while Bulgaria had fragmented into little kingdoms that then fell under Ottoman domination. The fragile Serbian kingdom of Stephen Dushan had also fallen apart as the Ottomans thrust into the heart of the Balkans.

It had proved almost impossible for the Orthodox Christian Balkan states to join forces with Catholic Christians to the north. In fact, while many of the ruling elites looked northwards for help, most ordinary people apparently preferred Ottoman-Islamic domination to that of the Catholic Hungarians who seemed to be the only viable alternative.

Within the fragmented relics of the Byzantine Empire confusion reached epidemic proportions.

A depiction of the Field of Blackbirds – the battle of 1389 at Kosovo Polje – which was a decisive victory for the Ottomans over the shaky kingdom of Serbia.

Most of the emperors were now vassals of the Ottoman sultan and everywhere there was hostility between the military and civilians, ruling elites and common people. Furthermore, the crushing of peasant and urban revolts had left large parts of Thrace and Macedonia almost uninhabited except for a few fortified towns.

In contrast, Ottoman expansion was carefully planned and carried out with utter conviction. The first real Ottoman capital had been Brusa in Anatolia but after 1362 Sultan Murad I made Adrianople – which he renamed Edirne – the base from which the greatest wave of Ottoman conquests was launched.

Despite the setback at Gallipoli in 1366, by 1370 the Turks were on the move again. Murad defeated a Serbo-Bulgarian army and the Bulgarian capital of Sofia fell in 1382. Macedonia and Thessaly fell next, and then the armies marched northwest into Serbia. Nis was besieged and captured, then the Serbian army was decisively defeated at Kosovo Polje in 1389, though Murad did not live long enough to savour it. He fell under an assassin's sword immediately after to be succeeded by his son Beyezit I.

Anatolia was not ignored either. Under Beyezit a similar policy of expansion took place as a succession of independent Seljuk emirates became amalgamated into the growing Ottoman

Empire. Despite the humiliating defeat of the Serbs, Beyezit was not convinced the Ottoman position was secure, and in 1393–4 he summoned his Christian vassals to a council, at which they swore oaths of allegiance in the feudal manner. For Byzantium it looked as though their whole world was turning Muslim about them, and Emperor Manuel II appealed to the West for a crusade – and for once, the West heard.

Saved by Tamerlane

In 1394 Beyezit laid siege to Constantinople, but was obliged to raise it two years later when news arrived that 100,000 European crusaders stood on his Danube frontier. The sultan raised the siege and marched his army north. On 25 September 1396 the Ottomans and crusaders met at Nicopolis in what was the first serious encounter between a western Catholic army and the Ottomans, and the outcome hardly augured well for the future. The Turks massacred the Christians, in so doing effectively ended any further possibility of Western intervention on behalf of the Byzantine Empire. However, Constantinople was spared for the time being as Beyezit consolidated his gains.

Europe was spared from further conquest by the appearance of a Mongol army on the eastern border of Anatolia. The invaders were led by Timur-i Lenk (Timur the 'Lame', better known as Tamerlane or Tamurlane) and when they captured the town of Sivas he had the garrison put to the sword, including Beyezit's eldest son. The Ottoman sultan left Europe to lead the counterattack, but Timur defeated him at Ankara in 1402. Beyezit was captured in the battle and committed suicide in captivity three years later.

The Mongols reached the Aegean coast before returning to the Asian steppes, leaving the Ottoman emirs and Beyezit's successors to pick up the pieces of their empire, a process that was to last for a decade of dynastic struggle. Constantinople had been granted a reprieve, but when Sultan Mehmet I emerged as the undisputed ruler of a united Ottoman Empire, even to the most optimistic the final fall of Constantinople could only be a matter of time.

The mosque and medical complex of Beyezit II, late 15th century, Edirne. The former Adrianople became the new capital of an expanding Ottoman Empire and its cutlural centre.

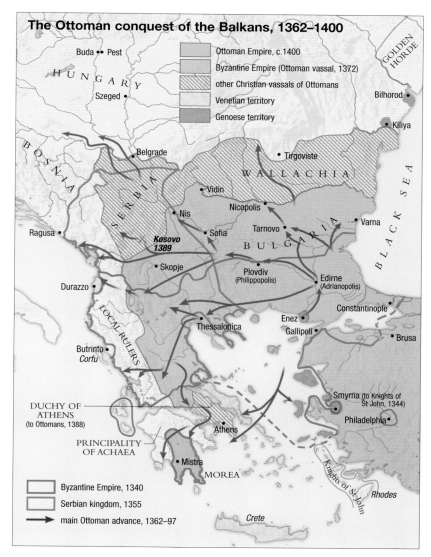

The Ottoman conquest of the Balkans, 1362–1400

- Ottoman Empire, c.1400
- Byzantine Empire (Ottoman vassal, 1372)
- other Christian vassals of Ottomans
- Venetian territory
- Genoese territory

GOLDEN HORDE

HUNGARY
Buda •• Pest
Szeged •
Bilhorod •
Kiliya •

BOSNIA
Belgrade •
Tirgoviste •
WALLACHIA
SERBIA
Vidin •
Nicopolis •
Ragusa •
Nis •
Tarnovo •
Varna •
Kosovo 1389
Sofia •
BULGARIA
BLACK SEA
Skopje •
Plovdiv (Philippopolis) •
Edirne (Adrianopolis)
Durazzo •
Constantinople •
LOCAL RULERS
Thessalonica •
Enez •
Gallipoli •
Brusa •
Butrinto •
Corfu
Smyrna (to Knights of St John, 1344)
DUCHY OF ATHENS (to Ottomans, 1388)
Athens •
Philadelphia •
PRINCIPALITY OF ACHAEA
• Mistra
MOREA
Knights of St John
Rhodes

- Byzantine Empire, 1340
- Serbian kingdom, 1355
- → main Ottoman advance, 1362–97

Crete

The Trials of Manuel II

When Manuel II came to the throne in 1391 the Byzantine Empire was so in name only. It consisted of some outposts in Greece – the Despotate of Morea – and the immediate environs of Constantinople. If any recovery was to be possible, it needed someone much stronger than vacillating John V, and Manuel II Palaeologus appeared to be this man.

These two images point up the continuing isolation of Byzantine art from that of the European Renaissance. The Italian fresco *Procession of the Magi* by Benozzo Gozzoli (**below**) presents one of the magi as Manuel's son John VIII. It contrasts starkly with the typically Byzantine iconic representation of his father on the facing page.

Manuel was aged five in 1355 when his father John V offered to send him to Avignon and the care of Pope Innocent VI to be raised as a Catholic. It was another of John's attempts to raise support from a crusade to save Byzantium, and it failed. He was 16 when John left him as a hostage at the court of King Louis I of Hungary in yet another unsuccessful plea for Catholic military aid; but Manuel had returned to Constantinople in the following year, 1367. In 1371 John made Manuel governor of Thessalonica, which aroused Andronicus IV's anger at his father's obvious preference for the younger son.

Manuel was bound as a vassal of the Ottomans by John's agreement with Murad, made in 1372, and both father and son frequently found themselves campaigning with the Turks. Manuel was with Murad in Anatolia in May 1373 when Andronicus rebelled against his father, which resulted in the three-year civil war and his eventual imprisonment. In turn, Manuel suffered imprisonment with John at his brother's hand in 1376, to be freed by the Venetians three years later (*see page 163*). With Andronicus out of the picture, Manuel was crowned as co-emperor in 1379, and returned to his province of Thessalonica. Here he continued to resist Turkish expansion, despite its vassalage to the sultan, and even scored some victories, which were an embarrassment to John and led to their estrangement.

In spite of his spirited defence, Thessalonica was gradually reduced until it consisted only of the city, and this fell in 1387. Manuel was still in exile on the island of Lemnos at the time of Murad's death in 1389. In Genoa his nephew John VII was trying to raise an insurrection against John V. But he found a better ally in the new Sultan Beyezit I (r.1389–1402), who tired of the Palaeologi squabbling and wanted a tractable vassal on the Byzantine throne. With the assistance of a small Turkish force, young John overthrew his grandfather, who barricaded himself in one of the city wall fortresses.

It was Manuel II, having recruited ships from the Knights of St John, who effected John VII's eviction from the city and his father's rescue. Beyezit was furious – at both co-emperors, and demanded their service, which they reluctantly gave. Their punishment was to assist in the final capitulation of Philadelphia, the last Byzantine stronghold in Asia Minor. And so Manuel was a virtual prisoner of the sultan when John V died in February 1391.

An appeal to the West

He may have been his father's son but Manuel – now in the prime of life – was not his father's shadow. Knowing that Beyezit, as Byzantium's suzerain, would almost certainly appoint John VII as *basileus*, Manuel made good his escape early in March and was welcomed in the capital with enthusiasm. Beyezit left him in relative peace until a Bulgarian insurrection brought the sultan back to Europe in 1393. After a swift retribution,

Beyezit called all his Christian vassals to his camp at Serres. As well as the emperor, these included his brother Theodore, despot of Morea, his father-in-law Constantine Dragash and his hated nephew John VII. Beyezit tongue-lashed them for their various disobediences, and when they were let go Manuel was convinced he had narrowly escaped with his life.

When he was summoned again shortly afterwards, Manuel flatly refused his suzerain, and in the spring of 1394 a massive Turkish army marched against Constantinople. Beyezit ordered a complete blockade by land and sea, and almost brought the great city to complete famine. However, the citizens were spared not by their own hands or any relief force, but by Beyezit's notorious impatience. He soon lost interest in the siege, and although it was to continue spasmodically for several more years,

Constantinople was essentially free again.

The emperor now made an impassioned appeal to the West, which resulted in the crusade of 1396, and the disastrous Christian defeat at Nicopolis. Consequently, Beyezit renewed the siege in the following year, but once again the mighty walls resisted his attempts to break in, and the Turkish army drifted away to more imperative tasks. Manuel wasted no time; he needed the West and knew that only a personal visit to the European courts would be likely to result in further assistance against the Turks. In 1399 he reconciled himself to his nephew, made him regent – John VII would simply take it if it was not official – and travelled to Europe.

John's mission did not succeed as he had hoped, but as it turned out, it was no longer so vital. Beyezit had been captured by Tamerlane in 1402, and the Ottoman Empire thrown into disarray.

Emperor Manuel Palaeologus kneels in supplication at the feet of the Archangel Michael.

Tamerlane's Legacy

Tamerlane was born in 1336 into the Barlas clan, which dominated a small region south of Samarkand. These Turks or Turco-Mongols were members of the military elite of the Jagatai Khanate. In a series of ruthless campaigns, Tamerlane and his army overran large areas of central Asia, Russia, Iran, the Middle East and India, and only Tamerlane's death stopped the Mongols from invading China.

Tamerlane's wars were marked by savage massacres and cruelties that even exceeded those of his Mongol predecessors. Another feature of Tamerlane's epic conquests was the fragility of the state he created. Having been born and raised to power in the borderland between the nomadic

Mongol infantry and cavalry in combat; from a 14th-century manuscript.

steppes of central Asia and the settled, urbanised lands of Transoxania, Tamerlane was a man of both cultures. His state and his highly effective army were similarly mixed. Even when it came to the legal system, Tamerlane relied on two traditions; the Mongol laws of Genghis Khan and the *sharia* religious law of Islam.

Despite the apparent sophistication of the administration Tamerlane put in place, his empire failed to take root in conquered territories even during his own lifetime. He had to reconquer many provinces more than once and was never able to consolidate his hold much beyond his own homeland of Transoxania. Nevertheless, the Timurid dynasty survived until the end of the 15th century.

After Beyezit's capture in 1402 and his probable suicide, Tamerlane's horde descended on the Ottoman capital of Brusa and burned it. Then they turned on Smyrna – which had been in the hands of the Knights of St John since 1344 – and the last Christian enclave in Asia Minor was left a smoking ruin in December 1402. Had Tamerlane remained longer in Asia Minor he might have dealt the Ottomans a deathblow, but in the spring of 1403 he led his nomadic horde back to Samarkand. And then in the following year he set out on a conquest of China; fortunately for the Chinese he died on the journey, the victim of a fever.

One effect of Tamerlane's lightning conquest was to drive great numbers of Ottomans across the Hellespont into Europe to join those already there. Oddly enough, at first this was viewed as a benefit – if the Mongols attacked Constantinople, the more there were to resist them the better. Only when Tamerlane had vanished did the Byzantines wonder whether they were, if anything, worse off. However, circumstances had greatly altered. Even before his leisurely return from the 42-month visit to Europe, Manuel II was greeted by the news that Beyezit's eldest surviving son, Prince Suleiman, had taken over the European provinces. Tolerant and easy-going, Suleiman preferred compromise to the battlefield, and offered to return the city of Thessalonica, the Thracian Chaldice and Mount Athos, a length of the Black Sea coast as far as Varna, and three important Aegean islands. More astonishingly, he released Byzantium from vassalage and undertook to accept Manuel as his suzerain. In return he asked only to be allowed to rule over Thrace from the palace at Edirne (formerly Adrianople).

Ottoman civil war

When he had left for Europe leaving the troublesome John VII behind, Manuel had promised him the overlordship of Thessalonica on his return. True, this was in Turkish hands, but Manuel presumed on its recapture when he came back with a European army. Now, without such bloody effort, the city was back in Byzantine hands thanks to the Turks and he was able to fulfil his promise. John settled in Thessalonica with every sign of contentment, and died there in September 1408.

Into the vacuum of Beyezit's death came civil war between his four surviving sons. Prince Isa, who had managed to establish himself at ruined Brusa, was driven out by his brother Mehmet,

Tamerlane attacks the Ottomans, 1400–03

Varna

Mesembria

Sinope

EMPIRE OF TREBIZOND

CANDAR

Sultan Beyezit I is captured, dying later in captivity

Edirne

In Tamerlane's first assault on the Ottoman Empire in 1400, Sebastea is destroyed. Events in Mesopotamia then demand his attention.

Anatolian Ottomans escaping from Asia are welcomed by Byzantines as an extra defence against a Mongolian invasion of Europe.

Constantinople

Chubuk Plain 28 July 1402

Sebastea

Thessalonica

Gallipoli

Mt. Athos

Brusa

Ancyra

GERMIYAN

Tamerlane returns to Anatolia in 1402, determined to reduce the Ottomans.

Scyros, Sciathos & Scopelos

SAHIPATA

SARUHAN

HAMID

KARAMAN

Smyrna

LADIK

ACHAEA

Athens

AYDIN

Philadelphia

Knights of St John evicted

MOREA

Mistra

Attaleia

who later murdered him. Then in 1404 another prince, Musa, declared war on Suleiman in Edirne. Suleiman crossed to Asia Minor and captured Brusa, but was forced to abandon the city and return to Thrace in 1409 where – encouraged by Mehmet – Musa had invaded. Suleiman now appealed to his suzerain for assistance, and unwillingly, Manuel was dragged into the Ottoman civil war.

When Musa emerged the victor in 1411, having strangled Suleiman, there was panic in Constantinople; Musa was well known for his hatred of Christians and he soon readied yet

another siege. There was only one solution left to Manuel: he made a treaty with Mehmet to help him overthrow his surviving brother. Utilising Byzantine vessels, Mehmet shipped a large army to Thrace, and after several inconclusive skirmishes Musa was brought to heel, and himself strangled on 5 July 1413.

Mehmet remained true to the pact he had made with Manuel, honouring the provisions of Suleiman's treaty in every point, and for a while the empire was at peace with its Ottoman neighbours. But Manuel had little confidence in the long-term ambitions of the Turks.

Byzantine Empire

Ottoman Empire

Tamerlane's conquest

other Christian state

territory returned to Byzantium, 1403

Tamerlane's advance

fleeing Ottomans

LADIK non-Ottoman emirates temporarily restored by Tamerlane

Although Turks and Mongols originated from the same geographic region north of China, the two races had little love for each other. However, the Mongol invasions of the 14th century made little impact on the Ottomans of Asia Minor, until the arrival of Tamerlane. Having already conquered the Mongolian Empire of the Ilkhans – who had supplanted the Seljuks in central Asia – Tamerlane swept into Anatolia.

A Shrinking Empire

At 63 Manuel II Palaeologus was still energetic and healthy, and determined to leave to his son John VIII an empire – crumbling as it might be – as firmly based as he could make it. Between 1414 and 1416 he visited Thessalonica and Morea, governed by two of his sons, Andronicus and Theodore, where he strengthened the fortifications and built a six-mile defensive wall across the Isthmus of Corinth. These were measures against any Turkish incursions; but the Ottomans were never far away.

Bronze medal of John VIII Palaeologus, by Pisanello. The medal was struck in about 1439 on the occasion of John's visit to Italy for the Council intended to unite the two Churches.

Facing: The Byzantine ruins at Mistra still evoke the pleasant atmosphere of this last enclave of the empire in its decline.

Mehmet and Manuel II enjoyed good relations, which meant that the emperor could spend time on diplomacy, and dream again of a union between the Greek and Latin Churches. Such a possibility existed because the Great Schism that had rent apart the papacy had come to an end in 1417. Once again, Manuel was to be disappointed, but in consequence of his overtures his son Theodore was married to the daughter of the count of Rimini and John married, with reluctance, Sophia of Montferrat. John was then crowned as co-emperor with his father in 1418, and began taking over much of the government.

Unfortunately, when Mehmet died in May 1421 John VIII favoured the claims of a pretender named Mustapha (who falsely claimed to be a son of Beyezit) over Mehmet's son Murad II. Mustapha attempted an invasion of Asia Minor but was easily defeated; however, Murad was enraged at what he saw as Byzantine treachery and determined to take Constantinople by storm. Murad was well aware of the supposed impregnability of the city's walls, so his engineers built a massive rampart from the Marmara to the Golden Horn, from which his siege engines bombarded the capital.

Only two things saved Constantinople. Murad II, a very superstitious man, had claimed the city would fall to him on 24 August 1422, and when – thanks to the stirring defence – it did not, he withdrew. He had another reason. Manuel had been intriguing to place the late sultan's youngest son, also Mustapha, on the Ottoman throne during Murad's absence. On learning of the conspiracy, Murad was forced to hurry back to Asia Minor to avoid another civil war.

John's shrunken empire

Manuel suffered a stroke towards the end of the year, although he hung on in a weakened state. In the months before his death, his son Andronicus, who was suffering a fatal disease, handed Thessalonica over to Venice, since it was clear Constantinople was in no position to protect the tiny province; he then retired to Morea as a monk and died there four years later. And John undertook his own mission to the West, but received the usual answer: only after submitting to the Roman Church would any assistance against the Turks be considered. On his return, deeply disillusioned, John accepted the price of peace with Murad – the return of those parts of the Marmara and Black Sea coast ceded by Suleiman. Shortly after his son's return, Manuel died in July 1425.

John VIII's empire now consisted of Constantinople and the city's northern approaches. The cities of Selymbria and Heraclea on the Sea of Marmara, and Mesembria and Archialus on the Black Sea were held by John's younger brother Constantine in fief from Murad, who could take them back whenever he liked. With the deprivations it had suffered over the past 150 years, the capital had become seriously underpopulated, perhaps no more than 50,000 – hardly enough to mount a defence of the still-mighty land walls of Theodosius. With economic decline came famine through the intermittent food supply system, and the malnourished

inhabitants were vulnerable to constant epidemics. The churches were largely shells, whole tracts of once-prosperous housing had been torn down after war damage and allowed to return to fields to grow food; even the imperial palaces were in disrepair.

By contrast, life in Greek Morea was pleasant. Ruled by four despots – more of Manuel's sons – there was factional unrest from the local population, which although mostly Greek, resented rule form a distance. In the south lay the city of Mistra, founded by William of Villehardouin in 1249. He had surrendered it to Byzantium 12 years later, together with Monemvasia. As the Latins retreated Mistra had expanded, and it was where John VI Cantacuzenus had sent his son Manuel, the first despot of the Morea, in 1349. Over the next 60 years Mistra had grown into an intellectual and cultural centre, easily able to rival the declining Constantinople.

But the writing was on the wall for Morea, when after seven years as a Venetian outpost, Thessalonica fell to Murad in March 1430.

Morea in the 1400s

The Final Days

The last two emperors of Byzantium did their best to save a state that rapidly shrunk to the confines of the great Theodosian Wall. But the situation they inherited was beyond all hope. Devouring itself from within, threatened without, by the inevitable end Constantinople was scarcely capable of independent action.

Portrait of John VIII Palaeologus by the school of Gentile Bellini.

John VIII's turbulent reign was spent in political turmoil. In pursuit of the Palaeologi dream of union between the Churches in return for Western aid, he followed his father's footsteps to Italy in company with Joseph II, Patriarch of Constantinople. After a year of gruelling sessions at Rome and Florence, the exhausted Orthodox prelates gave in to almost every point on the Roman agenda except for the Metropolitan of Ephesus, who had given in on absolutely nothing, but was forbidden a veto by the emperor. The Decree of Union was publicly proclaimed in Florence cathedral on 5 July 1439, first in Latin by Cardinal Giuliano Cesarini, and then in Greek by the Metropolitan of Nicaea.

General revulsion greeted John's return to Constantinople, and open rebellion from the patriarchs of Jerusalem, Alexandria and Antioch, who declared the Greek signatories as traitors. In 1442 the emperor's younger brother Demetrius – the ever-ambitious despot of tiny Mesembria – made an attempt at the throne in the name of Orthodoxy; but failed and ended up in prison.

'The predicted fall of Constantinople' by an unknown Turkish artist depicts the Ottoman army surrounding the city in preparation for the final assault in 1453.

However, to an extent John succeeded in rousing a crusade. Pope Eugene IV and Cardinal Cesarini persuaded the Serbs and Hungarians – alarmed at continual Turkish gains – to march.

The expedition under the command of John Hunyadi of Transylvania made immediate progress, destroying a Turkish army near Nis and taking Sofia. Murad II, who had problems of his own in Anatolia, hastened to Bulgaria and negotiated a ten-year truce, before returning to Asia Minor. But the pope, furious that what had been gained might be lost, ordered them to renege. Hunyadi pushed across the Balkans towards Varna, and then south towards the Bosphorus. And there, on 10 November 1444, outnumbered three to one, the last ever Christian crusade fell: Hunyadi escaped but

Cesarini died on the field. Byzantium was now truly alone, and a chastened John VIII renewed his vassalage to Murad.

In Morea, Constantine, who had taken over the despotate from his brother Theodore, faced renewed Turkish aggression, and the Greeks were forced back to Mistra, which was spared only after a furious battle that claimed 22,000 Greek

lives. On 17 October 1448 a second battle of Kosovo between the Hungarians and Turks ended in Hunyadi's defeat; and John VIII died 11 days later, on 31 October.

A new Turkish Sultan

Of Manuel's three surviving sons – Constantine, Demetrius and Thomas – John had nominated Constantine, but for his support of Orthodoxy Demetrius had followers in the city and he contested Constantine for the throne. But their mother, Empress Helena, declared for her older son and found backing in the younger Thomas. Demetrius backed down. Since Byzantium no longer had any ships, when Constantine XI Palaeologus arrived in Constantinople on 12 March 1429, he was transported in a Venetian vessel. The Turks, too, had a new ruler. Murad II died in February 1451 and was succeeded by his son, Mehmet (Mohammed) II (r.1451–81).

Mehmet was only 19, but already a seasoned veteran in the Turkish court politics. He wasted no time in stamping his authority on his viziers and showed his mettle in having Murad's infant son murdered in his bath. But knowing that his youth would inevitably lead to dissent among the Turkish nobility, he determined to keep them busy with the final reduction of Constantinople. In April

1451 he began building the castle of Rumeli Hisar (Strait Cutter) on the Bosphorus, which was designed to cut Constantinople off from any possible relief. In August he sank a Venetian ship that refused to stop and decapitated the crew.

Constantine had sent out final desperate appeals to the West for help, but indecision ruled the debate over what could be done. In the event Pope Nicholas V dispatched three Genoese ships, which he chartered and provisioned at his own expense, and made it safely into the Golden Horn to join their fellow Genoese, who knew their fate was now joined with that of the city they had so long economically pillaged.

Constantine also sent indignant embassies to Mehmet II. The sultan's patience was tried, and when the third company of Greek envoys came before him, Mehmet had them beheaded. This was his answer, and he emphasised it by beginning the construction outside Galata of massive bronze siege guns. By the end of March 1453 the guns were in place in front of the city and Turkish forces sealed Constantinople off from the outside world. The defenders strengthened their defences, drew the great chain across the entrance to the Golden Horn… and waited.

On 5 April 1453, Mehmet called on the Byzantines to surrender. When no answer came by the next day, he ordered his guns to open fire.

Left: A portrait of Sultan Mehmet II attributed to Costanza da Ferrara, c.1470.

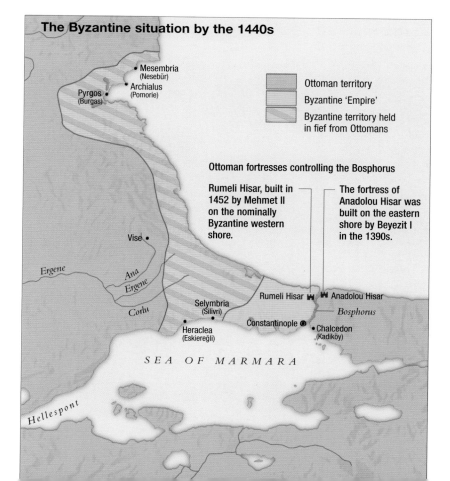

The Byzantine situation by the 1440s

Ottoman territory

Byzantine 'Empire'

Byzantine territory held in fief from Ottomans

Ottoman fortresses controlling the Bosphorus

Rumeli Hisar, built in 1452 by Mehmet II on the nominally Byzantine western shore.

The fortress of Anadolou Hisar was built on the eastern shore by Beyezit I in the 1390s.

Mesembria
(Nesebür)

Archialus
(Pomorie)

Pyrgos
(Burgas)

Visé

Ergene

Ana
Ergene

Corlu

Selymbria
(Silivri)

Heraclea
(Eskiereğli)

Rumeli Hisar

Anadolou Hisar

Bosphorus

Constantinople

Chalcedon
(Kadiköy)

SEA OF MARMARA

Hellespont

1453: Into the Abyss

For one thousand and forty years the great Theodosian Wall had kept at bay Constantinople's invaders: Goths, Huns, Slavs, Bulgars, Russians, Turks and any number of rebels. Now the huge defensive edifice faced its most determined threat. Mehmet II was the most implacable foe the Greeks had ever fought – and they were so few against so many.

Constantine XI had little to comfort him, though there were some small mercies. Late in January a single ship from Genoa arrived, under the command of Giovanni Giustiniani Longo, a member of a leading Genoese family. With him came some 700 of his countrymen – appalled at western pusillanimity – to aid Constantine. But this was offset by the defection a month later of the same number of Italians,

Below: The Turkish army camps before Constantinople; from an illustration of 1455 by Jean Mielot.

who secretly slipped away in seven Venetian ships to Tenedos. When he ordered a census of fighting men towards the end a March, the figure was worse than he could have imagined: 4,983 Greeks and a little less than 2,000 foreigners. These to defend 14 miles of walls against an estimated 100,000 Turks.

The first Ottoman assault was probably launched on 7 April, when irregulars and volunteers advanced, supported by archers and handgunners. However, they were met at the outer rampart and driven back with relative ease by what amounted to no more than 7,000 defenders. In fact the Byzantine artillery was notably effective until their largest cannon exploded, after which Byzantine guns were limited to an anti-personnel role.

As the siege progressed, Mehmet had most cannon taken off the Ottoman ships and mounted ashore to bombard enemy vessels that were defending the chain across the Golden Horn. Work was also speeded up on the construction of a wooden slipway from the Bosphorus to the Golden Horn. By 22 April it was complete, and under the cover of an artillery bombardment 72 of the Ottomans' smaller ships were hauled across the hills on rollers before being slid into the Golden Horn. Having lost control of the waterway, troops had to be withdrawn from other areas to man this threatened sector, and the investment of Constantinople was complete.

On 26 May Mehmet toured the army while heralds announced that a final assault would take place in three days' time. Celebration bonfires were lit and there was continuous feasting in the Ottoman camp. The Byzantines saw so many torches that some hoped the enemy were burning their tents before retreating – it had happened often before.

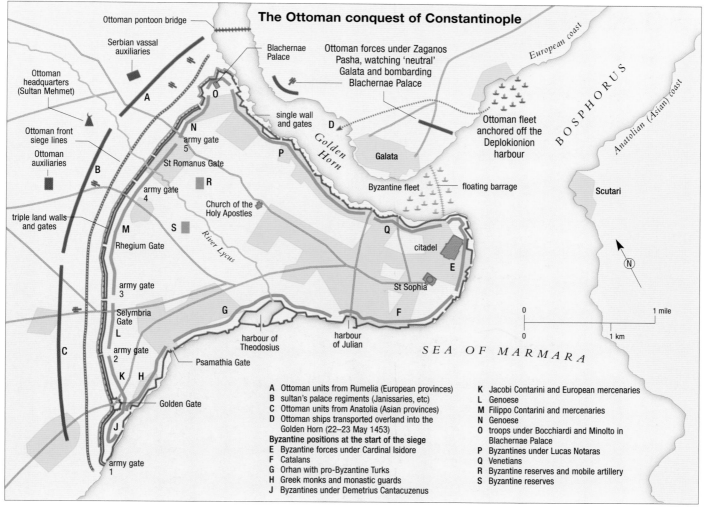

The Ottoman conquest of Constantinople

Ottoman pontoon bridge

Serbian vassal auxiliaries

Ottoman headquarters (Sultan Mehmet)

Ottoman front siege lines

Ottoman auxiliaries

triple land walls and gates

Blachernae Palace

single wall and gates

army gate 5

St Romanus Gate

army gate 4

Church of the Holy Apostles

Rhegium Gate

River Lycus

army gate 3

Selymbria Gate

army gate 2

Psamathia Gate

Golden Gate

army gate 1

harbour of Theodosius

harbour of Julian

Ottoman forces under Zaganos Pasha, watching 'neutral' Galata and bombarding Blachernae Palace

Golden Horn

Galata

Byzantine fleet

floating barrage

Ottoman fleet anchored off the Deplokionion harbour

citadel

St Sophia

European coast

BOSPHORUS

Anatolian (Asian) coast

Scutari

N

SEA OF MARMARA

0 ———— 1 mile
0 ———— 1 km

A Ottoman units from Rumelia (European provinces)
B sultan's palace regiments (Janissaries, etc)
C Ottoman units from Anatolia (Asian provinces)
D Ottoman ships transported overland into the Golden Horn (22–23 May 1453)
Byzantine positions at the start of the siege
E Byzantine forces under Cardinal Isidore
F Catalans
G Orhan with pro-Byzantine Turks
H Greek monks and monastic guards
J Byzantines under Demetrius Cantacuzenus

K Jacobi Contarini and European mercenaries
L Genoese
M Filippo Contarini and mercenaries
N Genoese
O troops under Bocchiardi and Minolto in Blachernae Palace
P Byzantines under Lucas Notaras
Q Venetians
R Byzantine reserves and mobile artillery
S Byzantine reserves

The final assault

About three hours before dawn on 29 May there was a ripple of fire from the Ottoman artillery and Turkish irregulars swept forward. Their main attack focused around the battered walls next to the Gate of St Romanus. Despite suffering terrible casualties, few of them retreated until, after two hours of fighting, Mehmet ordered a withdrawal. Ottoman ships also tried to get close enough to erect scaling ladders.

After another artillery bombardment it was the turn of the provincial troops. These marched forward carrying torches but were hampered by the narrowness of the breaches in Constantinople's defences. More disciplined than the irregulars, they occasionally pulled back to allow their artillery to fire, and during one such bombardment a section of defensive stockade was brought down. Nevertheless this second assault failed.

The only fresh troops now available to Mehmet were his own palace regiments, including the famous Janissary infantry. All sources agree that these advanced with terrifying discipline, slowly and without noise or music. The third phase of fighting lasted an hour before

some Janissaries found that a small postern door had not been properly closed after a previous Byzantine counterattack. About 50 soldiers broke in and raised their banner on the battlements. They were, however, in danger of being wiped out when the Ottomans had a stroke of luck.

Giovanni Giustiniani Longo commanded the most threatened sector of the fortifications, but when he was mortally wounded, panic spread among the defenders, and the Janissaries took the inner wall. Word spread that the Ottomans had also broken in via the harbour, and the defence collapsed.

While some Byzantines fled for the ships and tried to fight their way through the Turkish blockade, the rest were slaughtered in the streets. Constantine XI Palaeologus, the last Byzantine emperor, died defending his city. About noon, Sultan Mehmet the Conqueror, as he was thereafter called, rode though his prize to the church of St Sophia, where he prayed, and marked the end of a Byzantine Empire that had survived the fall of Rome by almost a thousand years.

Facing top: In suitably dilapidated state, obverse and reverse of a billon coin of Constantine XI Palaeologus – among the very last coins of the Byzantine Empire.

After the Fall

The whole of Christendom received the news of the fall of Constantinople with horror. And yet Western Europe, which had done so little to help and much damage, was largely unaffected. The Italian mercantile city-states suffered from the immediate curtailment of trade, but the rest of Europe would have to wait a little longer to feel the full impact of the Ottomans' victory.

Refugees who escaped the city carried the stories with them: of the brave emperor who had died fighting for his people; or that Constantine had escaped to fight another day; of the merciless Turks. Few today believe that Constantine XI managed to extricate himself, and though the Turks showed little mercy to the defenders, the fate of Constantinople was less unkind than the survivors made out.

Among those who escaped were several of the Palaeologi, John and Demetrius Cantacuzenus, two Comneni, two Lascaris and many other members of distinguished families. Some settled on Chios to where they were first taken on a Genoese ship; others stopped off at Monemvasia in Morea, Corfu and Italy. But the influx was so great at the northern end of the Adriatic that Venice became the chief city of the Byzantine diaspora.

Those nobles who had neither perished nor escaped were brought before Mehmet II on the day after the conquest. The ladies were given their freedom, except for the most beautiful, whom the sultan kept for his own pleasure – along with a number of their more attractive sons. The men were largely redeemed from their captors by ransoms paid by the sultan.

Those of the proletariat who had escaped the initial massacre were organised as a self-governing commune within the Ottoman Empire under a leader elected by themselves. In the absence of any Greek nobility, the community elected the patriarch to lead them. In recent decades there had often been no incumbent of the see – the last had been Gregory III, who had resigned three years previously and fled to Italy, but since he was a unionist with attachments to Rome, Mehmet would have disallowed him anyway. Instead he found the leader of the pro-Orthodoxy movement, a monk named George Scholarius who had been sold into slavery and was working as a menial in a Turkish household in Edirne. Scholarius was enthroned as patriarch in January 1454 in the Church of the Holy Apostles (St Sophia was already reconsecrated as a mosque).

Ambassadors of the neighbouring Christian states poured into Constantinople seeking the best advantage possible from Mehmet, but to little long-term gain. The Knights of St John faced the sultan's forces in 1480, but held on until 1520, when Mehmet's son Suleiman the Magnificent took Rhodes by storm. Morea, already ravaged by the antagonism of the despot brothers Demetrius and Thomas Palaeologus, fell in 1460. On 15 August 1461 David Comnenus, last emperor of Trebizond, surrendered the last throne of the Byzantine world to Mehmet.

The Ottomans were supreme.

The Ottoman Empire and southern Europe, c.1500

Ottoman Empire
by 1389
by 1402
by 1464
by 1500
Ottoman vassal by 1500

POLAND

LITHUANIA

KHANATE OF CRIMEA

Dniepr

Dniester

Buda • • Pest

Transylvania

• Jassy

MOLDOVIA

Ottoman vassal
intermittently after 1456)

Bilhorod

Kaffa

Danube

H U N G A R Y

Mures

Brassó •

Kiliya

(to Genoa until c.1460)

• Kherson

• Pécs

Banat

WALLACHIA

Tisa

BLACK SEA

• Belgrade

(Ottoman vassal, end of
14th century, thereafter
intermittently a Hungarian
vassal)

• Bucharest

Danube

Bosnia

Morava

Nicopolis

• Varna

REPUBLIC OF
RAGUSSA

• Nis

B u l g a r i a

• Mesembria

Serbia

O

Ragusa

MONTENEGRO
(Ottoman vassal from end
of the 15th century)

• Sofia

T

(to Genoa until c.1460)

Amasra
(Amastris)

Plovdiv
(Philippopolis)

T

O

R u m e l i a

Edirne
(Adrianople)

Istanbul
(Constantinople)

Albania

M

Ankara
(Ancyra)

• Durazzo

A

Salonica
(Thessalonica)

N

E

M

P

I

R

E

Corfu
(to Venice)

• Janina

• Larissa

A E G E A N
S E A

Epirus

Thessaly

Lesbos

*Ionian
Sea*

Negroponte

Chios
(to Genoa)

Izmir
(Smyrna)

Cephalonia

Corinth

• Athens

Ikaria

Samos
(to Genoa)

Zante
(to Venice)

M o r e a

DUCHY OF
NAXOS
(to Venice)

Bodrum

• Mistra

Knights of St John

Rhodes

Rhodes

Major Italian states, 1454
Duchy of Milan (Visconti family)
Republic of Venice
Republic of Genoa
Republic of Florence
Papal States
territories of the Kingdom of Aragon
southern/eastern boundary
of the Holy Roman Empire

Sea of Crete

• Candia

CRETE
(to Venice)

Sultan and Caesar

The relationship between the Ottoman Empire and the Islamic Turco-Mongol khanates of southeastern Russia and the steppes was very important. In some ways it mirrored the earlier one between the Romano-Byzantine empire and the pagan steppe states of the medieval period.

The organisational skills of Mehmet II brought the early Ottoman Empire to its peak. This portrait, attributed to Venetian Renaissance painter Gentile Bellini, shares in common with the portrait on page 174 a serenity that belies the sultan's ruthless nature in conquest, but perhaps hints at the mercy and tolerance he could show towards the defeated and their religion.

The Ottoman conquest of Constantinople in 1453 and the subsequent mopping up of remaining relics of the Byzantine Empire also changed the political, strategic and economic situation around the Black Sea. The impact on the Ottoman Empire itself was profound. The *ghaza* or struggle with neighbouring Christian states now focused on the Ottoman sultan's own actions rather than on the autonomous frontier heroes of earlier days.

More immediately, however, Sultan Mehmet II reconstructed his new capital. The fortifications were repaired and Constantinople (hereafter generally known as Istanbul) was repopulated with Christian Greeks, Muslim Turks and others. Some were encouraged by tax privileges but many were forced to settle in the largely empty city. This rapid growth then led to food shortages, which in turn prompted the Ottoman conquest of grain-producing regions north of the Black Sea.

Mehmet II wanted to make Istanbul a multi-faith centre for all Peoples of the Book: Muslims, Christians and Jews alike. This grand imperial statement would create a crossroads where the cultures of East and West, Europe and Asia, could meet and mingle. Furthermore, Mehmet declared himself to be the new *Qaysar* or Caesar, the legitimate heir to the Roman and Byzantine empires, with a claim to territory far beyond the Ottoman Empire's existing frontiers. This was widely accepted, not only by Mehmet's Turkish and Muslim subjects, but by Greek scholars such as George of Trebizond, who wrote to Mehmet in 1466: 'No one doubts that you are the Emperor of the Romans. Whoever is legally master of the capital of the Empire is the Emperor, and Constantinople is the capital of the Roman Empire.'

New balance of power

The conquest of Constantinople cut Italian trade through the Hellespont and Bosphorus to the Crimea, and there was soon a steady emigration away from the Genoese Black Sea colonies. Many Armenians moved to the Ukraine or Poland, some Italian craftsmen went as far as Moscow, and within little more than 20 years Genoa's possessions beyond the Bosphorus had been lost to the Ottomans.

Following the fall of Constantinople a series of other campaigns confirmed Ottoman domination of the Balkans, although a clash with Hungary led to them suffering a reverse outside Belgrade. Wallachia moved firmly beneath Ottoman suzerainty and even Moldavia was theoretically tributary to the sultan after 1456. On the other hand Stephen the Great came to throne of Moldavia the following year and spent much of his reign competing with the Ottomans for domination over neighbouring Wallachia.

The consolidation of Ottoman power had already strangled the link between the Mongols and the Mamluk sultanate of Egypt, having a profound impact on both. The Mongol Golden Horde was in decline during the 15th century,

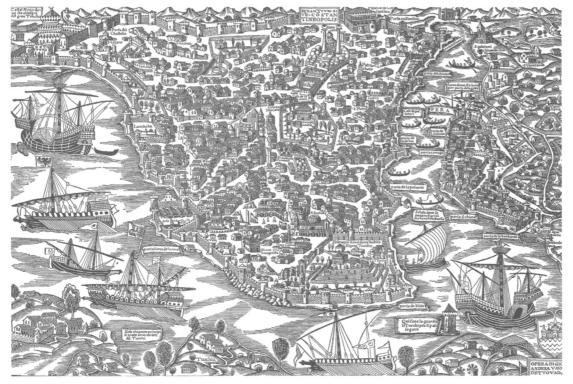

Constantinople after its capture by Turks; from original plans drawn in 1522. The Sea of Marmara is on the picture's left, with the Bosphorus running along the bottom and the Golden Horn rising vertically to the right of centre. On its right shore is the former Genoese enclave of Galata.

having already been defeated and largely absorbed by the Khanate of the Crimea in 1502. The Giray Khans of the Crimea were themselves descended from Genghis Khan's son Jochi. At first they were vassals of the much larger Golden Horde, but in the early 15th century they achieved independence.

Thereafter the Khans of the Crimea ruled over a substantial part of what are now the eastern Ukraine and southern Russia, as well as the Crimean peninsula itself. Their khanate proved to be the most enduring of all the states

that emerged from the fragmentation of the Mongol 'world empire'.

The Crimean Khanate and the Ottoman Empire also became natural allies, first against the Golden Horde and later against the rising power of Russia. It was, however, a lopsided relationship, with the Ottoman sultans by far the stronger partner. They regarded the khans of the Crimea as their vassals and imposed direct Ottoman rule over the coastal enclaves, which had once been Byzantine and then Genoese.

The growth of Venice, 1390–1454
Venice was the main beneficiary of Byzantine wealth, both acquired through trade and looted since 1204. The vast increase in the republic's wealth fuelled aggressive expansion at the expense of the once-powerful Visconti family who ruled the Duchy of Milan.

Venice in 1390

Venice in 1454

The Byzantine Cultural Legacy

Although the Byzantine Empire ended with the fall of Constantinople in 1453, the influence of Byzantine culture was felt elsewhere, particularly in Italy, where it has been described as one of the sources of inspiration for the artists and architects of the Renaissance.

The impact of Byzantine artistic style is clearly seen here in this *St Matthew* altarpiece by the Florentine painter Andrea di Cione, known as Orcagna (c.1308–68). With its lavish use of gold, the remote and immobile figures and glowing colours, it represents a reversion from Giotto's naturalism to the iconic ideals of Byzantine art.

Following the sack of Constantinople by the crusaders in 1204 and its recovery, the Byzantine Empire was no longer a source of religious and secular patronage. Many Byzantine artists, thinkers and artisans sought employment with their new Italian overlords (principally in Venice and Genoa), while others enjoyed the patronage of Muslim rulers. And so even before the fall of Constantinople, Byzantium had exercised a considerable influence over the Renaissance in Italy, both through its vast resources of preserved Latin and Greek classical literature and its artistic style, which naturally impacted most heavily on Venetian painters. The classical texts had already exercised a humanist approach among Byzantine philosophers, and this movement soon impacted on Italian scholars, such as the poet Francesco Petrarca (Petrarch, 1304–74). After the fall, the Greek diaspora continued in greater degree to spread Byzantine culture in Europe.

The greatness of Byzantine art, claimed early 20th-century Philhelene Robert Byron, lay in its Roman body, Greek mind and its mystical, oriental soul – his 'Triple Fusion'. These three strands are to be seen in almost every example of Byzantine art and architecture; from the exotic orientalism of Theophilus's Tzykanisterion pleasure palace to the magnificent mosaics of the cathedral of Cefalù in Sicily.

Religious architectural masterpieces such as St Sophia and the church of St John of the Studion combined spacious domed structures with a wealth of internal decoration: mosaics, marble decoration and ornamental metalwork, and traces of their former sumptuous nature can still be seen. Both were built during the reign of Justinian I; a period that is now regarded as a golden age of Byzantine religious art and architecture.

By the time of the collapse of the Roman Empire a particular form of Greek religious art had developed, which drew inspiration from regional Greek traditions. By the sixth century this had merged with Middle Eastern forms, which were more mystically symbolic, to create a uniquely Byzantine style that appeared in several forms, particularly as icons, mosaics or illuminations in Greek manuscripts.

Mosaics evolved into a particularly Byzantine art form; the majority of works were religious, but some secular examples remained. Byzantine mosaic artists were particularly fond of portraiture, although artistic traditions veered towards a formal, eastern style of depiction. In most examples the rigid figures are portrayed facing the viewer, a style which was repeated in both iconography and illuminated works.

Philosophical immigrants

Even before the iconoclast controversy the range of Byzantine visual arts was narrow, essentially restricted to the great mystery of the Christian faith. Byzantine painters received simple instruction: to represent the spirit of God. This formidable challenge – met time and again to a sublime degree in the East – was one which Western artists seldom attempted. In Venice, it was Byzantine architectural styles and the modes of decoration that commanded most attention – influences that inspired a generation of Venetian Renaissance painters, who nevertheless preferred the humanist thinking of Byzantine philosophers,

such as George Gemistos Plethon, to following the two-dimensional representation of Byzantine art.

Plethon, who stayed for several years in Turkish Edirne (Adrianople), studied Aristotle, Zoroastrianism and Jewish cabalistic philosophy. The orthodox of Constantinople considered his lectures on Platonism subversive, and his friend, Manuel II Palaeologus, suggested he would be happier in Mistra. From Greece, he later accompanied John VIII on his visit to Italy, and greatly impressed the scholars of Rome and especially Florence. In 1439 his lectures on the differences between the work of Plato and Aristotle were eagerly received and prompted the comment that Plethon had brought the spirit of Plato from the Byzantine Empire to Italy.

The warmth of his reception soon encouraged a veritable flood of Byzantine writers and philosophers to escape the sinking ship of Constantinople for the new learning centres of Europe, and it was this aspect of Greek culture that had the greatest impact on the Renaissance.

The other important contribution Byzantium made to the Renaissance was in the area of applied art. As a consequence of the emphasis on two-dimensional representation seen so clearly in icons, three-dimensional sculpture was rare in Byzantine art (the bronze Lions of St Mark, looted from Constantinople in 1204 and transported to Venice, are famous exceptions). More commonly, carving was restricted to miniature relief in the form of book covers, decorative boxes or metalwork. Ivory was also a popular material, and methods of decoration included the use of enamelled metal or glass, fine metalwork and ivory relief. These influences found their expression in Renaissance decoration, a more rationally organised elaboration of detail than the previously popular Gothic styles.

Through the export of its ancient culture, the Byzantine Empire made its own unique contribution to the emerging modern Europe.

Christ Pantocrator in the cathedral of Cefalù, Sicily is a sumptuous example of Byzantine mosaic work that became an inspiration to many early Renaissance artists in Italy.

Glossary

acolythus Chief of the Varangian Guard; the modern word 'acolyte' is derived from it.

aeteriarch Chief of the barbarian mercenaries.

anchorite An eremetic (hermit) monk who lives in isolation from the community.

basileus Greek for 'king', originally any king in the Greek-speaking areas of the Roman Empire. Heraclius adopted it to replace the old Latin title of Augustus, and it came to mean 'emperor'.

basilissa An empress. Empresses were also called *kyria* or *despoina*.

basilopator Honorific to describe the 'father' of an emperor, although a basilopator was not necessarily the emperor's natural father.

bey Turkish word for a provincial governor. Ottoman provinces or small semi-autonomous states were therefore referred to as *beyliks*.

catepanos Governor of a naval theme, a title developed after the tenth century.

caesar Title used for a subordinate co-emperor or heir-apparent. It lost importance when the titles of *sebastocrator* and *despotes* were created. The feminine form is *caisarissa*.

cenobite A monk who lives with other monks, working as directed within the monastery and for the local community.

Chi-Rho The Christian symbol adopted by Constantine the Great on his labrum (standard). They are the Greek letters 'C' and 'H', the first letters of Christ's name.

chronocrator, cosmocrator *Lit,* 'ruler of time' and 'ruler of the world', titles later emperors gave themselves.

comes 'Count', a title derived from *comitatensis*, or companions of the emperor – effectively his administration, and also an infantry military rank of senior command. It fell into disuse after Justinian I.

conostaulos Chief of the Frankish mercenaries.

deme Any political faction, or party.

despotes The highest title after the emperor, created by Manuel I Comnenus in the 12th century. A despot was usually the ruler of a despotate, such as the Despotate of Morea. A despot's wife was termed a *despoina*.

diocese Term given to the major divisions of the Roman Empire by Diocletian (r.284–305), later adopted by the Church as the patrimony of a bishop.

domesticus (*Domestikos*) The *domestikoi* were originally imperial guards, who became generals in the themes. They included: **megas domesticus** (grand domestic), overall commander of the army; **domesticus tou scholae** (domestic of the *scholae*), the commander the *scholae*, originally a replacement for the praetorian (or imperial) guard, later a recruiting position; **domesticus tou thema** (domestic of the themes), one of two commanders of the military themes, one for Europe and one for Asia; **strategos**, a military commander of a theme equivalent to 'general', who often also had the title of *dux*; **protospatharios**, commander of the imperial guard, with the **spatharios** as his subordinate; **protostrator**, a later term for the commander of the army; **stratopedarch**, commander of the army in the field, who also possibly had legal powers.

drungarios A naval officer of lower rank.

dux *Lit.* 'leader', now 'duke'. Originally the title given to commanders of cavalry in the late imperial Roman army, it evolved into a general honorific for many military commands.

exarch Title given to the proconsul or viceroy of a province at some remove from the central authority, who wielded absolute power over the civilian and military administration.

excubitorii The Imperial Guard at the time of Anastasius and Justinian, effectively replacements for the praetorian guard of imperial Rome.

foederati Roman name for barbarians allowed to settle within the Empire in return for the men giving service as allies in the legions. Later used to describe all foreign mercenary soldiers.

ghazi A Muslim warrior who has fought successfully against infidels.

hyperpyron *Lit.* 'highly refined', a gold coin introduced to replace the debased *nomisma* by Alexius I Comnenus.

logothete Secretary in the extensive bureaucracy; there were several levels within the hierarchy: **megas logothetes** (grand logothete, and the title referred to in this book as simply 'logothete'), chief logothete, responsible for the legal system and treasury; **logothetes tou dromou** (posta), head of diplomacy and the postal service; **logothetes ton oikeiakon** (domestic), head of Constantinople's security and the local economy; **logothetes tou genikou** (general logothete), responsible for taxation; **logothetes tou stratiotikou** (military logothete), a civilian in charge of distributing pay to the army.

megas dux 'Grand duke', equivalent of lord high admiral, commander of the Byzantine naval themes, and likely one of the few who knew the secret of the composition of Greek Fire.

megas drungarius Subordinate to the megas dux in charge of the naval officers.

merarches Commander of a cavalry division in the army.

Millon The milestone in Constantinople from which all distances were measured.

mitata A community of foreign merchants, bankers, and their families, servants, etc, segregated from the local population of a city. Synonymous with 'ghetto', the word later derived by the Venetians.

monophysitism (Greek *monos*, 'one' and *physis*, 'nature'). The belief that Christ has only one nature, as opposed to the orthodox, or Chalcedonian position, which states that Christ has two natures, one divine and one human.

monothelitism A compromise developed to bridge the gap between monophysitism and the orthodox Chalcedonian position. It was rejected by the Chalcedonians, despite at times having the support of the emperors.

nomisma Greek word for the Latin *solidus*, a gold coin struck at 72 to the Roman pound (4.48gm); pl. *nomismata*.

Outremer The collective name given to the Crusader States of the Mediterranean coast from Syria to Palestine; from old French, meaning 'overseas'.

parakoimomenos An imperial bodyguard of the palace.

pontifex maximus Chief priest of the pagan Roman state religion.

porphyrogenitos Later emperors used this word, meaning 'purple-born', to indicate that they were born to a reigning emperor, and were therefore legitimate.

Pragmatica Sanctio 'Pragmatic Sanction'; a government decision in a matter (Greek, *pragma*) involving

community or public interest. Later, an expression of will by a ruler defining the limits of his own power or regulating the succession.

protocentarchos, kentarchos Commanders of a smaller division of the army in the field.

praetorian prefect Old Roman title for the commander of the imperial guard, later commander of the entire army of the eastern portion of the Empire. It was abolished in the 7th century to be replaced by *domesticus*.

protovestiarios A (usually) minor relative of the emperor who took care of his wardrobe, especially on military campaigns, and the emperor's personal finances.

Saracen Originally a member of the nomadic people of the Syrian and Arabian deserts at the time of the Roman Empire, but later used to describe any Arab and specifically a Muslim who opposed the crusades.

sebastocrator 'Majestic ruler', title created by Alexius I as a combination of autokrator and sebastos. Essentially a meaningless title, it signified only a close relationship with the emperor. The feminine form is sebastokratorissa.

sebastos 'Majesty', title originally equivalent to Augustus used by early emperors. Under Alexius I it became less important. The feminine form is sebasta.

taktika Books of dignities, which outlined in great detail the complex pecking order of the Byzantine court, bureaucracy and army.

theme A provincial division of the Empire, based on military principles.

trisagion The three-part refrain in the orthodox Byzantine liturgy of 'Holy God, Holy and Mighty, Holy and Immortal'.

Family Trees

Families of Diocletian, Constantine the Great, Valentinian and Theodosius

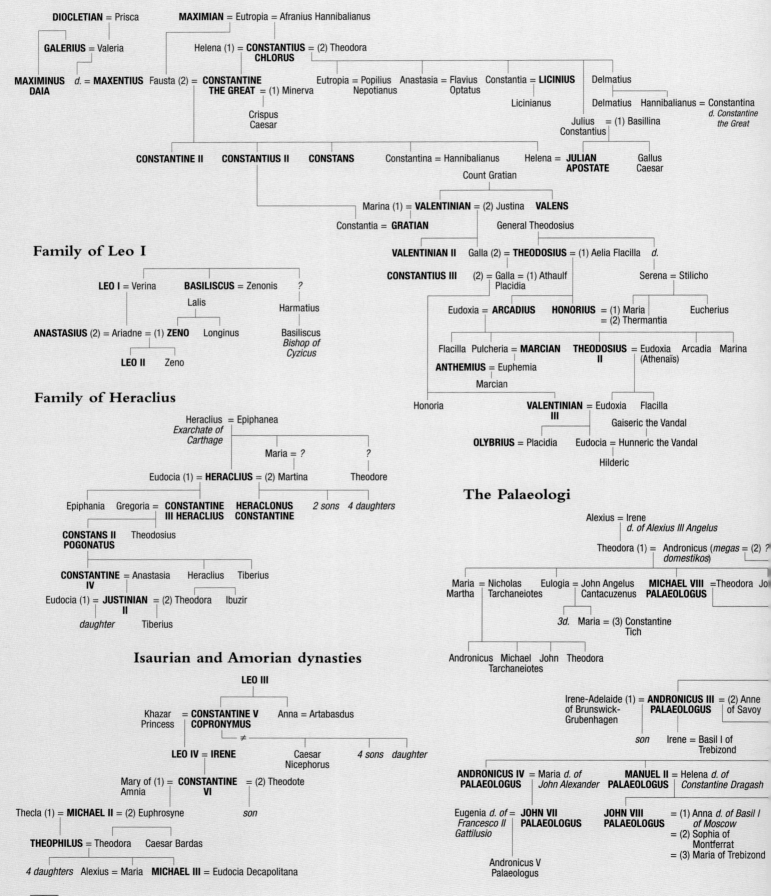

DIOCLETIAN = Prisca   **MAXIMIAN** = Eutropia = Afranius Hannibalianus

GALERIUS = Valeria

Helena (1) = **CONSTANTIUS CHLORUS** = (2) Theodora

MAXIMINUS DAIA   d. = **MAXENTIUS**   Fausta (2) = **CONSTANTINE THE GREAT** = (1) Minerva   Eutropia = Popilius Nepotianus   Anastasia = Flavius Optatus   Constantia = **LICINIUS**   Delmatius

Crispus Caesar

Licinianus   Delmatius   Hannibalianus = Constantina *d. Constantine the Great*

Julius Constantius = (1) Basillina

CONSTANTINE II   **CONSTANTIUS II**   **CONSTANS**   Constantina = Hannibalianus   Helena = **JULIAN APOSTATE**   Gallus Caesar

Count Gratian

Marina (1) = **VALENTINIAN** = (2) Justina   **VALENS**

Constantia = **GRATIAN**   General Theodosius

VALENTINIAN II   Galla (2) = **THEODOSIUS** = (1) Aelia Flacilla *d.*

CONSTANTIUS III   (2) = Galla = (1) Athaulf Placidia   Serena = Stilicho

Eudoxia = **ARCADIUS**   **HONORIUS** = (1) Maria = (2) Thermantia   Eucherius

Flacilla   Pulcheria = **MARCIAN**   **THEODOSIUS II** = Eudoxia (Athenaïs)   Arcadia   Marina

ANTHEMIUS = Euphemia

Marcian

Honoria   **VALENTINIAN III** = Eudoxia   Flacilla

Gaiseric the Vandal

OLYBRIUS = Placidia   Eudocia = Hunneric the Vandal

Hilderic

Family of Leo I

LEO I = Verina   **BASILISCUS** = Zenonis   ?

Lalis   Harmatius

ANASTASIUS (2) = Ariadne = (1) **ZENO**   Longinus   Basiliscus *Bishop of Cyzicus*

LEO II   Zeno

Family of Heraclius

Heraclius = Epiphanea *Exarchate of Carthage*

Maria = ?   ?

Eudocia (1) = **HERACLIUS** = (2) Martina   Theodore

Epiphania   Gregoria = **CONSTANTINE III HERACLIUS**   **HERACLONUS CONSTANTINE**   2 sons   4 daughters

CONSTANS II POGONATUS   Theodosius

CONSTANTINE IV = Anastasia   Heraclius   Tiberius

Eudocia (1) = **JUSTINIAN II** = (2) Theodora   Ibuzir

daughter   Tiberius

Isaurian and Amorian dynasties

LEO III

Khazar Princess = **CONSTANTINE V COPRONYMUS**   Anna = Artabasdus

≠

LEO IV = **IRENE**   Caesar Nicephorus   4 sons   daughter

Mary of Amnia (1) = **CONSTANTINE VI** = (2) Theodote

Thecla (1) = **MICHAEL II** = (2) Euphrosyne   *son*

THEOPHILUS = Theodora   Caesar Bardas

4 daughters   Alexius = Maria   **MICHAEL III** = Eudocia Decapolitana

The Palaeologi

Alexius = Irene *d. of Alexius III Angelus*

Theodora (1) = Andronicus (*megas domestikos*) = (2) ?

Maria Martha = Nicholas Tarchaneiotes   Eulogia = John Angelus Cantacuzenus   **MICHAEL VIII PALAEOLOGUS** = Theodora   Jo[hn]

3d.   Maria = (3) Constantine Tich

Andronicus   Michael   John   Theodora Tarchaneiotes

Irene-Adelaide (1) = **ANDRONICUS III PALAEOLOGUS** = (2) Anne of Savoy
of Brunswick-Grubenhagen

son   Irene = Basil I of Trebizond

ANDRONICUS IV PALAEOLOGUS = Maria d. of John Alexander   **MANUEL II PALAEOLOGUS** = Helena d. of Constantine Dragash

Eugenia d. of Francesco II Gattilusio = **JOHN VII PALAEOLOGUS**   **JOHN VIII PALAEOLOGUS** = (1) Anna d. of Basil I of Moscow = (2) Sophia of Montferrat = (3) Maria of Trebizond

Andronicus V Palaeologus

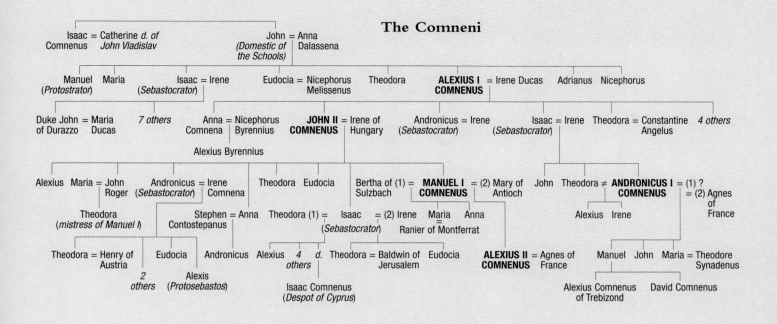

The Comneni

Isaac = Catherine d. of John Vladislav
Comnenus

John = Anna Dalassena
(Domestic of the Schools)

Manuel (Protostrator) — Maria — Isaac = Irene (Sebastocrator) — Eudocia = Nicephorus Melissenus — Theodora — **ALEXIUS I COMNENUS** = Irene Ducas — Adrianus — Nicephorus

Duke John of Durazzo = Maria Ducas — 7 others — Anna Comnena = Nicephorus Byrennius — **JOHN II COMNENUS** = Irene of Hungary — Andronicus = Irene (Sebastocrator) — Isaac = Irene (Sebastocrator) — Theodora = Constantine Angelus — 4 others

Alexius Byrennius

Alexius — Maria = John Roger — Andronicus = Irene Comnena (Sebastocrator) — Theodora — Eudocia — Bertha of Sulzbach (1) = **MANUEL I COMNENUS** = (2) Mary of Antioch — John — Theodora ≠ **ANDRONICUS I COMNENUS** = (1) ? = (2) Agnes of France

Theodora (mistress of Manuel I) — Stephen Contostepanus = Anna — Theodora (1) = Isaac (Sebastocrator) = (2) Irene — Maria = Ranier of Montferrat — Anna — Alexius — Irene — Manuel — John — Maria = Theodore Synadenus

Theodora = Henry of Austria — 2 others — Eudocia — Alexis (Protosebastos) — Andronicus — Alexius — 4 d. others — Isaac Comnenus (Despot of Cyprus) — Theodora = Baldwin of Jerusalem — Eudocia — **ALEXIUS II COMNENUS** = Agnes of France

Alexius Comnenus of Trebizond — David Comnenus

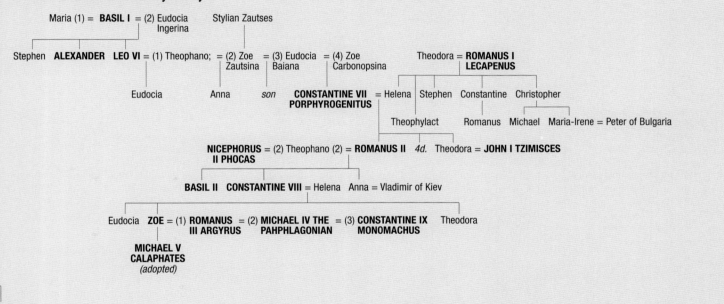

The Macedonian Dynasty

Maria (1) = **BASIL I** = (2) Eudocia Ingerina — Stylian Zautses

Stephen — **ALEXANDER** — **LEO VI** = (1) Theophano; = (2) Zoe Zautsina = (3) Eudocia Baiana = (4) Zoe Carbonopsina — Theodora = **ROMANUS I LECAPENUS**

Eudocia — Anna — son — **CONSTANTINE VII PORPHYROGENITUS** = Helena — Stephen — Constantine — Christopher

Theophylact — Romanus — Michael — Maria-Irene = Peter of Bulgaria

NICEPHORUS II PHOCAS = (2) Theophano (2) = **ROMANUS II** — 4d. — Theodora = **JOHN I TZIMISCES**

BASIL II — **CONSTANTINE VIII** = Helena — Anna = Vladimir of Kiev

Eudocia — **ZOE** = (1) **ROMANUS III ARGYRUS** = (2) **MICHAEL IV THE PAHPHLAGONIAN** = (3) **CONSTANTINE IX MONOMACHUS** — Theodora

MICHAEL V CALAPHATES (adopted)

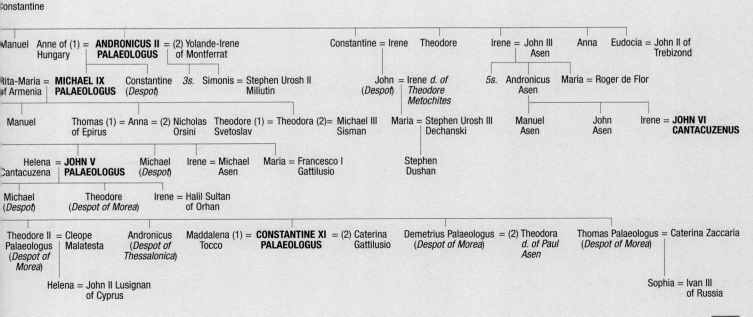

Constantine

Manuel — Anne of Hungary (1) = **ANDRONICUS II PALAEOLOGUS** = (2) Yolande-Irene of Montferrat — Constantine = Irene — Theodore — Irene = John III Asen — Anna — Eudocia = John II of Trebizond

Rita-Maria of Armenia = **MICHAEL IX PALAEOLOGUS** — Constantine (Despot) — 3s. — Simonis = Stephen Urosh II Miliutin — John (Despot) = Irene d. of Theodore Metochites — 5s. — Andronicus Asen — Maria = Roger de Flor — Irene = **JOHN VI CANTACUZENUS**

Manuel — Thomas (1) = Anna = (2) Nicholas Orsini of Epirus — Theodore (1) = Theodora (2) = Michael III Sisman Svetoslav — Maria = Stephen Urosh III Dechanski — Manuel Asen — John Asen

Helena = **JOHN V PALAEOLOGUS** — Michael (Despot) — Irene = Michael Asen — Maria = Francesco I Gattilusio — Stephen Dushan
Cantacuzena

Michael (Despot) — Theodore (Despot of Morea) — Irene = Halil Sultan of Orhan

Theodore II Palaeologus (Despot of Morea) = Cleope Malatesta — Andronicus (Despot of Thessalonica) — Maddalena (1) = **CONSTANTINE XI PALAEOLOGUS** = (2) Caterina Gattilusio — Demetrius Palaeologus (Despot of Morea) = (2) Theodora d. of Paul Asen — Thomas Palaeologus (Despot of Morea) = Caterina Zaccaria
Tocco

Helena = John II Lusignan of Cyprus

Sophia = Ivan III of Russia

List of Emperors

306–324	Constantine I	} Joint Emperors	
312–324	Licinius		
324–337	Constantine I	Sole Emperor	
337–340	Constantine II	} Joint Emperors	
337–350	Constantius II		
337–350	Constans		
350–361	Constantius II		
361–363	Julian Apostate		
363–364	Jovian		
364–375	Valentinian I	} Joint Emperors	
364–378	Valens		
375–383	Gratian	} Joint Emperors	
379–392	Theodosius I		
383–392	Valentinian II		
392–395	Theodosius I		

	EAST		WEST
395–408	Arcadius	395–423	Honorius
408–450	Theodosius II	423	Constantius III
		423–425	Johannes
450–457	Marcian	425–455	Valentinian III
		455	Petronius Maximus
		455–456	Avitus
457–474	Leo I	457–461	Marjorian
		461–465	Libius Severus
		467–472	Anthemius
		472	Olybrius
		472–474	Glycerius
474	Leo II	474	Julius Nepos
474–491	Zeno	474–476	Romulus Augustulus
[475–476	Basiliscus]		
491–518	Anastasius I		
518–527	Justin I		
527–565	Justinian I – nephew of Justin I		
565–578	Justin II – nephew of Justinian I		
578–582	Tiberius II Constantine – adopted by Justin II in 574		
582–602	Maurice Tiberius – son-in-law of Tiberius II		
602–610	Phocas – overthrew Maurice		
610–641	Hercalius		
641	Constantine III } – son of Heraclius		
	Heraclonus } – son of Heraclius, half-brother of Constantine III		
641–668	Constans II Pogonatus – son of Constantine III		
668–685	Constantine IV – son of Constans II		
685–695	Justinian II Rhinometus – son of Constantine IV		
695–698	Leontius – general under Justinian II		
698–705	Tiberius III Apsimar – overthrew Leontius		
705–711	Justinian II Rhinometus – restored		
711–713	Philippicus Bardanes – usurping soldier		
713–715	Anastasius II – elected by Senate, secretary to Philippicus		
715–717	Theodosius III – proclaimed by troops		
717–741	Leo III the Isaurian		
741	Constantine V Copronymus – son of Leo III		
742	Artabasdus – rival Emperor, son-in-law of Leo III		
743–775	Constantine V Copronymus – restored		
775–780	Leo IV the Khazar – son of Constantine V		
780–797	Constantine VI – son of Leo IV		
797–802	Irene – wife of Leo IV, mother of Constantine VI		
802–811	Nicephorus I – logothete under Irene		
811	Stauracius – son of Nicephorus I		
811–813	Michael I Rhangabe – son-in-law of Nicephorus I, brother-in-law of Stauracius		
813–820	Leo V the Armenian – general under Michael I		
820–829	Michael II the Amorian – son-in-law of Constantine VI		
829–842	Theophilus – son of Michael II		
842–867	Michael III – son of Theophilus		
867–886	Basil I the Macedonian		
886–912	Leo VI the Wise – son of Basil I		
912–913	Alexander – son of Basil I		
913–959	Constantine VII Porphyrogenitus – son of Leo VI		

920–944	Romanus I Lepacenus – father-in-law of Constantine VII
959–963	Romanus II – son of Constantine VII
963–969	Nicephorus II Phocas – married widow of Romanus II
969–976	John I Tzimisces – brother-in-law of Romanus II
976–1025	Basil II Bulgaroctonus – son of Romanus II
1025–28	Constantine VIII – son of Romanus II, brother of Basil II
1028–34	Romanus III Argyrus – son-in-law of Constantine VIII
1034–41	Michael IV the Paphlagonian – married widow of Romanus III
1041–42	Michael V Calaphates – cousin of Michael IV
1042	Zoe and Theodora – daughters of Constantine VIII
1042–55	Contantine IX Monomachus – married widow of Michael IV
1055–56	Theodora – restored
1056–57	Michael VI – chosen by Theodora
1057–59	Isaac I Comnenus – overthrew Michael VI
1059–67	Constantine X Ducas – chosen on retirement of Isaac I
1068–71	Romanus IV Diogenes – married widow of Constantine X
1071–78	Michael VII Ducas – son of Constantine X
1078–81	Nichephorus III Botaneiates – married widow of Michael VII
1081–1118	Alexius I Comnenus – nephew of Isaac I
1118–43	John II Comnenus – son of Alexius I
1143–80	Manuel I Comnenus – son of John II
1180–83	Alexius II Comnenus – son of Manuel I
1183–85	Andronicus I Comnenus – grandson of Alexius I, nephew of John II
1185–95	Isaac II Angelus – great-grandson of Alexius I
1195–1203	Alexius III Angelus – brother of Isaac II
1203–04	Isaac II Angelus and Alexius IV – restored, father and son
1204	Alexius V Murzuphlus – son-in-law of Alexius III
1204–22	Theodore I Lascaris – son-in-law of Alexius III
1222–54	John III Ducas Vatatzes – son-in-law of Theodore I
1254–58	Theodore II Lascaris – son of John III
1258–1261	John IV Lascaris – son of Theodore II
1259–82	Michael VIII Palaeologus
1282–1328	Andronicus II Palaeologus – son of Michael VIII
1328–41	Andronicus III Palaeologus – grandson of Andronicus II
1341–91	John V Palaeologus – son of Andronicus III
1347–54	John VI Cantacuzenus – father-in-law of John V
1376–79	Andronicus IV Palaeologus – son of John V
1390	John VII Palaeologus – son of Andronicus IV
1391–1425	Manuel II Palaeologus – son of John V, brother of Andronicus IV
1425–48	John VIII Palaeologus – son of Manuel II
1449–1453	Constantine XI Palaeologus – son of Manuel II

The Latin Emperors of Romania

1204–05	Baldwin I of Flanders
1206–16	Henry of Hainault
1217	Peter of Courtenay
1217–19	Yolanda
1221–28	Robert of Courtenay
1228–61	Baldwin II
[1231–37	John of Brienne]

The Despotate of Epirus

1204–15	Michael I
1215–24	Theodore

Emperors/Despots of Thessalonica

1224–30	Theodore
1230–40	Manuel
1240–44	John
1244–46	Demetrius

Despots of Epirus

1237–71	Michael II
1271–96	Nicephorus
1296–1318	Thomas
1318–23	Nicholas Orsini
1323–55	John Orsini
1335–40	Nicephorus II

Sebastocrators of Thessaly

1271–96	John I
1296–1303	Constantine
1303–18	John II

Abbasid Caliphs of Baghdad

786–809	Harun al-Rashid
809–813	Amin
813–833	Mamun
833–842	Mutasim
842–847	Wathik
847–861	Mutawakkil
861–862	Muntasir
862–866	Mutazz
866–869	Muchtadi
869–892	Mutamid
892–902	Mutadid
902–908	Muktafi
912–932	Muqtadir
932–934	Kahir
934–940	Radi
940–943	Muttaki
943–946	Mustakfi
946–974	Muti
974–991	Tai
991–1031	Kadir
1031–75	Kaim

Seljuk Sultans of Rum

1063–72	Alp Arslan
1072–92	Malik-Shah
1092–1107	Kilij Arslan I

Patriarchs of Constantinople

bold indicates mentioned in text

337–39	Paul I (341–42; 346–51)
339–41	Eusebius of Nicomedia
342–46	Macedonius I (351–60)
360–70	Eudoxius of Antioch
370–79	Demophilus
379	Euagrius
380	Maximus
379–81	Gregory I the Theologian
381–97	Nectarius
398–404	John I Chrysostom
404–05	Arsacius of Tarsus
406–25	Atticus
426–27	Sisinnius I
428–31	Nestorius
431–34	Maximianus
434–46	Proclus
446–49	Phlabianus
449–58	Anatolius
458–71	Gennadius I
471–88	**Acacius**
488–89	Phrabitas
489–95	Euphemius
495–511	Macedonius II
511–18	Timotheus I
518–20	**John II of Cappadocia**
520–35	Epiphanius
535–36	Anthimus I
536–52	Menas
552–65	Eutychius (577–82)
565–577	John III Scholasticus
582–595	John IV Nesteutes
596–606	Cyriacus
607–610	Thomas I
610–638	Sergius I
638–641	Pyrrhus I
641–653	**Paul II**
654–666	Peter
667–669	Thomas II
669–675	John V
675–677	Constantine I
677–679	Theodore I
679–686	George I
687–693	Paul III
693–705	Callinicus I
705–711	Cyrus
712–715	John VI
715–730	Germanus I
730–754	Anastasius
754–766	Constantine II
766–780	Nicetas
780–784	**Paul IV**
784–806	**St Tarasius**
806–815	Nicephorus I
815–821	Theodotus of Cassiteras
821–836	Antony I
836–843	John VII Grammarian
843–847	**Methodius I**
847–858	**Ignatius (867–877)**
858–867	**Photius (877–886)**
886–893	Stephan I
893–901	Antony II Cauleas
901–907	**Nicholas I Mysticus (912–25)**
907–912	Euthymius I Syncellus
925–928	Stephan II of Amasea
928–931	Tryphonlus
933–956	Theophylactus
956–970	Polyeuctus
970–974	Basil the Scamandrian
974–980	Antony III Studites
984–996	Nicholas II Chrysoberges
996–998	Sisinnius II
999–1019	Sergius II
1019–25	Eustathius
1025–43	Alexus I Studites
1043–58	Michael I Cerularius
1059–63	Constantine III Likhoudes
1064–75	**John VIII Xiphilinus**
1075–81	Cosmas I
1081–84	Eustathius Garidas
1084–1111	Nicholas III Grammaticus
1111–34	**John IX Agapetus**
1134–43	Leon Styppes
1143–46	Michael II Kurkuas
1146–47	Cosmas II Atticus
1147–51	Nicholas IV Muzalon
1151–53	Theodotus II
1153	Neophytus I
1154–56	Constantine V Chliarenus
1156–69	Luke Chrysoberges
1170–77	Michael III of Anchialus
1177–78	Chariton
1179–83	Theodosius I Borradiotes
1183–86	Basil II Carnaterus
1186–89	Nicetas II Muntanes
1189–90	Leon Theotokites
1190–91	Dositheus
1191–98	George II Xiphilinus
1198–1206	John X Camaterus
1207–13	Michael IV Autoreianus
1213–15	Theodore II Eirenicus
1215	Maximus II
1215–22	Manuel I Charitopoulos
1222–40	Germanius II
1240	Methodius II
1240–44	*vacant*
1244–55	Manuel II
1255–59	**Arsenius Autoreianus (1261–67)**
1260–61	Nicephorus II
1267	Germanus III
1267–75	Joseph I Galesiotes
1275–82	John XI Bekkos
1283–89	Gregory II Cyprius
1289–93	Athanasius I (1303–09)
1294–1303	John XII
1310–14	Nephon I
1315–20	John XIII Glykys
1320–21	Gerasimus I
1323–34	Jesaias
1334–47	John XIV Kalekas
1347–50	Isidore I
1350–54	Callistus I (1355–63)
1354–55	Philotheus Kokkinos (1364–76)
1376–79	Macarius (1390–91)
1379–88	Neilus Kerameus
1389–90	Antony IV (1391–97)
1397	Callistus II Xanothopoulos
1397–1410	Matthew I
1410–16	Euthymius II
1416–39	**Joseph II**
1440–43	**Metrophanes II**
1443–50	**Gregory III Mammas**
1450–53	Athanasius II (*bishop*)
1453–56	**Gennadius II Scholarius (1458, 1462–63, 1464)**

Popes of Rome

(excludes anti-Popes)

bold indicates the pope is mentioned in book

337–52	St Julius I
352–66	Liberius
366–84	St Damasus I
384–99	St Siricius
399–401	St Anastasius I
401–17	**St Innocent I**
417–18	St Zosimus
418–22	St Boniface I
422–32	St Celestine I
432–40	St Sixtus III
440–61	**St Leo I**
461–68	St Hilarius I
468–83	**St Simplicius I**
483–92	**St Felix III (II)**
492–96	St Gelasius I
496–98	Anastasius II
498–514	St Symmachus
514–23	**St Hormisdas**
523–26	St John I
526–30	Felix IV (III)
530–32	Boniface II
533–35	John II
535–36	St Agapitus I
536–37	**St Silverius**
537–55	Vigilius
556–61	Pelagius I
561–74	John III
575–579	Benedict I
579–590	Pelagius I
590–604	**St Gregory I**
604–606	Sabinianus
607	Boniface III
608–615	St Boniface IV
615–618	St Adeodatus
619–625	Boniface V
625–638	**Honorius I**
638–640	Severinus
640–642	**John IV**
642–649	**Theodore I**
649–653	**St Martin I**
654–657	St Eugene I
657–672	St Vitalian
672–676	Adeodatus II
676–678	Donus
678–681	**St Agatho**
681–683	St Leo II
684–685	St Benedict II
685–686	John V
686–687	Conon
687–701	St Sergius I
701–705	John VI
705–707	John VII
708	Sisinnius
708–715	Constantine
715–731	**St Gregory II**
731–741	**Gregory III**
741–752	St Zacharias
752	Stephen (II)
752–757	**Stephen II (III)**
757–767	St Paul I
768–772	Stephen III (IV)
722–795	**Hadrian I**
795–816	**Leo III**
816–817	Stephen IV (V)
817–824	Paschal I
824–827	Eugenius II
827	Valentinus
827–844	Gregory IV
844–847	Sergius II
847–855	Leo IV
855–858	Benedict III
858–867	**Nicholas I**
867–872	Hadrian II
872–882	**John VIII**
882–884	Marinus I
884–885	Hadrian III
885–891	Stephen V (VI)
891–896	Formosus
896	Boniface VI
896–897	Stephen VI (VII)
897	Romanus
897	Theodore II
898–900	John IX
900–903	Benedict IV
903	Leo V
904–911	Sergius III
911–913	Anastasius III
913–914	Lando
914–928	John X
928	Leo VI
928–931	Stephen VII (VIII)
931–935	John XI
936–939	Leo VII
939–942	Stephen VIII (IX)
942–946	Marinus II
946–955	Agapitus II
955–964	John XII
963–965	Leo VIII
965–972	John XIII
973–974	Benedict VI
974–983	Benedict VII
983–984	John XIV
985–996	John XV
996–999	Gregory V
999–1003	Silvester II
1003	John XVII
1004–09	John XVIII
1009–12	Sergius IV
1012–24	Benedict VIII
1024–32	John XIX
1032–44	Benedict IX (1047–48)
1045–46	Gregory VI
1046–47	Clement II
1048	Damasus II
1049–54	**Leo IX**
1055–57	Victor II
1057–58	Stephen IX (X)
1059–61	**Nicholas II**
1061–73	Alexander II
1073–85	Gregory VII
1086–87	Victor III
1088–99	**Urban II**
1099–1118	**Paschal II**
1118–19	Gelasius II
1119–24	Calixtus II
1124–30	Honorius II
1130–43	**Innocent II**
1143–44	Celestine II
1144–45	Lucius II
1145–53	Eugene III
1153–54	Anastasius IV
1154–59	**Hadrian IV**
1159–81	Alexander III
1181–85	Lucius III
1185–87	**Urban III**
1187	**Gregory VIII**
1187–91	Clement III
1191–98	Celestine III
1198–1216	**Innocent III**
1216–27	Honorius III
1227–41	Gregory IX
1241	Celestine IV
1243–54	Innocent IV
1254–61	Alexander IV
1261–64	**Urban IV**
1265–68	**Clement IV**
1268–71	*vacant*
1271–76	Gregory X
1276	Innocent V
1276	Hadrian V
1276–77	John XXI
1277–80	Nicholas III
1281–85	**Martin IV**
1285–87	Honorius IV
1288–92	Nicholas IV
1294	Celestine V
1294–1303	Boniface VIII
1303–04	Benedict XI
1305–14	Clement V
1316–34	John XXII
1334–42	Benedict XII
1342–52	Clement VI
1352–62	**Innocent VI**
1362–70	**Urban V**
1370–78	Gregory XI
1378–89	Urban VI
1389–1404	Boniface IX
1404–06	Innocent VII
1406–15	Gregory XII
1415–17	*vacant*
1417–31	Martin V
1431–47	**Eugene IV**
1447–1455	**Nicholas V**

INDEX